ROUTLEDGE LIBRARY EDITIONS: ARTIFICIAL INTELLIGENCE

Volume 6

SIMULATING SOCIETIES

SIMULATING SOCIETIES
The Computer Simulation
of Social Phenomena

Edited by
NIGEL GILBERT AND JIM DORAN

LONDON AND NEW YORK

First published in 1994 by UCL Press Ltd.

This edition first published in 2018
by Routledge
2 Park Square, Milton Park, Abingdon, Oxon OX14 4RN

and by Routledge
711 Third Avenue, New York, NY 10017

Routledge is an imprint of the Taylor & Francis Group, an informa business

© 1994 Nigel Gilbert and Jim Doran

All rights reserved. No part of this book may be reprinted or reproduced or utilised in any form or by any electronic, mechanical, or other means, now known or hereafter invented, including photocopying and recording, or in any information storage or retrieval system, without permission in writing from the publishers.

Trademark notice: Product or corporate names may be trademarks or registered trademarks, and are used only for identification and explanation without intent to infringe.

British Library Cataloguing in Publication Data
A catalogue record for this book is available from the British Library

ISBN: 978-0-8153-8566-0 (Set)
ISBN: 978-0-429-49236-5 (Set) (ebk)
ISBN: 978-0-8153-4926-6 (Volume 6) (hbk)
ISBN: 978-1-351-16512-9 (Volume 6) (ebk)

Publisher's Note
The publisher has gone to great lengths to ensure the quality of this reprint but points out that some imperfections in the original copies may be apparent.

Disclaimer
The publisher has made every effort to trace copyright holders and would welcome correspondence from those they have been unable to trace.

Simulating societies
The computer simulation of social phenomena

Edited by

Nigel Gilbert
University of Surrey

Jim Doran
University of Essex

© Nigel Gilbert and Jim Doran 1994

This book is copyright under the Berne Convention.
No reproduction without permission.
All right reserved.

First published in 1994 by UCL Press

UCL Press Limited
University College London
Gower Street
London WC1E 6BT

The name of University College London (UCL) is a registered trade
mark used by UCL Press with the consent of the owner.

ISBN:
1-85728-082-2 HB

British Library Cataloguing in Publication Data.
A catalogue record for this book is available from the British Library.

Typeset in Baskerville.
Printed and bound by
Biddles Ltd, Guildford and King's Lynn, England.

Contents

	Preface	vii
	Contributors	ix
1	Simulating societies: an introduction *Jim Doran & Nigel Gilbert*	1
2	Simulation of complex organizational processes: a review of methods and their epistemological foundations *Ann C. Séror*	19
3	The evolution of technologies *Klaus G. Troitzsch*	41
4	Simulating the emergence of social order from individual behaviour *Andrzej Nowak & Bibb Latané*	63
5	The architecture of society: stochastic simulation of urban movement *Alan Penn & Nick Dalton*	85
6	Multi-agent simulation as a tool for studying emergent processes in societies *Alexis Drogoul & Jacques Ferber*	127
7	Simulating fishermen's society *F. Bousquet, C. Cambier, C. Mullon, P. Morand, J. Quensiere*	143

CONTENTS

8 Simulating prehistoric hunter-gatherer societies 165
Steven Mithen

9 The EOS project: modelling Upper Palaeolithic social change 195
Jim Doran, Mike Palmer, Nigel Gilbert, Paul Mellars

10 Learning to co-operate using cultural algorithms 223
Robert G. Reynolds

11 The simulation of trade in oligopolistic markets 245
José Castro Caldas & Helder Coelho

12 Mind is not enough:
the precognitive bases of social interaction 267
Rosaria Conte & Cristiano Castelfranchi

References 287
Index 301

Preface

In April 1992, the first international symposium on "Simulating Societies" was held at the University of Surrey, Guildford, England. This book includes revised versions of most of the papers that were delivered to the symposium, which has now become an annual event.

The symposium marked a resurgence of interest in the use of simulation to develop and test ideas and theories about society and social phenomena. Simulation had a brief vogue in the late 1960s as social scientists began to realize the opportunities that the development of the digital computer had brought about. But simulation technology was then rather crude and better adapted to, for example, modelling the movement of goods along a production line than developing useful, let alone realistic, models of human societies. While the idea of simulation continued to attract some interest over the following two decades, especially in economics, it has been advances in the field of artificial intelligence that has inspired the recent rapid and worldwide renewed interest in the simulation of social phenomena.

Many researchers, several of whom are represented in this volume, realized that the sets of autonomous, communicating and pseudo-intelligent "agents" that scientists interested in the burgeoning field of distributed artificial intelligence (DAI) experiment with could be used to simulate groups or societies of people. For the first time it became possible to envisage social scientists experimenting with societies (of computational agents) rather than having to rely on observation of social events. This book describes some of the first, tentative steps that are being taken in this direction. We are now at the very beginning of what may prove to be a long, fascinating and profitable period of exploration, to see how far one can go towards reproducing the features of human societies in computer simulations.

PREFACE

The symposium on "Simulating Societies" held at the University of Surrey was partially supported by the Johnson Wax Foundation and by the Department of Sociology at Surrey. It was held as one of the Sociology Department's regular series of "Conferences on Sociological Theory and Method". We are very grateful to the University and to the Johnson Wax Foundation for their support.

Nigel Gilbert
Jim Doran
July 1993

Contributors

François Bousquet is a water science engineer and is preparing a doctoral thesis on the modelling of the interaction between people and their environment at the Laboratoire d'Informatique Appliquée, ORSTOM-Bondy, France. His interests include ecological and social modelling, complexity and multi-agent simulation.

José Castro Caldas is a lecturer at ISCTE (Management Science Institute) in Lisbon, Portugal. He received his BSc in economics and MSc in mathematics applied to economics and management from the Technical University of Lisbon. Currently he is preparing a PhD thesis on distributed artificial intelligence and the simulation of interaction among economic agents. He is also teaching operations research and decision support systems at ISCTE. His research interests include multi-criteria decision theory and related topics in operations research and distributed artificial intelligence applied to economics.

Christophe Cambier is a computer scientist at LAFORIA at Paris University. He is working on a thesis on multi-agent simulation applied to ecological and social interaction.

Cristiano Castelfranchi is a researcher at the Institute of Psychology of the National Research Council of Italy. He has been the head of the Project for the Simulation of Social Behaviour since 1988. He is the author of several books on social and cognitive modelling. In 1992 and 1993 he was programme chairman of the European Workshop on Modelling Autonomous Agents in a Multi-Agent World (MAAMAW).

Helder Coelho is professor of computer science (artificial intelligence) at the Technical University of Lisbon. He received his BSc and MSc from the

CONTRIBUTORS

Technical University of Lisbon and his PhD from Edinburgh University. He is project leader of the AI group at INESC in Portugal. Dr Coelho has authored many papers and books on information technologies and computing science and his research interests include distributed artificial intelligence, knowledge engineering, multi-modal intelligent interfaces and expert systems for public administration and legal reasoning.

Rosaria Conte is a researcher at the Institute of Psychology of the National Research Council of Italy, working on a project on the Simulation of Social Behaviour. Her research interests include both the formal study and the computer simulation of social interaction.

Nick Dalton is a lecturer at the Bartlett School of Architecture and Planning, University College London. He is the senior computer programmer in charge of software development for the Unit for Architectural Studies and has written software which is being used around the world for configurational analysis of buildings and cities.

Jim Doran read mathematics at Oxford, became a specialist in artificial intelligence at the University of Edinburgh and is now professor at the University of Essex. Throughout his career he has applied statistical and computer methods in archaeology. His particular interest is in the simulation of societies using the concepts and techniques of distributed artificial intelligence.

Alexis Drogoul is a PhD student in the AI Laboratory of University Paris VI, within the MIRIAD team. He is currently working on a thesis on the emergence of organizational structures within multi-agent systems. His interests include reactive agents, distributed problem solving and multi-agent simulation.

Jacques Ferber is professor at University Paris VI where he leads the MIRIAD team, which conducts research on DAI in its AI Laboratory. His interests include actor languages, distributed problem solving (with the Eco-Problem-Solving model) and multi-agent simulation.

Nigel Gilbert is professor of sociology at the University of Surrey. He is a founder member of the Social and Computer Sciences research group at Surrey, which applies insights from the social sciences to the design of information technology. His interests include social simulation, natural language interaction with computer systems, and statistical methods for social research.

CONTRIBUTORS

Bibb Latané is professor of psychology at Florida Atlantic University in Boca Raton, Florida. With degrees from Yale and Minnesota, he has taught at Columbia, Ohio State and UNC. Past president of the Society for Personality and Social Psychology and the Midwestern Psychological Association, he currently organizes eight scientific conferences a year for the Nags Head Conference Centre.

Paul Mellars took his BA and PhD in archaeology at Cambridge, where he is currently reader in palaeolithic archaeology. His research has been concerned mainly with the problems of the behavioural transition from anatomically "archaic" to "modern" populations in Europe. He recently held a British Academy research readership to undertake a general study of the archaeological evidence for Neanderthal behaviour, to be published by Princeton University Press.

Steven Mithen is lecturer in prehistoric archaeology at the University of Reading. Following a first degree in archaeology, he took an MSc in biological computation and then returned to archaeology for doctoral research at St John's College, Cambridge, and postdoctoral research at Trinity Hall. His current work involves a field project studying Mesolithic hunter-gatherers in the southern Hebrides and the computer simulation of mammoth extinction.

Pierre Morand is a bio-mathematical researcher with the Niger Central Delta research team located in ORSTOM-Bamako in Mali. He is working on the modelling of fish population dynamics and statistical analyses of fishermen's activities.

Christian Mullon is director of the ORSTOM environmental modelling laboratory. His background is in mathematics.

Andrzej Nowak received his PhD in 1986 in psychology at the University of Warsaw. He is especially interested in inter-disciplinary work, applying methods of physics to social and cognitive psychology. His recent work includes formal models of social processes, in particular modelling the emergence of public opinion, neural networks, especially models of self-control in neural networks, and applications of dynamical systems to cognitive and social behaviour. He is a director of the Center for Complex Systems in the Institute for Social Studies at the University of Warsaw and also has a post in the Faculty of Psychology at the University.

Mike Palmer gained a BA in archaeology and an MSc in computer sci-

CONTRIBUTORS

ence at the University of Newcastle upon Tyne. Since then he has been a senior research officer at the University of Essex, assisting in the development of DAI models of the emergence of social complexity.

Alan Penn is an architect and lecturer at the Bartlett School of Architecture and Planning, University College London. As research manager for the Unit for Architectural Studies, he is involved in range of empirical and computing research projects aimed at the development of methods for representing and understanding the social effects of spatial design.

Jacques Quensiere manages the multi-disciplinary Niger Central Delta research team located in ORSTROM-Bamako in Mali. He is an ecologist.

Robert G. Reynolds is an associate professor in computer science at Wayne State University. He received a PhD in computer science from the University of Michigan. His thesis concerned the use of evolutionary learning algorithms, genetic algorithms, to model the evolution of incipient agriculture in the Oaxaca Valley, Mexico. He has also studied the evolution of co-operative behaviour and the emergence of hierarchical decision systems.

Ann C. Séror is associate professor of management at Université Laval in Quebec, Canada. She completed her doctoral studies at the Krannert Graduate School of Management, Purdue University, and has taught at Vanderbilt University. Her current research interests include qualitative and quantitative research methodologies for the social sciences, trans-cultural organizational analysis and the management of information technology transfer.

Klaus G. Troitzsch is professor of social science informatics at Koblenz-Landau University. Having taken a first degree in political science, he gained some experience in politics as a member of the state parliament of Hamburg and after taking his PhD returned to scientific work when the Institutes of Computer Science and Social Science Informatics were founded at Koblenz in 1978–9. His research interests cover mathematical modelling and computer simulation in the social sciences.

Chapter 1
Simulating societies: an introduction

Jim Doran & Nigel Gilbert

This book is concerned with a particular approach to the study of societies, primarily human societies, that has been fruitful in the past and appears likely to be even more so in the future. This is the use of precisely specified simulation models, often formulated and run on computers, to recreate and study essential aspects of societies. The central advantage of precise modelling is that when results are obtained they are obtained objectively and repeatably. The disadvantage is that drawing any conclusions at all becomes a technically more demanding task.

Although the chapters that follow have this modelling theme in common, the work they report relates to a variety of disciples – economics, anthropology, archaeology and social psychology, among others – and this inevitably creates potentially confusing divergences of presentation and understanding. This introductory chapter is intended to help overcome these difficulties by presenting the concepts, procedures and problems that are intrinsic to all modelling (and simulation) wherever it is applied.

In this chapter we will explain what we mean by modelling and by computer simulation, and suggest that there is one simple and unified modelling framework which encompasses the various modelling traditions. We will also identify the special problems and opportunities associated with modelling or simulating societies, especially human societies, and suggest how the work described in the rest of the book sits within this framework.

1.1 An example: simulating the Mayan collapse

We begin by describing a typical example of simulating a society that will serve to introduce a number of the points we wish to make.

SIMULATING SOCIETIES: AN INTRODUCTION

Within the time period AD 750 to AD 900 the mesoamerican Classic Maya culture, as viewed through the archaeological record, "collapsed". That is, those characteristics of advanced society that the Classic Maya culture had earlier displayed (most notably monumental buildings, sophisticated art and large apparently well organized populations) disappeared abruptly from the archaeological record. Many have tried to explain why the collapse occurred. It is easy to speculate about possible reasons: invasion by "barbarians" from outside, disease, earthquake, peasant rebellion, climatic change and so on. However, no simple explanation has been accepted as convincing in accord with the details of the available evidence.

Alongside more traditional attempts to deploy scholarship and insight, computer simulation and mathematical modelling techniques have been invoked more than once in the search for an explanation for the end of Mayan civilization. Thus, in a well known study, Hosler et al. (1977) conducted a simulation based on the ideas of "systems dynamics" (following the influential work of Jay Forrester 1968). Their starting point was a verbal model of the Mayan collapse put forward by Willey & Shimkin (1973) that hypothesized a disastrous deviation-amplifying feedback loop between (a) increasing ritual and public building, intended to enhance the prestige of the elite, and (b) the consequent decline in commoner food production that lowered its prestige. Hosler et al. quantified these and other elements of the Mayan socio-economic system and specified recurrence equations determining their interacting behaviour over time. They then tracked the Mayan system though history, varying assumptions and parameters, and showed that a collapse could be made to occur within their model, and that alternative behaviour by the ruling elite could have delayed the collapse for a while at least.

There are a number of problems with this study that are typical of such simulations. It did not address certain seemingly fundamental issues. For example, it said nothing about spatial factors in Mayan society, or about warfare. And there were many assumptions of detail that were not well grounded given the limited archaeological evidence available. It is worth underlining that the Hosler et al. model was studied by simulation, not by analysis. That is, the authors were not able to reason directly from their equations to conclusions about the behaviour of the model. They had to use a computer to work systematically through simulated time. This inevitably meant that certain possible system trajectories were left unexamined.

Lowe (1985) attempted to strengthen the Hosler et al. model by using a systems dynamics formulation for *each* of the Mayan polities and adding another component concerned with the "domino" effect between polities (using the technical repertoire of epidemic theory to create this part of their formal model). This brought the spatial dimension into play, but the model began to seem unduly cumbersome, although Lowe was persuasive in matching his simulation results to the available data. He also performed a limited sensitivity analysis; that is, he explored the consequences of variations in his basic assumptions and parameter settings in order to identify those that were particularly critical.

Doran (1981), starting from the same initial verbal model as Hosler et al., adopted an artificial intelligence (AI) perspective and concentrated directly on the dynamics of the interaction between the Mayan elite and commoners, viewed as a two-agent system in the AI sense. He particularly considered the circumstances in which the relationship between the agents might initially arise and then break down. Although this model was not formalized in detail, it did indicate a quite different approach which has the advantage of directly addressing the notion that the relationship between the Mayan elite and commoners involved aspects of dialogue, manipulation and conflict.

The studies we have just outlined illustrate a number of key issues that we shall return to later in this chapter. The emphasis of a modelling or simulation study (we shall clarify the distinction shortly) is often on gaining insight into some system which is (or was) "out there" in the world but is relatively inaccessible. More than one model may be targeted at the same phenomena. There is a theoretical context regarding both the target system (e.g. the social dynamics of early states) and the model (e.g. the theory of epidemics). Most models embody many detailed assumptions and adjustable parameters. Obtaining convincing evidence to support the assumptions and set the parameters of a model may be very difficult, and completing a simulation study may be very laborious because of the effort needed to implement a model specification as a computer program and because of the computational load of systematically tracking through the many alternative possible behaviours inherent in the model.

Mayan studies have moved on significantly since the computer-based studies sketched above were conducted, and there have been developments that can also tell us something about modelling human societies and its pitfalls. It now seems that the Mayan "collapse" must be seen in the context of a shift of dominance and population from one part of the region (the Southern Lowlands of the Yucatan Peninsula) to another (the Northern Lowlands). Thus, according to Sabloff (1990: 145), "There was no massive, overall collapse but a partial one, leading to large-scale demographic, political, and economic rearrangements. The Classic tradition did not die out entirely, but its focus shifted from the Southern to the Northern Lowlands." Further, the earlier interpretations of the evidence are now beginning to look strongly and unduly influenced by their authors' own cultural background. " . . . it has been noted that many of the leading Maya scholars in the first half of this century were themselves upper class or upper middle class in background and either unconsciously or unapologetically transferred their Western European elite values onto Maya culture." (Sabloff 1990: 53).

These latest developments in Mayan studies indicate something very important, if rather obvious, about formal modelling. Models are targeted at a certain part of reality and are created in a certain theoretical context. If the targeting or the theory is wrong, then the models are all too likely merely to confirm error.

1.2 Key concepts in modelling and simulation

1.2.1 Modelling

There are many and various definitions of modelling. The notion we shall use is a simple one. We wish to acquire knowledge about a target entity T. But T is not easy to study directly. So we proceed indirectly. Instead of T we study another entity M, the "model", which is sufficiently similar to T that we are confident that some of what we learn about M will also be true of T.

Put like that, modelling seems a rather daunting and implausible business. What, for example, does "sufficiently similar" mean? From where do we get a "sufficiently similar" M? There are no simple answers to these questions. Some degree of prior understanding of the target system and of the range of potential models may suggest that one of the latter can be revealing about the former. And, having provisionally selected or designed a model, we can very likely confirm or revise our choice by comparing characteristics or behaviour of the model with known characteristics or behaviour of the target not explicitly incorporated into the model.

It should be clear that both targets and models may be dynamic – themselves changing with time. Indeed, since we are concerned with human and other societies in this book, for us this is essential. That means that we shall think of a model as comprising

STRUCTURE + BEHAVIOUR

KEY CONCEPTS IN MODELLING AND SIMULATION

At a moment in time the model has structure. With the passage of time the structure changes and that is behaviour.

Our view of modelling places no restriction on the nature of models. The requirement is merely that they should be effective within the modelling procedure. So we might use a sparrow as a model of an eagle, or a pile of sand as a model of a mountain, or a computer as a model of a human mind, or an ant colony as a model of a human city.

Models are autonomous, precisely because they are themselves entities in the world. And one entity may function as a model for many different target systems. Further, there is in principle no logical problem with the concept of a model of a model.

1.2.2 Simulation

Now we explain what we mean by "simulation". Suppose that we have located or constructed a model of some target of interest to us. Clearly, we wish to know the behaviour of the model. How? We may set the model running (possibly in special sets of circumstances of our choice) and watch what it does. It is this that we refer to as "simulation" of the target. As will appear, if the model is a computational process within a computer, then simulation is a matter of executing that process and we speak of computer simulation.

Simulation contrasts with a second, analytic, way of obtaining the behaviour of a model. This is by reasoning directly from knowledge of its structure. The reasoning may be informal and subjective or, if the model is specified or is describable in some formal language (a language of mathematics or a formal logic, say), we may be able to infer something about its behaviour from the specification or description from formal reasoning. Either way, the model's behaviour need not be observed directly at all. This analytic approach is very desirable, but only rarely is it possible. Simulation is the norm as far as this book is concerned.

1.2.3 Models and model specifications

As we have indicated, it seems important to distinguish between a "model" and a "model specification". The relationship between them is much like that between a house and an architect's plans. A model specification may exist without the corresponding model. The properties and behaviour of the model could be determined just from the specification. Of course, without the model itself, simulation as we have defined it is not possible. Accordingly, we shall view a set of mathematical equations or a computer program as a specification or description of an abstract process which may in turn be a model of something of interest to us. In this light a computer is a device for turning a model specification (a computer program) into a "running" model, i.e. a simulation – the computational process itself. (Our use of the word "specification" here is a little different from the usual computer science usage.)

There may be many model specifications, all of which are equivalent in that they describe the same abstract process. The obvious example is a set of computer programs, written in different programming languages, that specify the same computational process.

Formal model specifications typically contain variables, which change as part of the model's behaviour (or which express varying outside influences upon the model), and also parameters: values set at the beginning of the simulation that, in effect, enable one model description to specify a whole range of particular models. This is not only convenient, it also greatly increases the scope of any conclusions about behaviour inferred directly from the specification – but, sadly, the process of inference is liable to become correspondingly much more difficult to carry through. Also, parameters mean that simulating the model becomes a much more complex and laborious business, because all possible behaviours corresponding to all possible parameter combinations must now be explored.

1.2.4   The multiplicity of models

It should be clear that there is not just one model for any particular target. There may be a potentially infinite number of models with some degree of plausibility. An eagle may be modelled by a sparrow, a robin, a moth, a tiger moth, a mathematically specified abstract process and so on; and recall the three models described earlier which were used to study Mayan dynamics.

It is usually possible to classify this multitude of models in various ways. Some models will be relatively concrete, some abstract. Some will be much more complex than others, and different models will relate to different aspects of the target system. For example, we may have a very simple and abstract or a very complex and detailed model of an eagle; and one model may concentrate upon the eagle's ability to fly, while another may focus on its digestive tract.

KEY CONCEPTS IN MODELLING AND SIMULATION

A particularly important dimension of variation is the degree of "lumping" or "aggregation" that models embody, that is, the extent to which multiple elements of the target are expressed by single elements of the model. This is well illustrated by the three models of Mayan society sketched earlier. Doran's model distinguished just two main components in the society, the elite and the commoners. Lowe's model, on the other hand, was structured primarily in terms of a dozen or so interacting polities. And the model of Hosler et al. isolated a number of particular variables: "number of monuments", "number of commoners", "food per commoner" and so on.

1.2.5 The validity of models

The most important characteristic of models is the degree to which they may be trusted. A model that can be relied upon to reflect the behaviour of its target is said to be "valid". It is less obvious that models may be untrustworthy in different ways. A model may, to a greater or lesser extent:

- generate spurious behaviours by indicating that in certain circumstances the target will do X when this is not so;
- not generate correct behaviours by failing to indicate that in certain circumstances the target will do Y;
- generate behaviours that, although correct, are insufficiently discriminating to be useful, by indicating that in certain circumstances the target will do Z which, however, could be any one of X_1, X_2 or X_3 (e.g., a bomb will be planted somewhere in the city, but there is no information as to where).

Attention is often focused upon the first of these possibilities, but the others may be equally damaging if not understood and controlled. Also, of course, there are degrees of validity. For example, a model may generate spurious behaviour only rarely (which may be acceptable) or it may habitually do so (which presumably will not be acceptable).

If it is often the case that there are many alternative models available, as we have suggested in this and the preceding section, how can a choice be made between them? We shall return to this key question shortly.

1.3 Modelling procedure

We shall now review the main issues and stages in a standard modelling procedure as a context for further discussion. We shall not go into detail –

many excellent texts on simulation and modelling are available (e.g. Zeigler 1976, 1990; Shannon 1975; Pooch & Wall 1993).

1.3.1 Aims

There are different reasons for modelling. The aim may merely be to construct a model that is valid at least to some degree – that is, whose behaviour does match that of the target in at least some significant respects. By constructing such a model, we may hope to gain new insights into the target itself. Such modelling is exploratory in nature, often involves theory building, and is the type of modelling mainly at issue in this book.

Alternatively, the aim may be to predict reliably the behaviour of the target in certain key conditions which may or may not be under our control. For example, we may wish to know what will happen to traffic if a new pedestrian precinct is created in a city centre, or the likely consequences on patient care of a power failure in a hospital. Modelling of this type is relatively well focused and is usually conducted within a stabilized theoretical context.

The contrast between exploratory and focused modelling is not absolute. Recall the studies of the Mayan collapse. The primary modelling aim was clearly to gain new insight. However, it is possible to envisage such models being used to predict where an archaeological excavation might prove fruitful, or, indeed, to predict collapse in certain circumstances in some closely similar existing social system.

We should mention in passing a third possibility: model building as part of design. In this case the model is built as a forerunner of the real thing. One might, for example, construct a reduced-scale model of a proposed new aircraft as a means of partially testing the design. Although important, this possibility will not be a concern of this book.

1.3.2 Traditions of modelling and types of model

Modelling as a scientific technique is not fully unified. There are different modelling traditions, some associated with particular disciplines, and different types of model specification.

Most model specifications involving time have in common that the structure of the model is specified and so is the way in which that structure changes through time. A specification therefore takes the form:

$$S_0 \text{ and } T(S_n) \to S_{n+1}$$

MODELLING PROCEDURE

where S_0 is the initial structure of the model at time 0, S_t is the structure of the model at time t, and T is a transition function between structures. Successive applications of T to S_0 and its successors generate a model trajectory.

Commonly, the model structure is a set or vector of numeric variables, and the transition function consists of one or more statements about the dependence of variable values at time $t + 1$ on values at time t. This implies a specification with a traditional mathematical flavour. However, the specification of structure and behaviour does not have to be in numerical terms and often should not be. Structure may be expressed as a set of relationships (e.g. "part of", "connected to", "alongside"), and the transitions may be changes to those relationships. In this case the model begins to look more purely symbolic and is likely to be based in formal logic.

Important different types of model (specification) include the following:

I Fully numerical differential and recurrence equations. The non-linear models of chaos theory are a subcategory.

II Stochastic and statistical models. These are like the models of type I, but involve stochastic elements. Transitions are uncertain, with the uncertainty expressed in terms of probability distributions. ·

III Models of the traditional operations research variety. These are commonly of type II but are often designed for computer simulation and specified using dedicated computer programming languages. A noteworthy subtype is that of "next event" simulation models, where simulation time is advanced to the next significant event rather than in fixed increments.

IV Artificial intelligence models and specifications. These are usually primarily symbolic rather than numeric and are often, but by no means always, concerned with aspects of cognition. Subtypes are:

   (a) qualitative simulation models: these are akin to models of type I but are partially symbolic, involving only a restricted range of numeric values. In AI work they are typically used to model physical systems for expert system purposes, but their use for social modelling has been suggested. We mention them because they stand between traditional numeric models and fully non-numerical AI models.

   (b) multiple-agent (DAI) models: these are structured as multiple intercommunicating "agents" each of which is a complex knowledge-based system. Models of this type are often created within software called "DAI testbeds", analogous to the dedicated simulation programming languages mentioned above under III. In spite of their complexity, which makes them difficult to use, multiple-agent models are attractive because they seem more able to "mirror" societies and groups of people than their alternatives;

(c) formal logic specifications: the structure of these models is usually expressed with a language of first-order logic, and temporal transitions and model implications are captured by corresponding inference rules. The emphasis of such models tends to be strongly on the expressive power and other properties of the formal system itself, and on its ability to capture the essence of the target.

For illustration we may refer back to the models for Mayan society discussed earlier. The model of Hosler et al. was of type I, Lowe's model was of type II and Doran's of type IV(b).

These different model types are clearly related. Thus, it is entirely possible to embed numeric values within symbolic relational structures, and to update them as the structure is updated. In fact, it seems that DAI type models can embed all the other types, although it is not, of course, necessarily sensible to do such a thing. Recent years have seen a convergence between AI modelling methods and those of operations research (see e.g. Zeigler 1990).

1.3.3 The modelling process

In standard practice, model specification involves the following steps in order:

- Considering what is known about the target and clarifying modelling objectives
- Choosing the aspects of the target to be modelled
- Choosing the type of model to be deployed (including the level of abstraction of the model and the technical repertoire and the formal language in which it is to be specified)
- Establishing the detailed content and specification of the model
- Verifying that the model is as intended
- Validation: checking the model as specified against already available data
- Deriving the model's behaviour: the two possibilities are direct inference from the specification or by simulation
- Sensitivity analysis: determining the relative significance of the various assumptions embodied in the model
- Relating the results back to the target, interpreting them and assessing their validity

MODELLING PROCEDURE

− Reporting the conclusions

Each of these steps can present considerable problems, some of which we shall now discuss.

1.3.4 Problems of modelling

There are well known difficulties often encountered with the modelling procedure. Perhaps the most fundamental is how to choose between different types of model in a particular problem context. Our initial Mayan example illustrated that there may be a choice between, say, a nonlinear mathematical model, a model with stochastic components or an AI-type model. What criteria enable us to choose between them?

There is no simple standard criterion. What can be said, rather obviously, is that a model must be so structured and sufficiently detailed as to be able in principle to answer the questions to be asked of it. There is little point in designing a model whose behaviour cannot even express the alternative answers of interest. Equally, there seems little merit in models that go beyond the needs of the questions to be answered in the detail they encompass. Indeed, there are good reasons to avoid such models. Detail for its own sake merely confuses and generates labour. So there is a "principle of minimality" to be followed. What is needed is the simplest model that will do the job.

This puts great weight on a clear statement of objectives, for it is they that should determine the type and complexity of model to be used. But very often the question of which model to use is not even posed, and a modeller adopts whatever he or she happens to be familiar with. Alternatively, the modeller has a prior belief that certain features of the target are the really significant ones (e.g. positive feedback loops, mental models) and goes for a model that makes it easy to express that prior belief.

Closely related is the question of the detailed assumptions, deterministic or stochastic, that may reasonably be built into a model. Assumptions should be at least plausible and preferably well grounded in empirical evidence. For example, if a certain variable is assumed to be distributed according to the Poisson distribution with mean 1.5, there should be some evidential justification for that assumption. However, this may be very hard to achieve for complex models. If several related assumptions cannot be justified, they should be replaced by simpler and rather more aggregated assumptions.

Many models involve explicit "constraint" assumptions. These assume that the outcome of some elements of behaviour within the model may be

11

SIMULATING SOCIETIES: AN INTRODUCTION

predicted by asserting that one or more constraints will always be satisfied (e.g. concerning an agent's choices, the outcome of negotiations, the effects of an explosion). An example of such an assumption is the "rational man" of economic models: we assume that in all circumstances an agent will act in its own best interest, and we make no attempt to specify just how it comes to choose its actions. Typically, constraint assumptions are based on hypotheses rather than on specific evidence.

What if a model requires many low-level assumptions, but there is no evidence to support them? Perhaps unexpectedly, this is not necessarily fatal. It may be that low-level assumptions may be at least partially justified by their joint higher-level consequences. Consider, for example, a computer-based model that captures the chess play of a human grand master. This behaviour is so difficult to achieve that whatever assumptions are made in the model's creation immediately gain plausibility. However, it is clearly dangerous to rely heavily upon this type of justification.

The plausibility, by whatever arguments, of the assumptions built into a model strongly influences the degree of confidence that may be placed on the relevance of its behaviour to that of the target system. Also crucial is the degree of experimental validation of the model and the extent to which its behaviour has been fully explored and understood. Little can be learned from an inadequate sample of the model's behaviour. If a model embodies implausible assumptions and cannot be validated, then nothing can be learned from it about the target – though much may be learned about the properties of the model itself and that may be useful.

The last difficulty we shall mention here concerns the interpretation of behaviour obtained from a model even when the model has been experimentally validated and its individual assumptions justified. Just because the model is *only* a model, it will always be possible to dispute any parallel claimed between its behaviour and that of the target. They are, after all, two different things. More importantly, perhaps, it may well be that the observations to be made relate to complex patterns of events in the model and that the interpretation of these patterns may be ill defined and controversial. Thus, where one observer sees a clear and significant "collapse", another may see only an uninteresting "decline". A deeper version of this last problem concerns the "emergence" or otherwise of macro-level phenomena from micro level events (see Sec. 1.6). Just what constitutes "emergence", and just when it occurs, has proved to be highly controversial.

MODELLING PROCEDURE

1.3.5 Particular problems of computer simulation

Computer simulation presents its own particular difficulties that should be mentioned in passing. First, a computer-based model is likely to involve relatively many detailed assumptions, with the attendant problems discussed in the preceding section. A particular hazard for the computer-based modeller is to succumb to the richness of representation available and to fall into what may be called the "trap of verisimilitude" – to put plausible detail into the model program not because it is required, but just because it is plausible. (The complementary trap for the mathematical modeller may be called the "trap of tractability": to subordinate everything to being able to do something analytic with the model.)

Then there are decisions to be made about the choice of hardware and software platform. It is easy to be misled into using a simulation package (or DAI testbed) that is conveniently to hand but is actually quite inappropriate to the task. Whatever the language used, programs must be debugged and checked to do what they are intended to do (verification). This may be difficult and time-consuming, especially if a pseudo-random number generator is used to implement stochastic variables. Finding a suitably reliable and efficient pseudo-random number generator may itself be difficult.

Commonly, the computational load of running a particular trial of a simulation will be quite substantial. Conducting a soundly structured experiment, with balanced trials of particular combinations of parameter settings, suitably replicated, may take very substantial computer power indeed, especially in the case of some of the artificial intelligence models. Even the problem of viewing the experimental results, prior to interpreting them, can be very time-consuming unless there is good program support for tracking selected variables.

1.3.6 Models and theories

In the foregoing discussion we have neglected an important issue: the relationship between modelling and theory. Theory impacts upon modelling in important ways that need to be distinguished and considered.

By (established) theory we mean an agreed body of concepts and relationships between them, together with agreed processes of inference, and possibly conclusions linking structure to behaviour. It is important to recognize that *two* bodies of theory are at issue in any modelling exercise: one associated with the target, and the other associated with the model. For example, there may be a body of theory associated with a particular social system (early states, say), and a quite different body of theory associated with the mathematical equations used to specify its model (how to solve partial differential equations, say). Sometimes one of the two theoretical domains is given undue dominance in a modelling study. For example, a mathematical argument may be the centre of interest, with the associated application little more than initial motivation; alternatively, an elaborated piece of social theory may dominate with a minor piece of statistical modelling thrown in to make weight.

Those aspects of the target deemed relevant to the goals of the study are likely to be strongly determined by (target-oriented) theory, in the sense that there will be certain presuppositions about what is and what is not of importance. Limitations of target-oriented theory will lead to uncertainty about what are the right questions to ask, and hence to problems in choosing relevant and informative models.

On the other hand, in order to express target phenomena in a suitable model, it is necessary to know how versions of those phenomena can be created (to some acceptable degree of approximation) out of the available elements. It is therefore necessary to have some general theoretical understanding of how relevant phenomena may be synthesized. (Here model-oriented theory is at issue.) This may not be easy. For example, to construct within a model an inference process of a certain type (say, non-trivial multi-agent planning) may be beyond the state of the art. Indeed, merely to generate a particular sequence of values for some variable without explicitly listing them may be intractable. Put otherwise, there are sometimes *no* plausible models to choose from, at least none that can be precisely specified. In such a case, either the modelling exercise must be abandoned or an element of new theory building must be associated with model selection.

These issues of theory seem particularly relevant when modelling and simulating societies, as will appear in the next section.

1.4 Issues in modelling and simulating societies

There are special problems associated with modelling and simulating societies. For a start, there is the question of just what we mean by a society. One partial definition is that a society is any relatively isolated interacting collection of individuals, where the individuals are relatively "complex". Clearly, by this definition not all societies are composed of human beings. There is a myriad of societies of living organisms, there are societies of computers,

ISSUES IN MODELLING AND SIMULATING SOCIETIES

and robot societies are escaping from the pages of science fiction. Nevertheless, our focus is on human societies.

What is special about modelling or simulating human societies? The following list of characteristics of human societies must have an impact upon simulation:

(a) *Environment* – Human societies are embedded within, interact with, and are to some degree determined by, their environment. This environment will be physical, but may well include other human societies and even be dominated by them.

(b) *Complexity* – Whatever else they are, human societies are highly complex. This suggests that either a model must itself be complex (with all that implies for the difficulty of study), or the process of extracting the theoretical essentials to be embodied in the model must be particularly successful. It follows also that there are many alternative views of the society possible, e.g. micro and macro level, with different views suggesting very different model contents.

(c) *Distribution* – Human societies are spatially distributed. They are also distributed by way of internal grouping and functional specialization. So models that use concepts of distributed processing seem to have particular relevance.

(d) *Agency/cognition* – Human societies comprise individuals that have cognitive abilities, notably "rationality", awareness of others and of the society around them. This suggests that models that capture aspects of human cognition, for example mental models, planning and reflexivity, may be appropriate.

(e) *Communication* – Central to human social activity is natural language and other communication. Communication enables information sharing and co-ordinated action, which is the essence of society.

If these are accepted to be some of the fundamental characteristics of human societies, it seems to follow that a proposed model of human society that fails to express one or more of them must be correspondingly limited in its ability to provide answers to our questions.

Non-human societies fail to display one or more of the foregoing characteristics. For example, except in very limited ways, they do not include "rational" agents communicating in natural language. Although communication is present in many non-human societies, e.g. an ant community, a computer network, it is the use of natural language, with its richness of expression and content, that is special. To the extent that non-human societies are relatively simple, modelling them is somewhat easier than modelling human societies.

15

Unfortunately, there is a major problem in modelling human societies. There is no agreed theory of human societies to guide the modeller, no theory that will identify clearly and without controversy the key elements to be incorporated in the models or even the key considerations to have in mind as the model is designed. It is this that simulation might help to alleviate. Part of the problem is that we ourselves are within human society and therefore have great difficulty in seeing it clearly. That is one reason why archaeology and anthropology are prominent in this book. These disciplines are better placed than the other social sciences to attempt an external view of societies and are correspondingly receptive to simulation approaches (e.g. Doran 1991).

1.5 The work presented in this book

The chapters that follow cover a wide range of both social applications and model types. Two of the chapters, those of Séror (Ch. 2) and of Mithen (Ch. 8) are partly in the nature of reviews. Séror addresses social simulation in general (and therefore takes this introductory chapter further) and in particular focuses on the notion of a "garbage can" model for an organization. In such a model the organization is viewed as "a system of independent, exogenous flows of problems, solutions, decision-makers and choice opportunities". Mithen is much more specialized in the application he considers (hunter–gatherer societies). But the instances of modelling work he discusses, including notably his own and that of Reynolds (see also Ch. 10), illustrate well the diversity of approaches that are possible.

Troitzsch (Ch. 3) reports work with a model specified as a set of differential equations that express the interactions between, and hence predict the dynamics of, subpopulations within a general population. Different variants of his model relate to micro and macro levels of society. Nowak & Latané (Ch. 4) are concerned with social influence in a population and use computer simulation as a "derivation machine" to establish the "emergent group level consequences" of their micro-level specification of individuals. Penn & Dalton (Ch. 5) report studies of urban movement. Their computer simulation studies relate the mental maps that individuals have of their urban environment and observed population movements in towns and cities.

A number of the chapters are strongly influenced by the techniques and concepts of artificial intelligence studies. Thus Reynolds (Ch. 10) deploys insights from machine learning studies to formulate and test a "dual inheritance" model of cultural evolution, seeking to capture the interaction between the genetic and cultural levels. He uses an anthropological case study to demonstrate the validity of a simple version of his model.

A group of chapters apply methods associated with "distributed" artificial intelligence. Drogoul & Ferber (Ch. 6) explain how such methods may be used in simulation work and stress that they enable a bridge to be built between micro and macro perspectives on society. They describe a simulation of an ant colony. Bousquet et al. (Ch. 7) report a study of a fishing society located on the Niger delta in Mali that uses a similar approach. Doran et al. (Ch. 9) also use DAI methods, to address the development of relatively complex forms of society in the late Upper Palaeolithic period in southwestern France, and emphasize the significance of the interaction between agents' internal models of society and society itself. Caldas & Coelho (Ch. 11) are concerned with modelling an oligopoly from an economic perspective, and use laboratory experiments with human subjects to guide AI-based modelling. Their particular interest is to capture and to study the implications of bounded rationality.

Finally, Conte & Castelfranchi (Ch. 12) report work in another DAI tradition. Within a formal (rather than computational) framework, they show how knowledge of objective relations between agents in their environment can predict certain cognitive social actions of the agents, for example "influencing", and can predict certain social relationships between the agents, for example forms of co-operation and aggression.

1.6 Discussion

A number of points should be made about the work sketched in the last section and reported in detail in the remainder of the book:

- There are a diversity of types of model used and a diversity of types of application found for them. But there is little discussion of the criteria for choosing between different types of models in different circumstances.
- There is a recurring emphasis on the relationship between micro and macro views of society. A link is often made in the work reported between what happens within agents, and the macro behaviour that the simulated society shows.
- There is much use of artificial intelligence techniques, in particular with the idea that experimentation with a multiple-agent system model can

support crossing the bridge from the micro to the macro, using some notion of "emergence".

- A further idea associated with the use of artificial intelligence techniques is that they enable the modeller to work with the notion of "bounded rationality". That is, it is possible to build into a model individuals with an incomplete and possibly faulty knowledge of their world, and with heuristic or downright irrational ways of using their imperfect knowledge.
- In traditional terms, the studies are often methodologically incomplete. Most have *not* been carried through to a thorough validation of the model, and to a systematic study of it including sensitivity analysis.
- The methodological incompleteness of the studies can be linked to a lack of two kinds of theory: insufficient agreed theory about human or other societies, and insufficient artificial intelligence (and other) theory with which to build the models.

Following up this last point, progress in science, including social science, consists largely in the identification of precise models that are useful, valid and tractable. We see in the work presented here the beginning of that process of identification.

Chapter 2
Simulation of complex organizational processes:
a review of methods and their epistemological foundations

Ann C. Séror

This chapter reviews the literature on methodologies for the simulation of complex social behaviour and evaluates the ways in which they have been used in recent research in archaeology, economics, psychology and sociology. Special attention is paid to the theoretical framework appropriate to the methodology, and to the epistemological assumptions underlying the research strategy.

The applications of simulation methodologies considered here are drawn from macro and micro-organization analyses in the organization sciences, economics and psychology, as well as archaeology and sociology. Taken together, these applications and examples are exploratory, descriptive, explanatory, predictive and evaluative, depending on their specific research objectives; and they demonstrate a wide variety of strengths and limitations with regard to their respective objects. Recommendations focus on the fit between the research object and the design of a simulation methodology that integrates societal, organizational and individual levels of analysis by interfacing structural equation, stochastic process and dynamic systems models and artificial intelligence methodologies. The usefulness of new expert systems approaches to simulation will be emphasized as they capture the rule-based behavioural dynamics of organizational decision processes.

In the past five years few journal articles have reported applications of simulation methodologies to the study of organizations and society. The articles that have been published focus on computer-based manufacturing systems (Chaharbaghi 1991) and production and operations management (Scheller 1990; Berkley 1990; Rozenblit et al. 1990; Cedric 1990; Chaharbaghi et al. 1990), marketing and consumer research (Meyer et al. 1989; Krishnamurthi & Rangaswamy 1987), finance (Hiller 1991; Fox & Glynn 1989) and economics (Blundell et al. 1988; Caniglia 1988). Few articles

19

focus on organizations and organizational processes (Lant & Mezias 1990; Masuch & Lapotin 1989, Sterman 1989). The models discussed and tested in these studies represent organizational learning under varying conditions of environmental ambiguity (Lant & Mezias 1990) and ambiguous organizational choice under varying conditions of structure inspired by the "garbage can" metaphor (Masuch & Lapotin 1989), and examination of empirically derived decision rules yielding deterministic chaos (Sterman 1989).

The review of simulation methodologies presented in this chapter will show their usefulness in the analysis of organizational behaviour and suggest ways of integrating various approaches to study organization structures and processes.

2.1 Models and simulation of social systems

A model is a simplified and generalized image of reality (Meadows et al. 1982). Such abstract constructions can be built and evaluated only with respect to a specific reality and to the scientific or practical purposes they are conceived to serve. A social system is a set of actors, individuals or groups behaving in an interdependent pattern in order to adapt to environmental contingencies. The appropriate unit of analysis may be the individual, group, organization, society, nation or global economic and political community of nations. Models of social systems are designed to explore, describe, explain and predict system behaviours as well as to aid in prescribing appropriate policies for system leadership, co-operation and management.

Simulation models using computer technology have distinct advantages in certain situations over the bounded rationality of human reasoning powers (Meadows et al. 1982) :

- Some problems require a very precise answer from vast amounts of data under very limited time resources, such as the correction of a satellite orbit.
- The dynamics of social systems may involve a set of complicated interdependencies among a large number of components or units. Examples of such systems are complex production routines in manufacturing organizations and econometric forecasts of the behaviour of national economies.
- Interdisciplinary and multidisciplinary perspectives are necessary to analyze some policy problems such as public transportation investments and environmental impacts of new technologies.

MODELS AND SIMULATION OF SOCIAL SYSTEMS

- Errors resulting from incorrect decisions may be unacceptably costly or irreversible in terms of human life, such as in the management of spacecraft trajectories or air traffic control.

Simulation models focus particularly on system dynamics and they incorporate various epistemic views of the change or evolution of social systems. Models express change in several different ways: as growth, maturation or evolution of organisms or structures, as variations in exogenous variables operating upon or affecting a constant structure, as fluctuations resulting from random sampling or sampling of a given probability distribution, or as changes in the structural coefficients defining the model. The expression of change is closely related to the conception of time explicit or implicit in the model. For example, in neoclassical economic theory, social change takes place within a given social structure and may be considered mechanistic or Newtonian; on the other hand, in institutional economic theory, change is the result of changing social structure and is Darwinian or evolutionary in character (Radzicki 1990). In historical research the focus is not only on particular states of affairs but also on change over time; the emphasis is not forecasting future events but explaining complex problems over time. Meaning and reasons for actions are more prominent in explanation than physical causation (Ennals 1985). Dates are not significant in themselves, but their temporal sequence and coherence are critical.

These views of change are fundamental to the scientific objectives of simulation models and the research process. Requirements of the positivistic research process include explicit procedures which can be openly examined and criticized by the scientific community and replicated in subsequent studies. Simulation models serve this research process in several important ways (Meadows et al. 1982):

- The terms and assumptions of such models must be explicitly expressed. Definitions must be complete and underlying assumptions must be coherent. Specification of mathematical models assures the development of rigorous *a priori* frameworks.
- A priori specification of mathematical models assures their accessibility to scientific criticism and their replicability by other researchers.
- Simulation models are comprehensive in viewing the complexities of social processes, both in terms of their capacity to process a wide variety of information and in their analysis of interrelationships among variables over time.
- Given a complete set of assumptions and a fully specified model, simulation of complex processes may yield error-free results and conclusions.

As already stated, this may be particularly critical in technological decision-making or in social policy formulation where the risk of error is high and the cost of error cannot be recovered.

- Social experimentation using simulation models can explore a wide variety of conditions, variables, policies and underlying assumptions. The conduct of these experiments is less costly and more efficient than similar experimentation in the laboratory or the real world, provided that the phenomena under study are sufficiently well understood to be accessible to specification, and the limits of the procedure are made as explicit as the model itself.

The epistemological underpinnings of the scientific research process and its specific application in simulation models of social systems will be discussed on three dimensions: epistemological stance, scientific objective and validity. These dimensions will later be used to discuss the relation of the simulation models to reality. Two concepts of probability differentiate theory and reality (Voorrips 1987). First, the classical conception of the probability of an event is taken as a formal property of that event. It is the ratio of event occurrences to the number of possible occurrences, where each occurrence is equally possible. This conception of probability applies to theory. In consideration of reality, the probability of an event is the outcome of an infinite series of trials which might be observable in empirical reality. As Voorrips (1987: 70) states, "The link between abstraction and reality is the analogy between the "classical" and the "frequency" approach to probability." Models may be formal or empirical representations. The objective is to extend the applicability of a model to as many empirical realities as possible to demonstrate its generalizability.

The simulation methodologies discussed in this chapter will be presented according to theoretical or disciplinary perspectives which determine their assumptions and condition their interpretation. These perspectives have been selected for their potential for understanding the behavioural aspects of organizations and their environments as social systems, including internal structures and processes as well as the constraints of external environments. They conceive the social system in different ways: as an organized (or chaotic) collection of individual actors or decision-makers, as an holistic entity interacting with its environment, or as a global system of causal links and flows of economic goods broadly defined. The theoretical or disciplinary perspectives considered here are the garbage can model, the physical symbol system and institutional dynamics models. Simulation methodologies will be considered in light of these theoretical frameworks, their

MODELS AND SIMULATION OF SOCIAL SYSTEMS

underlying assumptions and epistemological foundations. In particular, the view of organizational or institutional systems and their representation in simulation models will be discussed.

2.1.1 The garbage can model

The garbage can model of organizational choice was elaborated as an alternative to the pervasive view of intentional organizational decision-making (March & Olsen 1986) and its tenets: a knowledge of alternatives and their consequences, consistent individual or collective preferences, and a set of decision rules. The major weaknesses of this view are its treatment of information and time as freely available resources, the assumption of goal consensus and negotiated conflict management, and the assumption of the unique determination of organizational decisions by environmental constraints.

The garbage can theory views the organization (anarchy) as a system of independent, exogenous flows of problems, solutions, decision-makers and choice opportunities. Association among these flows is determined by their arrival and departure times as well as by structural constraints on access to opportunities. Access is modulated by structural constraints and simultaneity. In the original model (Cohen et al. 1972) three decision structures were considered. In the first, *unsegmented*, structure any actor may participate in any choice opportunity. In the second, *hierarchical*, structure access to choice opportunities increases with level in hierarchy; and in the third, *specialized*, structure each actor has specialized participation in choice. This view of the organization implies the discovery of preferences through action, rather than preferences as an *a priori* basis for action. Actors in the organization are not aware of the organization's own processes which proceed on a trial-and-error basis. This model places its emphasis on the choice behaviour of the individual actor and on collective behaviour as its aggregate. Individual goals are held by individual actors, and organizational goals are simply defined as widely held individual goals. Choice opportunities are the result of organizational routines, external events or hierarchical instructions and are viewed by decision-makers as opportunities to achieve individual goals and satisfy individual preferences (Anderson & Fisher 1986).

Explanation of events in the garbage can model is temporal but not consequential, since choice opportunities are assumed to be exercised by virtue of their simultaneity at a particular point in time with problems, solutions and decision-makers. This conception of time is logical, but the manifestation of logical relations is not sequential; it is based on the random simul-

SIMULATION OF COMPLEX ORGANIZATIONAL PROCESSES

taneity of the model's elements. The passage from one choice opportunity to another is therefore not logical; logic is rather inherent in the exercise of choice under randomly occurring conditions of simultaneity among problems, solutions and decision-makers.

Simulations of organizational decision-making processes based on the garbage can model have included a number of variations in the model (March & Olsen 1986). The main parameters have been the structural characteristics of flows or problems; solutions and decision-makers and their access to choice opportunities; the assumptions concerning the flows (such as their random components), energy resources and deadlines; and the system-awareness of decision-makers. It is of interest to note that, where decision-makers become more aware of system processes, gaming may become more explicit among decision-makers.

In the original garbage can simulation (Cohen et al. 1972), the following were specified: a set of fixed parameters including the number of time periods (20) number of choice opportunities (10), number of decision-makers (10), number of problems (20), and solutions for choices; entry times for choices; entry times for problems; net energy load; organization access structure; organization decision structure; and energy distribution among decision-makers. All possible combinations of organizational dimensions were considered, with four combinations of choice and entry times yielding 324 simulation situations. The results reveal that important problems are more likely to be solved than unimportant ones; that important choices tend to be made more often by oversight and flight while unimportant choices are made by resolution; and that decision-makers and problems tend to track each other from choice to choice.

Anderson & Fischer (1986) varied the original garbage can model in three ways. First, individual decision-makers are vehicles to carry solutions and problems to choice opportunities; they are not an independent stream within the organization. Secondly, solutions are directly represented as organizational courses of action that influence problems. Thirdly, problems are individual and may or may not be shared by other organizational actors. Individual problems are justified by their identity with organizational objectives and they are distinguished from personal problems in the requirement of organizational resources for their solution. The Anderson–Fischer model was tested using a Monte Carlo method which allowed comprehensive sampling of the parameter space. The design of the experiment was a full factorial, with five organizational structures, two goal structures, three levels of choice density and three levels of technology yielding 90 cells, for

MODELS AND SIMULATION OF SOCIAL SYSTEMS

each of which there were 30 model runs. The total sample of observations was 2700; for each run there were 20 time periods, 10 individuals, 10 solutions, 21 goals and 10 choice opportunity types. The most striking result was the superior performance of undifferentiated organizational structure under conditions of neutral or favourable technology with relatively greater goal consensus and less conflict among decision-makers.

Carley (1986a,b) tested efficiency in a garbage can hierarchy using a simulation program (GARCORG). The organizational structure has four tiers (Padgett 1980) where the command flows downward and decisions flow upward through the hierarchy. Staff members occupy positions where information is received for analysis and decision-making. Information is characterized by amount and content, and these parameters may be modelled by either stochastic or deterministic processes. Carley's model, unlike Padgett's (1980), does not specify fixed organizational membership but provides for the hiring or firing of human resources as well as their transfer through a series of positions according to the availability of information concerning the issue at hand, the quality or content of the information and the saliency of the work as seen from the upper hierarchical (chief executive officer) level. Efficiency is measured by position valuation and availability of a competent staff member. The simulated movement of personnel is based on a mechanism which may be either deterministic or stochastic (for example, a Markov process).

The GARCORG program allows simulation of as many organizations as there are combinations of specified features. Since features are functionally independent, simulated observations on a particular organizational type may be averaged. The results of the simulation show, for example, that small differentiated organizations are more efficient than large undifferentiated organizations. The author points out that this simulation method is particularly useful for the comparison of different organizational scenarios specified on dimensions such as efficiency.

Masuch & Lapotin (1989) report an elaboration of the garbage can model of organizational choice based on artificial intelligence techniques to invoke a symbol driven decision-making process. This simulation considers each actor in a communication network making decisions according to search strategy, cognitive capacity, individual aspirations, preferences, workload and commitment. Perhaps the most original feature of the model is the determination of breadth and depth of search. The number of steps per decision is limited, and the search is terminated when the actor reaches that limit, thereby operationalizing bounded rationality.

SIMULATION OF COMPLEX ORGANIZATIONAL PROCESSES

All possible combinations of two parameters are explored, with other variables held constant at intermediate values, to some extent consistent with the original garbage can model. Some assumptions, such as the individual actor's ties with 20 per cent of an organization's members, are open to question, but their consequences can be examined because they have been made explicit. A Monte Carlo simulation design allowed exploration of the complete parameter space by 30 repetitions of 619 simulations over 20 time periods. Analyses of simulation data included step-wise regression to examine five dimensions of performance and analysis of variance to identify significant differences among types of organizations. The independent variables of the actors' commitment and cognitive capacity are the most significant in the regressions. Hierarchical authority relations appear to contribute to performance only if commitment is low.

All of the garbage can simulation models summarized here raise questions about their relation to reality (Anderson & Fischer 1986; Masuch & Lapotin 1989). Masuch and Lapotin suggest validation of such models by examining their underlying assumptions and their realism before testing specific predictions with empirical research. This suggestion places emphasis on theory elaboration supported with AI models and techniques to generate theoretical propositions and hypotheses for testing. The computer model is the instrument for theory development in this "top down" simulation approach. The examples of garbage can simulation studies show how models can be used to vary underlying assumptions and evaluate alternative organization structures under specified conditions.

2.1.2 The physical symbol system

The underlying metaphor of applications of artificial intelligence techniques and expert systems methods to organizational modelling is the physical symbol system (Newell & Simon 1976). A physical symbol system obeys the laws of physics, and may be created from engineered components.

A physical symbol system consists of a set of entities, called symbols, which are physical patterns that can occur and components of another type of entity called an expression (or symbol structure). Thus a symbol structure is composed of a number of instances (or tokens) of symbols related in some physical way. At any instant of time the system will contain a collection of these symbol structures. Besides these structures the system also contains a collection of processes that operate on expressions to produce other expressions:

processes of creation, modification, reproduction and destruction. A physical symbol system is a machine that produces through time an evolving collection of symbol structures. Such a system exists in a world of objects wider than just these symbolic expressions themselves. (Newell & Simon 1976: 116)

The physical symbol system is capable of two major functions: *designation*, which specifies access to an object via an expression, and *interpretation*, which carries out a process designated by an expression. The system must also satisfy other requirements of completeness and closure (Newell & Simon 1976): a symbol may be used to designate any expression; every process of which the machine is capable is designated by an expression; there exist processes for creating and modifying any expression; expressions are stable and exist until modified or deleted; and the system may contain an unbounded number of expressions.

From this description of the physical symbol system is derived the *physical symbol system hypothesis*, a law of qualitative structure specifying a general class of systems capable of intelligent action:

A physical symbol system has the necessary and sufficient means for general intelligent action. (Newell & Simon 1976: 116)

The implications of the physical symbol system hypothesis extend to individual and organizational behaviour. Organizational culture and language may be considered a set of symbols, and the physical symbol hypothesis contributes to linking organizational intelligence to both individual actors (Masuch & Lapotin 1989) and organizations themselves (Blanning 1991). This view of the organization is rather mechanistic; according to Blanning (1991), both organizations and intelligent machines are artefacts constructed by social actors to help them apply knowledge and experience to problem-solving. The expression of intelligence in the physical symbol system takes the form of heuristic search by generating and modifying symbol structures until a solution structure is identified. Heuristic search is necessary because of the limited resources available to support the problem-solving process. This feature of the physical symbol system makes it a particularly appropriate metaphor for organizations and organizational decision-making. The locus of the decision-making process may be viewed in three ways: within the individual decision-maker, as a property of the organization, or distributed among interacting organizational entities, individuals or groups.

In contrast to the process modelling originally used by engineers to represent production by strictly mathematical specification, expert systems approaches, with their heuristic rule-based manipulation of symbols, permit modelling of complex behaviour and decision-making processes that are inaccessible to mathematical identification. Applications and examples include historical explanation (Ennals 1985), reproduction of social structures (Banerjee 1986), foreign policy (Anderson & Thorson 1982), organizational decision-making (Blanning 1990) and design (Baligh et al. 1986), exchange (Hoffman et al. 1986; Doran 1987) and distributed knowledge-based systems in social networks (Doran 1989; Carlson & Ram 1990).

Ennals (1985) considers the historian's analysis and explanation of events consisting of explicit and implicit components. The data are explicit; they are the facts and rules that describe historical events and contexts. On the other hand, the historian's belief system is implicit, apparent in the framing or perspective of answers to questions based on data, and in the resolution of inconsistencies or conflicts in the data. The collaborative problem-solving system represents the dialogue of the historian with his or her evidence. Other information is not contained in the database but rather is elicited from the user and transferred to the system database. Other examples use logic programming to combine factual information and incorporate different possible outcomes of decision-making.

Another application (Banerjee 1986) presents an artificial intelligence model of reproduction of social structures based on a Piagetian concept of culture. According to this view, the major defining feature of social structure is the repetition of its component actions and behaviours. Social structure is derived from the cognitive processes and behaviours of individuals and groups. Central to Piaget's analysis is the concept of "action schemata" integrating behaviour and meaning. Human action is not simply a mechanical response to a stimulus, but reception of the stimulus signifies its assimilation in a schema manifested by the response. A collective set of integrated schemata constitute a shared system of meaning or culture (Piaget 1977), guiding the repertoire of possible behaviour. Social action schemata give rise to reproducing social structures and enduring patterns of social interaction.

Banerjee's (1986) computer model of social interaction includes three levels of hierarchy. The first level includes knowledge bases representing the preferences and causal beliefs of the subjects; the second level represents social action schemata deriving from constructs of stimulus, goal and act; the third level of hierarchy is the reproduction module with subjects' response to the previous round. Social action schemata guide action by identifying stimuli, matching goals, selecting actions to achieve goals, and monitoring the environment for goal achievement (reinforcement). Since schema

MODELS AND SIMULATION OF SOCIAL SYSTEMS

repetition occurs only after goal achievement, only socially successful schemata are repeated. Banerjee (1986) points out that this program cannot represent a creative process, but it does demonstrate that a knowledge base is sufficient for reproduction of social structures. The model also provides a tool for the study of relationships between beliefs and actions in structural evolution and social learning.

Anderson & Thorson (1982) show the application of artificial intelligence systems simulation to the development of theories of foreign policy behaviour of national governments or individual political actors. Such behaviour can be explained and modelled only through both teleological and causal explanation. Teleological explanation refers to the intentions, norms and customs that motivate a particular social behaviour; the significant dimension of the behaviour is its meaning. Causal explanation, on the other hand, makes reference to the deductive-nomological form; this explanation is founded in general laws relating prior conditions and their effects.

Foreign policy is defined as goal-directed activity by communities or states to adapt their own behaviour to the international environment and to affect the behaviour of other states in ways consistent with national or community goals. The goal-directed nature of foreign policy behaviour makes it particularly appropriate to rule-based simulation techniques. According to Anderson & Thorson (1982), the advantages of these techniques include the framing of a perspective from the point of view of the actor or decision-maker, the direct representation of context through a symbol processing system, and the active interpretation of a policy-making environment.

The simulation examples presented to illustrate foreign policy decision-making are interactive, giving the user the opportunity to manipulate an international environment and produce policy actions. The examples are composed of a set of independent decision rules of the form:

$$\text{CONDITION} \rightarrow \text{ACTION.}$$

The condition is a set of symbols describing the current environmental state defined as the ambient information structure (AIS). The action component of the decision rule results in modifications to the AIS and statements describing the actions taken in the simulation.

One of the simulations represents the policy-making behaviour of the government of Saudi Arabia. The hypothetical government receives information from the domestic environment simulated using difference equations, and manipulates parameters in these simulations in order to achieve goals. In addition, the simulated government interacts with its international environment by an interpretive methodology permitting integration of symbol content with its context. For example, the representation of "The US will sell arms to Israel" varies in its interpretation depending on the context of Arab–Israeli conflict. The most prominent feature of this simulation is its integration of causal and interpretive dimensions to portray complex foreign policy and provide a methodology for rigorous experimentation.

Blanning (1990) and Baligh et al. (1986) consider intelligent organizational models and organizational design using expert systems techniques within a functionalist perspective. Blanning examines the use of heuristic search techniques to model organizations. Expert systems techniques are used to describe organizational structures in a knowledge base, to express descriptions of organizational processes as meta knowledge, and to carry out intelligent inferencing and explanation to simulate and explain organizational decisions. The model is a collection of situation/action rules, with backward chaining to determine the decision steps to be taken. The organization is defined as a system of co-operating subunits. The organizational objective selected for illustrative modelling is the preparation of an estimate of the company's net income for the following year based on gross sales and total cost estimates prepared by marketing and manufacturing subunits. The sequence of events is determined by the availability of information. The simulation is interactive so that information not provided by any of the simulated organization subunits is requested from the system user.

In addition to information from organizational subunits and procedures for its integration, other information is helpful to make the simulation more realistic and to guide the decision-making process: the agreement of subunits on estimates and sequencing of consultations, the reliability of subunit information, the efficiency of the search process, and the justification of organizational recommendations. This additional information is modelled as a set of meta-rules. The model provides an explanation for its results by explaining the sequence of reasoning steps and by explaining requests for information. This explanatory capability may contribute to understanding of the ways organizations behave.

Baligh et al. (1986) develop an expert systems approach to the analysis of organizational design using contingency theory drawn from the models of Duncan (1972) and Perrow (1967). These two models are integrated and translated into a rule-based expert system relating structure, centralization, formalization and complexity to analysis of organization environments and technology by use of if–then rules. The special problems of this approach are the construction of an expert system from information gleaned from the literature, and the use of descriptive and explanatory theory for the simulation of organization designs and the formulation of prescriptive recommendations. These authors do not adequately demonstrate that statements describing the ways that observed organizations function can be presented as normative statements of the ways that organizations "should" function. Another difficulty in their approach is the use of complex constructs such as organization strategy in a goal-driven program with no database. The expert system application is more useful to simulate organizational designs emerging from environmental and technological conditions than to formulate normative recommendations.

The final set of examples of expert systems approaches includes exchange and distributed knowledge-based systems. The first example (Hoffman et al. 1986) focuses on the modelling of microeconomic systems integrating both mathematical process modelling of physical processes and expert systems approaches to capture behavioural dimensions. Emphasis is also placed on the use of expert systems as data generators to study the impact of institutional changes on bidder strategy. Both expert systems and process models require detailed knowledge about the problem domain for their specification, and they invoke transformation rules linking an initial state (inputs) to a goal state (outputs). In process models, these links are purely mathematical structures, while in expert systems models, they consist of pattern-based rules of action. In process models, data are generated from the solution of optimization problems over varying parameters.

In Hoffman's models of *first price sealed bid* and *English* auctions, the problem consists of two stages: the auction process and the decision process for bid determination. An auction is defined as a set of individuals bidding on an object for sale by an auctioneer. The process may be static, with one bid per bidder, or it may be dynamic, with cycles of revisions based on new information input during the process. The major strength of the expert system approach is its reliance on rules representing a wide variety of decision-making behaviour as well as optimal strategies for bid determination. This methodology is useful for simulation of varying bid strategies for theoretical comparisons among them and for their evaluation in light of empirical observations of naturally occurring bidding behaviour.

Other examples have been published in anthropological archaeology (Doran 1987, 1989; see also Chs 8 & 9 of this volume). The common objective of these models is to understand the organization and evolution of human cultural systems. Their application could include, for example, the study of resource distribution, warfare, or the social dynamics of emergence of chiefdoms (Doran 1987). TEAMWORK, EXCHANGE, and CONTRACT programs address the behaviour of multi-actor systems with differentiated contributions to a common task environment, concurrent goal-directed activities, requests among actors for information and action, and successive delegation of responsibilities. The CONTRACT model represents a socio-cultural system as a contract structure among its actors. Contracts are similar to exchange agreements, but without specified structure, and vary in value to actors involved. Contracts based on other contracts may create a hierarchical structure. A set of probabilistic rules determine the state of the system at which a contract may be added or deleted. Thus, the socio-cultural system is a function of co-operative structures and environmental variations derived from the aggregate of local behaviour and decisions (Doran 1987, 1989).

A final example (Carlson & Ram 1990) presents a system that specifies co-operation among multiple knowledge-based systems. The interactive program implements a hierarchical organization of problem solvers with top-down delegation of all user requests. The advantages of such a design are as follows (Carlson & Ram 1990: 271):

- modelling real-world knowledge that has natural, spatial or semantic separation;
- providing a modular architecture for large AI systems;
- integrating existing, heterogeneous knowledge-based systems;
- interconnecting multiple knowledge-based systems to solve a problem for which individual systems have incomplete knowledge, but collectively can develop a solution.

The construction of systems for narrow problem domains facilitates knowledge acquisition from specialized individual experts. The major problem of the approach is to integrate multiple simulated actors and co-ordinate their individual inferences in coherent decision-making. Through intention or commitment specified in a social belief profile, choices between equally likely alternative actions can be resolved within the network. The model represents the interaction of a profile of beliefs for each individual, practices defining the social belief profile for each community, and institutional rules and structures controlling multiple network channels of communication. The communities used to illustrate multiple community membership are American and Japanese culture, engineering and business disciplines, and academic and practitioner orientations. An actor resolves conflicts among belief profiles held by the communities of which he or she is a member by assigning priorities among community beliefs and those uniquely held by the

MODELS AND SIMULATION OF SOCIAL SYSTEMS

individual, such as moral or ethical beliefs. The control strategy suggested would select and establish communication channels among agents, activate communities and methods relevant to each actor's decision-making context, resolve conflicting methodologies among activated communities for individual actors, and derive inferences required for goal achievement.

These examples of expert systems approaches to the simulation of organizations and other social systems demonstrate the usefulness of the physical symbol system hypothesis for the representation and interpretation of individual and collective behaviour. These approaches provide a tool for theory development, experimentation with simulated social systems, data generation, and interpretation (Doran 1989). The physical symbol system hypothesis provides a conceptual framework for representation of theory for modelling and testing.

2.1.3 Institutional dynamics

Another theoretical perspective lending itself to a simulation methodology is institutional dynamics (Radzicki 1988, 1990): a synthesis of institutional economics and system dynamics. This approach is based on the holistic pattern model of explanation constructed from detailed empirical case studies, originally elaborated by John Commons (Wilber & Harrison 1978). Empirical case studies are researched by participant observers who seek the structural "themes" explaining the wholeness of the organization within its social and economic context. Pattern modelling is particularly accessible to system dynamics simulation methodologies. System dynamics is itself a quantitative pattern modelling process drawn from systems analysis, control theory and continuous simulation (Radzicki 1988).

The system dynamics view of organizations and societies is very similar to the institutional economists' view:

- Goal-seeking behaviour is exhibited by the system in interaction with its internal and external environments. For example, values, rules, customs, habits, incentives, moral and technological constraints, material and information flows and other factors influence the goals selected and the processes by which they are pursued.
- A consequence of goal-seeking behaviour is the existence of feedback structures for transmission and return of information.
- The principle of accumulation "uncouples" flows in system feedback loops through the existence of stocks, such as inventory in a production system.

SIMULATION OF COMPLEX ORGANIZATIONAL PROCESSES

- Bounded rationality characterizes the adaptive learning process, and a small number of information flows is considered at any given decision.
- The cumulative effects of negative (stabilizing) and positive (destabilizing) feedback cause system behaviour. In this sense, system causation is endogenous; it is not brought on by external variations or shocks, but by the way feedback structures process external events.
- Events and structure may be understood only in context.
- Systems evolve in a state of disequilibrium caused by conflict in pursuit of opposing or incompatible goals.
- Generic structures emerge when a particular combination of feedback loops gives rise to particular qualitative behaviour (e.g. damped oscillation) in a variety of different systems.
- Identification of generic structures directs the researcher's attention to the generation of a combination of loops in the analysis of new systems.

The foregoing set of dynamic system characteristics has certain consequences for a system's evolutionary adjustment to the environment. Socioeconomic systems adjust their structures to technological changes through endogenous closed-loop feedback. Structural adjustment to a new pattern of relationships can occur only if this pattern is recognized by system actors, and if some continuity is maintained between an existing pattern and the new pattern. Radzicki (1988, 1990) emphasizes the integration of qualitative variables as well as absolutely measurable parameters in institutional dynamics models. Table functions (Randers 1973), for example, permit subjective specification of relative changes in "metaphysical" dimensions and their effects on other variables. New applications of qualitative simulation methodologies are being developed which may prove promising for the specification of institutional dynamics models (Dolado 1992).

Special insights drawn from the study of deterministic chaos and self-organizing systems may also be specified in institutional analysis (Radzicki 1990). These modes of steady-state behaviour have been described in the institutional economics literature but there are few examples of their application to the study of organizations or other socioeconomic systems. Nevertheless, they are of particular interest to future research on social systems. Deterministic chaos is generated in the system model by destabilizing mechanisms, such as positive feedback, and by nonlinear constraints, such as human values. Systems specified in this way are very sensitive to their initial conditions, with the result that they cannot be used to predict future system states from initial states.

MODELS AND SIMULATION OF SOCIAL SYSTEMS

The theory of self-organizing systems is also based on a thermodynamically open system view (Prigogine & Stengers 1984). This view reconciles biological and physical system concepts of evolution. The total change in a system's entropy is the sum of the entropy from internal processes and negentropy imported from the environment. Three categories of such systems are considered: (1) systems in equilibrium, where $d_eS = -d_iS$ and total entropy production is zero ($dS = 0$); (2) systems near equilibrium, where $d_eS < d_iS$; and (3) systems far from equilibrium, where $d_eS < -d_iS$. The first two categories are characterized by maximum total entropy, uniformity and disorganization, while the third category of systems in a state far from equilibrium tend towards new structures of increased complexity and variety.

Radzicki (1990) presents an illustrative model of social revolution originally designed by Mosekilde et al. (1983). This model represents a society with two major political parties, hawks and doves, and a politically uncommitted group of "fence-sitters". The political composition of the society determines national budget spending. The major dynamic of the model is conversion of the uncommitted actors to one of the political parties, a process determined by three factors: the normal conversion rates for hawks and doves, a randomly generated stream of stochastic influences representing unpredictable behaviour, and social tension in the society due, for example, to the introduction of new technology, actions by another nation or internal economic strife. The third factor affects model behaviour only when a threshold for social tension is exceeded. Hawks and doves may also defect from their political parties and revert to uncommitted status. This simulation was run for 48 periods (months) and revealed three evolutionary periods. The first phase (periods 0–11) shows random fluctuations about the steady state arising from to random political behaviour. In the second phase, the threshold for social tension was exceeded, and a struggle for control of the society between hawks and doves ensued, represented by a "bandwagon" effect of self-reinforcing behaviour through positive feedback loops. In the third and final phase (periods 18–48), the doves gained control of the system through a self-organizing revolution. Dominance reverts to negative feedback loops, and a near-equilibrium state results. It is important to note that these simulation results are not robust, but are extremely sensitive to small parameter changes.

In a related stream of economics research (Sterman 1988, 1989), major preoccupations in developing the simulation methodology include the derivation of models from empirical evidence describing observed decision rules and the incorporation of action feedback permitting assessment of the rela-

SIMULATION OF COMPLEX ORGANIZATIONAL PROCESSES

tion between behaviour and environmental responses. Sterman (1989) simulated the capital investment decision specified by econometric estimation of a decision rule based on empirical data from a laboratory experiment with student subjects. Assumptions of the experimental and simulation methodology include perfect information for decision-making. The experiment and simulation show that chaos can arise from the behaviour of actual agents.

Suggestions for future research include modelling of micro-subsystems contributing to global system behaviour and specification of both deterministic and stochastic parameters to represent more accurately alternating periods of social stability and revolution (Radzicki 1990). Sterman (1987, 1989) suggests ways to relate experimental evidence and simulation methodologies. These strategies may begin with identification of formal decision rules or structural assumptions (Sterman 1987), or the starting point may be specification of a model from empirical data (Sterman 1989).

The comparison of results from laboratory experiments and behavioral simulation models does not validate the model as a representation of reality but does contribute to validation of underlying assumptions to show "people behave the same way the model presumes them to behave" (Sterman 1987: 1577).

The foregoing sections have presented three broad approaches to the understanding of behavioural aspects of organization and their simulation. Other approaches may also offer promising avenues for future research, such as the information processing view developed by Mack (1991) based on Malone (1987) and Galbraith (1977), the organizational learning perspective applied to strategic behaviour (Lant & Mesias 1990), and narrative positivism (Abbott 1990, 1992; Aminzade 1992; Griffin 1992; Quadagno & Knapp 1992).

The next section of the chapter will focus on comparison of the three major models: garbage can models, physical symbol systems and institutional dynamics.

2.2 Epistemological dimensions of simulation methodologies

The foregoing theoretical orientations with their simulation methodologies will be compared on three dimensions in order to discuss the relation between the theories, simulation methodologies and the reality they are constructed to represent:

EPISTEMOLOGICAL DIMENSIONS OF METHODOLOGIES

(a) *Epistemological stance* This dimension represents the continuum from interpretive to positivistic approaches to reality.

(b) *Scientific objective* The simulation framework seeks to explain and understand reality, or to predict future events and behaviour.

(c) *Validity* The relation between theory and empirical reality is evaluated in different ways, emphasizing formal models or empirical data as starting points for simulation procedures and their validation.

First, the fundamental epistemological stance and its core ontological assumptions vary from a view of reality as a social construction, embedded in context (interpretive), to a view of reality as a fully observable, measurable and objective phenomenon (positivist). The epistemological stance has profound consequences for the representation of human nature and conceptualization of time and causation. In the interpretive view the human being is a consciousness, a constructor of social reality and a manipulator; while in the positivist view the human being is a responder to the environment, either as a biological organism or as a machine. The garbage can model views the individual as a machine moving through the organizational decision process in an exogenous flow, subject to random simultaneity with organizational problems and solutions. When choice opportunities, problems and their solutions occur simultaneously, the individual decider *responds* by demonstrating problem-solving behaviour. In the original model, the individual decider is unaware of organizational processes or aggregate goals and preferences, but discovers these realities through a trial-and-error process. The relation among events is explained by simultaneity of organizational flows and the random presentation of exogenous organizational contingencies.

The physical symbol system obeys the laws of physics and may be created from engineered components. Physical symbol systems are made up of symbol structures performing the processes of designation and interpretation. These systems belong to a general class of systems capable of intelligent actions as stated in the physical symbol system hypothesis. Such systems are of particular interest because they may encompass aspects of both interpretive and positivist realities. Rule-based representations of decision-making specify both the subjective frame of the decider and the objective behaviour of the decider when a rule is applied or an action schema is reinforced. The production system, individual or organization possesses intelligence for adaptation to the environment or decision context. The process of rule-based decision-making is reversible and exogenously determined.

The thermodynamic open system of institutional dynamics views social systems as subject to endogenous change. The conception of time is Darwinian, and irreversible in nature. Change originates in the social structures of the model specification and may tend towards uniformity or towards higher orders of complexity and variety. Change is also a function of an actor's awareness of system dynamics in contrast to the garbage can view. The institutional dynamics simulation methodology is a holistic approach, focusing on the internal consistency of a detailed case study. It is a rigorously specified representation of a dominantly interpretive reality.

The second dimension, the *scientific objective* of the research process, is the explanatory or predictive relation of the model to its reality. The garbage can model and simulation examples show how data can be generated to explain organizational behaviour on specified dimensions or variables and to develop hypotheses to predict empirically observed behaviour: nomological theory is developed to compare organizational structures and processes and to develop scientifically useful general laws.

The physical symbol system hypothesis and examples of expert systems simulation methodologies show how the unit of analysis may vary from the individual decider to the institutional system. The research objectives are the explanation of relations between social values, beliefs and actions, and the prediction of the effects of values and beliefs upon social actions. The expert systems simulation examples integrate both teleological and causal explanation. Causality may be represented in the decision-makers' ideographic belief systems as well as in the deductive–nomological form founded on general laws relating prior conditions and their effects.

Institutional dynamics models are case-based, holistic representations of an internally consistent system. As suggested in Radzicki's (1990) example, simulations of chaotic systems are highly sensitive to initially specified conditions. The simulation is therefore not useful to predict future states from initial states of the system; the explanatory focus is on the dynamics of change from one mode of behaviour to another, such as the change from a chaotic to a non-chaotic model or pattern of behaviour. Such changes are the representation of the model's active structure that mimic the evolutionary behaviour of social systems. These changes are illustrated in Radzicki's (1990) example of transitions through three phases of system behaviour. When the evolution of a real social system closely approaches the evolutionary behaviour of the model, its specification is validated and the model may then be used to simulate the effects of policy decisions and other contextual variations.

It is of interest to note that the explanatory processes of expert systems and institutional dynamics models differ in fundamental ways. In the expert

CONCLUSIONS AND RECOMMENDATIONS

systems models, social structures and individual decision-making behaviour are reinforced and reproduced by a process of positive feedback, for example goal achievement. On the other hand, in institutional dynamics models positive feedback has a destabilizing effect, causing social "revolution" and higher-order structure with increased variety and complexity.

The third dimension, *validity* and its evaluation, further differentiates the simulation models presented here (Hogarth 1986). The garbage can model is a basis for "top-down" theory development and empirical testing. The simulation models can be used for the specification of a detailed parameter space and to generate data, particularly by Monte Carlo simulation techniques, for elaboration of theoretical hypotheses which may then be tested by empirical observation. Associations and causal relationships between model variables may be tested using a nomological–deductive research process.

The physical symbol system, on the other hand, requires knowledge engineering to elicit detailed rule-based decision-making routines from experts for each knowledge domain considered. Empirical data serve as a basis for specification of the rule-based system in this "bottom-up" development of theoretical frameworks from empirical reality. Integrated process models can combine nomological models of economic environments and rule-based representation of decision-making behaviour.

The institutional dynamics models demonstrate a holistic representation of a social system specified from a detailed empirical case analysis, identifying all interrelated factors that may affect the system. The validity of the model, which may incorporate elements of chaos theory or self-organizing systems, is then evaluated in terms of the extent to which its behaviour approaches the naturally occurring behaviour of the real social system. This evaluation is not focused on the degree to which the model predicts future states, but on the extent to which it replicates system alternation between stability and revolution.

2.3 Conclusions and recommendations

The theoretical perspectives and simulation methodologies presented in this chapter show particular promise for future research on social systems, particularly for modelling complex goal-directed behaviour. Simulation methodologies cannot be considered without an organizing theoretical framework which gives meaning to specified parameters and model dynamics.

SIMULATION OF COMPLEX ORGANIZATIONAL PROCESSES

These methodologies contribute to scientific inquiry in the following ways:

— They offer frameworks in which models of social systems can be specified with rigorous attention to explicit underlying assumptions. These frameworks may specify either nomological systems of relationships among variable dimensions as in the garbage can model, rule-based descriptions of decision-making behaviour, or detailed institutional dynamics models based on holistic pattern analysis of social system evolution.

— The relationship between theory and empirical reality is in some examples "top-down" and in others "bottom-up". The garbage can simulations show their usefulness as tools to generate theory and hypotheses for empirical testing, while the expert systems and institutional dynamics approaches rely on bottom-up model specification from empirical reality.

— The validation of these models of social systems depends on iterative verification with respect to empirical reality, whether this process is "top-down" or "bottom-up".

Simulation methodologies for the study of social systems should be designed to represent the particular characteristics of subsystems and the dynamics by which they interact. Such methodologies will be particularly appropriate in administrative sciences for the study of cultural differences among social organizations and the behavioral dimensions of new information technologies.

Chapter 3
The evolution of technologies

Klaus G. Troitzsch

The evolution of technologies may be considered in several ways, as other contributions to this volume show. My approach is based on the relations between different technologies and on the dependence of the number of people applying a certain kind of technology on that technology's success.

Modelling the evolution of technologies in a fragmented population requires a tool that allows the specification of a population as a whole with its properties, of several subpopulations with their properties, and of the individuals that make up the subpopulations. Moreover, it is necessary to specify the relations between the attributes of the objects at these three levels. For such purposes, members of my group have been developing a model specification and simulation tool (MIMOSE, an acronym for "Micro and multilevel modelling software environment") for the past four years.

We start from a simple model which was developed by the Ukrainian author Igor V. Chernenko for three populations using three different kinds of production processes. We then extend his model, thus generalizing it, first by introducing a variable number of subpopulations and their related technologies, then by analyzing the model on a micro, i.e. individual, level.

3.1 Basic assumptions

Chernenko (1989) analyzes how successive forms of social production evolved historically. The author enumerates three kinds of production process:
- "acquisitive" hunters' and gatherers' production,
- agrarian production,
- industrial production.

THE EVOLUTION OF TECHNOLOGIES

The focus of his analysis is on the quantities of products that are produced in the three sectors and the way the three sectors influence one another.

Generally speaking, he supposes that the increment in existing quantities of goods can be written as the difference between the quantities of goods produced (gains) and the losses arising from decomposition and decay, where gains are dependent on natural resources, on the existing quantity of goods of this kind and on the quantity of goods of other kinds needed to produce the gain. The following statements hold:

- The more natural resources that are available, the greater the gains will be.
- The greater the quantity of a certain kind of goods that already exist, the less the gains will be.
- The more auxiliary goods of other kinds that are available, the greater are the gains.

3.2 Formalization

Chernenko constructs three differential equations for quantities of goods:

$$\dot{x}_1 = \kappa_1 x_1 (\mathcal{N}_1 - x_1) - \phi_1 \tag{1}$$

$$\dot{x}_2 = \kappa_2 x_2 (\mathcal{N}_2 + \alpha x_3 - x_2) - \phi_2 \tag{2}$$

$$\dot{x}_3 = \kappa_3 x_3 (\beta x_2 - x_3) - \phi_3 \tag{3}$$

The variables and parameters of the equations have the following meaning:

x_1 the quantity of goods acquired by hunting and gathering

$\dot{x}_1$ the rate of change of x_1

$\mathcal{N}_1$ the total natural resources (capable of regeneration) exploitable by hunting and gathering

f_1 the losses resulting from decay of goods acquired by hunting and gathering

x_2 the quantity produced in the agrarian sector

$\mathcal{N}_2$ the total regenerating natural resources exploitable by agrarian production methods

αx_3 the relative increase of agrarian production arising from industrially produced goods supplied to the agrarian sector

f_2 the losses resulting from decay of goods produced in the agrarian sector

FORMALIZATION

x_3 the quantity of goods produced industrially

βx_2 the relative increase of industrial production arising from agrarian products supplied to the industrial sector

f_3 the losses arising from to depreciation of industrial products

Generally speaking, a differential equation for a certain kind of good is:

$$\dot{x}_i = \kappa_i x_i \left(N_i + \sum_{j \neq i} \alpha_{ij} x_j - \alpha_{ii} x_i \right) - \phi_i(x) \qquad (4)$$

where

N_i the natural resources (again taken as regenerating) necessary to produce goods of kind i

α_{ij} the effects of other kinds j of goods on good i

α_{ii} the saturation effect

The "net growth" or "excess production" (Eigen & Schuster 1979: 29–30)

$$\kappa_i x_i \left(N_i + \sum_{j \neq i} \alpha_{ij} x_j - \alpha_{ii} x_i \right)$$

may be written as one term, $G_i(x)$, so that Equation 4 can be stated more briefly as:

$$\dot{x}_i = \Gamma_i(x) - \phi_i(x) \qquad (5)$$

The total production at time t is called

$$C(t) = x_1(t) + x_2(t) + x_3(t) \qquad (6)$$

This system of differential equations has several stationary states. In these states, not only the rates of change of production, x_1, x_2 and x_3, but also the growth in total production, $\dot{C}$ become zero. The total production at a stationary state is called C_0.

As for losses resulting from decay and decomposition, Chernenko postulates that they are proportional both to the quantity of existing goods of this kind and to the gains in goods of all kinds. Hence, the loss functions are written as follows:

$$\phi_i(x) = \frac{x_i}{C_0} \left[\kappa_1 x_1 (N_1 - x_1) + \kappa_2 x_2 (N_2 + a x_3 - x_2) + \kappa_3 x_3 (\beta x_2 - x_3) \right] \qquad (7)$$

THE EVOLUTION OF TECHNOLOGIES

More generally we can write (cf. Eigen & Schuster 1979: 30, Eq (37)):

$$\dot{x}_i = \Gamma_i(x) - \phi_i(x) \qquad (8)$$

$$\Gamma_i(x) = \kappa_i x_i \left(\mathcal{N}_i + \sum_{j \neq i} \alpha_{ij} x_j - \alpha_{ii} x_i \right) \qquad (9)$$

$$\phi_i(x) = \frac{x}{C_0^i} \sum_k \Gamma_k(x) \qquad (10)$$

3.3   Chernenko's results

In Chernenko's model there are three stationary states:

1. $x_1 = C_0$ $x_2 = 0$ $x_3 = 0$

2. $x_1 = \dfrac{\kappa_2 C_0 + (\kappa_1 \mathcal{N}_1 - \kappa_2 \mathcal{N}_2)}{\kappa_1 + \kappa_2}$ $x_2 = \dfrac{\kappa_1 C_0 - (\kappa_1 \mathcal{N}_1 - \kappa_2 \mathcal{N}_2)}{\kappa_1 + \kappa_2}$ $x_3 = 0$

3. $x_1 = \mathcal{N}_1$ $x_2 = \dfrac{\mathcal{N}_2}{1 - \alpha\beta}$ $x_3 = \dfrac{\beta\mathcal{N}}{1 - \alpha\beta}$

Chernenko seems to suppose C_0 to be a monotonically increasing exogenous time-dependent function.

Depending on the parameters, exactly one of these stationary states is stable. If C_0 exceeds $\mathcal{N}_1 - \frac{\kappa_1}{\kappa_2}\mathcal{N}_2$ for the first time, then state 1 loses its stability, and state 2 becomes stable. A different threshold holds for the loss of stability at state 2, when state 3 becomes stable. It is interesting to see – and the same holds for the more general model in Equation 4 – that only the third stationary state, the one that has all populations present, does not depend on C_0. In this case, all "net growths" or "excess productions" vanish for non-vanishing population sizes. The question is: how and why does C_0 change?

Initially, Chernenko supposes that C_0 changes as it seems to have changed historically:

> We see that in the beginning of evolution the second and third sectors of production are practically absent. Afterwards the first aspect of production comes to saturation due to the limitation of the regenerat–ing capacity of natural resources, and the second aspect of production begins to evolve. Afterwards the evolution of the third aspect of production begins to the same extent as the exhaus-

AN ALTERNATIVE MACRO MODEL

tion of resources of agrarian production exceeds their regenerating capacity. (Chernenko 1989: 179)

A few lines later he switches to an explanation of the increase of C_0:

> For an explanation of the increase of C_0 we are compelled to postulate a selection of fluctuations which determine the direction of evolution. Those fluctuations will be selected that increase C_0. This selection may be explained as due to the competition between populations in which the [economically more effective and hence] more populous ones come off as victors. This also explains the fact that isolated tribes often remain in certain stages of evolution.
>
> (Chernenko 1989:180)

In this account, however, the mechanism by which fluctuations determine the direction of evolution remains unclear.

3.4 An alternative macro model

In the following we use a model slightly different from Chernenko's. We redefine the loss functions (cf. Eq. 7) as follows:

$$\phi_i(x) = \frac{x_i}{C}\left[\kappa_1 x_1(\mathcal{N}_1 - x_1) + \kappa_2 x_2(\mathcal{N}_2 + ax_3 - x_2) + \kappa_3 x_3(\beta x_2 - x_3)\right] \quad (11)$$

In this case $\dot{C} = 0$ for all x, since

$$\dot{C} = \sum_i\left(\Gamma_i(x) - \frac{x_i}{C}\sum_k \Gamma_k(x)\right) = \sum_i \Gamma_i(x) - \frac{\sum_i x_i}{C}\sum_k \Gamma_k(x) = 0 \quad (12)$$

Thus, we have the case of Eigen and Schuster's "constrained growth and selection" (1979: 30–31) where

$$C(t) = \sum_i x_i(0) = \text{constant}$$

As time goes by, the quantities of some goods might increase at the expense of others, leaving the total quantity of goods produced constant.

Only if the quantities of some goods are increased by external influences or if new goods are introduced from outside (but not at the expense of other goods) can $C = C_0$ increase too. By including results obtained by P. M. Allen (1976) – to whom Chernenko also refers – we can elucidate the growth mechanism. First, we identify the quantities of goods a subpopulation pro-

THE EVOLUTION OF TECHNOLOGIES

duces with the size of that subpopulation by the following argument. So far, no units of measurement have been given for the quantities of goods (which was no problem because there was no necessity to add quantities of goods of different kinds). Let us take the quantity of a subpopulation's goods produced per capita as the unit of measurement of this kind of goods. This is possible because the technology applied by a certain subpopulation is constant over time, so that the per capita production of each kind of good will be constant over time, too.

Second, we investigate the effect of a new and very small subpopulation entering the system, as did Allen (1976) for a predator–prey system in which mutations occurred within either the predator or the prey populations. Contrary to Allen, we are not interested in the circumstances in which a given mutation dies out or survives (i.e. what its parameters must be like), but in what happens when the introduction of new subpopulations with arbitrary parameters occurs very often.

To begin with, we postulate a single subpopulation i whose production (or size) follows Equation 4, i.e. $x_i > 0$, $x_k = 0$ for all $k \neq i$. The parameters in the equation represent the production technology applied by this subpopulation. At later points in time, new subpopulations will arise, initially with very small population and hence production sizes, but with new (and perhaps more or even less "effective") technologies, i.e. with different parameters. If a subpopulation is superior so far as its productivity is concerned, it will succeed and (some of) the less successful subpopulations will become extinct, or take over the new technology, or stagnate while the more successful subpopulation grows to become a great majority of the whole population.

Every now and then (more precisely, at exponentially distributed arrival times), a new population arises, thus making C_0 a stochastic, monotonically increasing time-dependent function.

In this model we need not specialize Equation 4 in order to anticipate the "law of history" as Chernenko must do. The evolution towards more and more efficient technologies that is observed historically will come about automatically; that is, the "law of history" is derived from simpler premises about mutation and selection.

We model Chernenko's "fluctuations" as new subpopulations arising stochastically. However, it is still not quite clear where these subpopulations come from. While it is not satisfactory to postulate the existence of fluctuations with a mean greater than zero as the model seems to require, a more justifiable model does not seem possible on the macro, i.e. subpopulation, level. It may be better to model the fluctuations as the result of a birth–death process *within* the subpopulations, that is on the micro (individual) level. But we shall postpone further elaboration of this idea until we have discussed the macro model in greater depth.

3.5 Simulation results

Chernenko's model as extended in this chapter has been programmed in MIMOSE and is reported in detail in Möhring & Strotmann (1993). In the simulation run reported below we used
– exponentially distributed resources N_i (i.e. with populations' capacity to exploit their natural resources varying from zero to infinity),
– uniformly distributed productivity k_i, and
– uniformly distributed coupling coefficients a_{ij}.

The results are plotted in Figure 3.1. This figure consists of graphs showing the subpopulation sizes and the total size during the first 1580 time steps (79 time units, one step being 0.05 time units). The total size C_0 fails to be a non-decreasing function of time because subpopulations of size less than 0.05 are removed. Figure 3.2 shows a magnification of the period from $t = 36$ to $t = 44$ (corresponding to the rectangular frame in Figure 3.1) to show some of the details discussed below.

During the simulated period 42 subpopulations came into being, two-thirds of which became extinct after five or fewer time units. A typical case is subpopulation #40 to which an arrow points in Figure 3.1. It is inserted

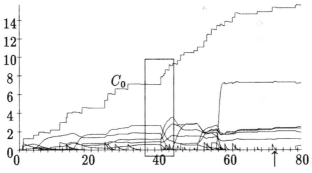

Figure 3.1 Results of a simulation run of the macro model with parameters specified as shown in §3.8 and subpopulations removed as soon as their size is < 0.05.

THE EVOLUTION OF TECHNOLOGIES

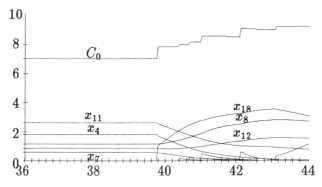

Figure 3.2 Results of a simulation run of the macro model with parameters specified as shown in §3.8 and subpopulations removed as soon as their size is less than 0.05 (magnification of Figure 3.1).

Table 3.1 Parameters of the main subpopulations at about $t = 40$.

(a) Sizes of the main populations

Time	Subpopulation					
	4	7	11	8	12	18
38.0	1.802	0.583	2.619	1.163	0.874	—
40.0	1.464	0.475	2.317	1.259	0.843	1.507
42.0	0.264	—	1.043	2.459	1.343	3.235

(b) N_i and k_i parameters of the main populations

Parameter	Subpopulation					
	4	7	11	8	12	18
N_i	1.445	0.342	0.661	0.127	2.172	0.943
k_i	0.692	0.702	0.914	0.965	0.717	0.865

(c) a_{ij} parameters of the main populations

Subpopulation i	Subpopulation j					
	4	7	11	8	12	18
4	0.314	0.696	0.495	0.034	0.907	0.066
7	0.840	0.755	0.682	0.067	0.096	0.192
11	0.909	0.947	0.506	0.255	0.874	0.361
8	0.598	0.450	0.369	0.657	0.891	0.990
12	0.198	0.965	0.119	0.507	0.794	0.701
18	0.868	0.572	0.502	0.867	0.609	0.247

MODELLING EVOLUTION ON THE INDIVIDUAL LEVEL

Table 3.2 Influence of parameters on lifetime.

Groups of subpopulations	n	means $\mathcal{N}_i$	k_i
Extant	6	4.130	0.701
Extinct, lifetime > 10	8	0.895	0.665
Extinct, lifetime < 10	28	1.619	0.349
All	42	1.840	0.460

into the system with an initial size of 0.625 at $t = 70.95$; thereafter it decreases exponentially in size until it has shrunk below 0.05 at $t = 72.15$ and is removed. In periods where no or few subpopulations are inserted by the random number generator, an equilibrium is achieved between the extant subpopulations. This is the situation in the periods from $t = 30.45$ to $t = 39.75$ (no additional subpopulation) and from about $t = 56$ to $t = 77$ (only very few additional subpopulations with small effects that can be seen quite distinctly at $t = 59.95$, 60.65, 66.80 and 79.95).

The insertion of successful subpopulations overthrows the prevailing equilibrium. To discuss this in more depth we need the detailed plot in Figure 3.2.

The most interesting event of this kind in this run seems to occur about $t = 40$, where subpopulation #18 comes into being (at $t = 39.75$), grows rapidly and causes subpopulations #4, #7 and #11 to decline suddenly. This is due mostly to the fact that the coefficients that describe how much #18 feeds on #4, #7 and #11 are quite high, while the coefficients describing how much #4, #7 and #11 feed on #18 are considerably lower. Subpopulations #8 and #12 survive at this time (and to the end of the simulation run) because the coefficients coupling them to each other and to #18 are all rather high (see Table 3.1).

The overall analysis of the constant attributes of the subpopulations and of their influence on the subpopulations' viability shows that higher $\mathcal{N}_i$ and k_i both seem to make a subpopulation stronger and more viable (see Table 3.2).

3.6 Modelling evolution on the individual level

On the individual level, we shall have to model the population growth with the help of individual birth and death rates. For the sake of simplicity, we shall model our individuals as if they were reproducing asexually. To make

THE EVOLUTION OF TECHNOLOGIES

our micro and macro models as similar as possible, we formulate the birth ("copying") rates using the positive parts and the death probabilities using the negative parts of the gains and losses of Equation 4.

Remember that in the macro model the overall growth of a subpopulation was described by

$$\dot{x}_i = \kappa_i x_i \left(\mathcal{N}_i + \sum_{j \neq i} \alpha_{ij} x_j - \alpha_{ij} x_i \right) - \phi_i(x) \tag{13}$$

$$= \kappa_i x_i \left(\mathcal{N}_i + \sum_{j \neq i} \alpha_{ij} x_j - \alpha_{ii} x_i \right) - \frac{x_i}{C_0} \sum_k \kappa_k x_k \left(\mathcal{N}_k + \sum_{j \neq k} \alpha_{kj} x_j - \alpha_{kk} x_k \right) \tag{14}$$

$$= \left[\kappa_i \left(\mathcal{N}_i + \sum_{j \neq i} \alpha_{ij} x_j \right) + \frac{1}{C_0} \sum_k \kappa_k \alpha_{kk} x_k^2 \right] x_i$$

$$\quad - \left[\kappa_i \alpha_{ii} x_i + \frac{1}{C_0} \sum_k \kappa_k x_k \left(\mathcal{N}_k + \sum_{j \neq k} \alpha_{kj} x_j \right) \right] x_i \tag{15}$$

Since all the factors of the terms in Equations 13–15 are non-negative, it seems reasonable to interpret the sum of the positive terms as the contributions of births to the net growth rate, and the negative terms as the contributions of deaths to the net growth rate.

Thus, the individual reproduction ("birth") rate in population i is

$$p_i^b(x) = \nu \left[\kappa_i \left(\mathcal{N}_i + \sum_{j \neq i} \alpha_{ij} x_j \right) + \frac{1}{C_0} \sum_k \kappa_k \alpha_{kk} x_k^2 \right] \tag{16}$$

and the individual death rate in population i is

$$p_i^d(x) = \nu \left[\kappa_i \alpha_{ii} x_i + \frac{1}{C_0} \sum_k \kappa_k x_k \left(\mathcal{N}_k + \sum_{j \neq k} \alpha_{kj} x_j \right) \right] \tag{17}$$

where n is a flexibility parameter; the lower n is, the slower will he population grow and decay.

We see immediately (compare Eq. 12) that

$$\sum_i x_i p_i^b(x) = \sum_i x_i p_i^d(x) \tag{18}$$

MODELLING EVOLUTION ON THE INDIVIDUAL LEVEL

On average, births and deaths are equally probable in the whole system. The coming into existence of new populations is now modelled in two steps. On the macro level, new populations arise, but with an initial size of zero. "Mutations" occur when an individual leaves his or her subpopulation to join another. (Note that, because the change occurs during the lifetime of the individual, this is not a mutation in the usual sense of the word.) Thus, a new population is empty when it starts and is not filled until an individual enters it. In a sense, we model the "genotype" to originate before its "phenotype"; the "plan" or "new technology" is conceived before it is realized. Moreover, a plan thathich has been given up by its population can be resumed by later individuals who decide to follow it – in the previous, macro approach, extinct populations were extinct for ever. (To save memory, we remove subpopulations with zero size after some time.)

An individual adopts another technology by the following mechanism. The system takes an individual from a source subpopulation according to the individual death rates and places it into a target subpopulation according to the individual birth rates. (Individual birth and death rates do not vanish for empty subpopulations.) Thus, mobility is modelled as occurring from a subpopulation with low relative growth to a subpopulation with high relative growth. In this case, explicit modelling of individuals is not a necessity, because the size of the target subpopulation can just be increased by one and the size of the source population decreased by one. However, this is not a desirable technique in a functional simulation language since it requires side effects; this is why the MIMOSE micro model contains an extra object type representing individual persons.

A second approach to modelling mobility is as follows. We take the right-hand sides of Equation 4 as representing the utilities of the technologies and determine the individuals' transition rates from one subpopulation into another by a positive semi-definite function of the difference of the two utilities. This approach has often been used by Weidlich's group for modelling migrations and similar processes (cf. e.g. Weidlich & Haag 1988) and is the approach we use in the MIMOSE specification of the micro model (Möhring & Strotmann 1993). One of MIMOSE's major advantages is that the main features of even a quite complex model can be presented in a few pages, allowing for easy comparison between related models and fast detection of similarities and differences. Of course, a certain familiarity with MIMOSE is necessary to enjoy these advantages to the full. Nevertheless, our actual simulations continue to be performed with the help of a considerably faster "C" program, using the simpler version of the mobility process.

THE EVOLUTION OF TECHNOLOGIES

The following discussion is based on a simulation (using the "C" program) in which the initial size of the first subpopulation is set at 500 and all later subpopulations come into existence with no members. The parameters for all the runs of the micro model reported in this chapter are:

N_i exponentially distributed with mean 0.5

k_i uniformly distributed in [0, 1]

a_{ij} uniformly distributed in [0, 0.3]

mean time between the arrivals

   of subsequent subpopulations   20 time steps

time between extinction of a subpopulation

   and its removal from the system   20 time steps

The runs differ only in the seed used for the random number generator.

3.6.1 Simulation run with total extinction

The run plotted in Figure 3.3 shows the total size $C(t)$ of the populations for about 186,000 time steps, by which time all the subpopulations were extinct. To give at least a vague notion of the meaning of "time step", consider that every two time steps about one birth and one death will occur within a population of about 500 persons in the model. If we take a real population with crude birth and death rates of about 12 per 1000 (6 per 500), one birth and one death will occur every two months and so one time step is approximately equivalent to one real-world month.

In all the runs carried out to date the macro state $C(t)$ seems to perform a random walk, which is not a surprise because the sum of the probabilities that the subpopulations should win or lose one member by birth or death is always zero. In the individual subpopulations, of course, the probabilities of winning or losing one of their members by birth, death or mobility do not equal zero, but this has no effect on the macro state of the population as a whole. Over the first 50,000 time steps of the simulation run shown in Figure 3.3, the autocorrelation function of the macro process looks much like the ACF of an ARIMA $(0, 1, 0)$ process; the same is true for the periodogram.

It is interesting to see that the entropy measure H, defined as

$$H = \frac{\sum_{i=1}^{n} \frac{x_i}{C} \log \frac{x_i}{C}}{\log n}$$

which we use to describe the complexity of the total population also seems to perform a random walk (see the lower part of Figure 3.3). The trajectory of

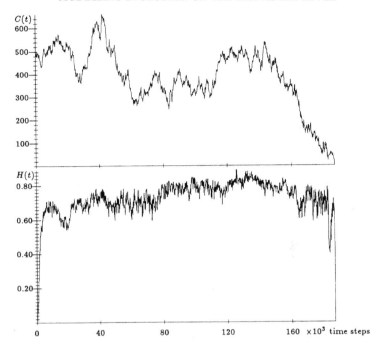

Figure 3.3 Total population size (top) and entropy (bottom).

the population as a whole through its C–H space (total size of the population plotted against its entropy measure) also looks much like a random walk.

A principle ("that the greatest amount of life can be supported by great diversification of structure") discovered by Charles Darwin (1987: 113) does not seem to apply for this version of an evolutionary process. With high complexity, and hence both high competition and high co-operation, we might have expected overall population growth. On the other hand, low complexity, when only one subpopulation survives, might slowly lead to the extinction of the overall population. Of course, even when there is only one active subpopulation, further subpopulations can come into existence and can even survive for some hundred steps (which would not be the case for an unfragmented population which must die out in the end).

This is why subpopulations coming late should have little chance of being successful against older and stronger subpopulations. This should not lead to the conclusion that total extinction is unavoidable. At least in the

THE EVOLUTION OF TECHNOLOGIES

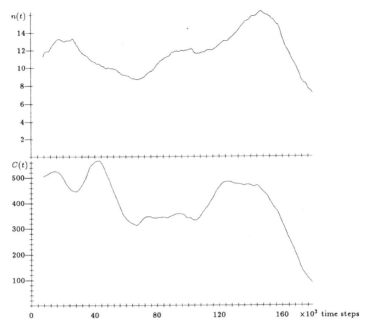

Figure 3.4 Number of extant subpopulations (top) and total population size (bottom).

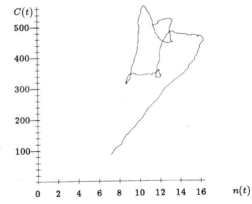

Figure 3.5 Number of extant subpopulations (horizontal) and total population size (vertical).

case of exponentially distributed N_i's, there is always a positive probability that another subpopulation grows up before the last surviving population dies out (while for uniformly distributed N_i the maximal possible value might have been generated at a certain time, such that populations with a more favourable N_i could not be generated any more: no further subpopulation would have a chance to grow).

Just before the whole population dies out, the number of extant subpopulations (a crude measure of the complexity of the population) seems to have some impact on the extinction process. The two graphs in Figure 3.4 show the number of extant subpopulations and the total size plotted against time, while Figure 3.5 plots them against one another. To hide part of the noise in these graphs, number and total size have been smoothed by moving averages over 15,000 time steps. When the extinction process begins, the number of extant subpopulations is at its maximum, and from this moment on the dependency of the total size on the number of extant subpopulations seems to be exactly linear (while previously it seems to be just random).

Figure 3.6 shows the sizes of the individual subpopulations during the run. As in the macro model, we can trace the fate of the subpopulations and explain their growth and decline with their coupling coefficients. The first frame inserted into Figure 3.6 contains the subpopulations #11, #98, #115, #910 and #1377, whose history may also be found in Table 3.3.

All the subpopulations mentioned (there are some others during the time interval we are looking at, but they soon vanish) have very high k_i's. Within the left frame of Figure 3.6, subpopulations #11 and #98 lose about one half of their members, while subpopulation #910 grows from zero and soon

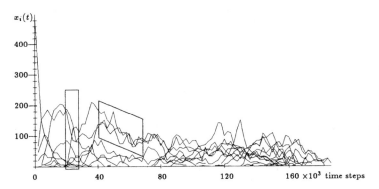

Figure 3.6 Individual populations.

THE EVOLUTION OF TECHNOLOGIES

Table 3.3 History and parameters of some subpopulations.

(a) Sizes of the subpopulations

Time step	Subpopulation				
	11	98	115	910	1377
18,000	168	202	75	—	—
20,000	190	178	87	5	—
22,000	169	124	74	62	—
24,000	138	86	55	125	—
26,000	83	82	31	131	—
28,000	100	81	33	113	—
30,000	108	61	14	140	7
32,000	103	59	8	140	19
34,000	93	69	3	176	42
36,000	97	43	—	211	58
38,000	116	40	—	203	100

(b) N_i and k_i parameters of the subpopulations

Parameter	Subpopulation				
	11	98	115	910	1377
N_i	0.391	0.145	0.633	0.415	0.092
k_i	0.991	0.936	0.961	0.959	0.982

(c) a_{ij} parameters of the subpopulations

Subpopulation i	Subpopulation j				
	11	98	115	910	1377
11	0.075	0.177	0.268	0.123	0.275
98	0.149	0.030	0.252	0.157	0.038
115	0.030	0.228	0.050	0.088	0.251
910	0.261	0.265	0.215	0.094	0.141
1377	0.068	0.049	0.237	0.279	0.038

exceeds #11 and #98. From the coupling matrix we see that #910 is fostered by both #11 ($a = 0.261$) and #98 ($a = 0.265$) while both of these subpopulations depend on #115 to which they are coupled by $a = 0.268$ and $a = 0.252$, respectively. Now #115 is weakened (beside other impacts we do not discuss here) by a feedback loop to #98, because the contribution of #98 to #115 is only 0.228. The decline of #11 is prevented by #1377, which comes into being between time steps 28,000 and 30,000, just in time to replace #115 as a main contributor to #11. This is why #11 survives up to time step 182,000, while #98 dies out at about time step 44,000. #1377's

MODELLING EVOLUTION ON THE INDIVIDUAL LEVEL

possible contributions ($a = 0.251$) come too late to prevent #115's extinction. #11, #910 and #1377 continue their co-operation for a long time. From about time step 40,000 onwards they decline jointly (see the second frame in Figure 3.6), bringing about a decrease in the total population from about 600 at time step 40,000 to about 300 at time step 60,000 (see Fig. 3.3 and the bottom of Fig. 3.4).

From this, we may conjecture that a high coupling of the major subpopulations may become dangerous for the population as a whole because the coupling can amplify a random drift downwards.

3.6.2 Simulation run without extinction

The second simulation run reported here is based on the same parameters as the run discussed above. It is documented to about 3,256,500 time steps, at which point the total population size is 3934 (its maximum was 4368 at

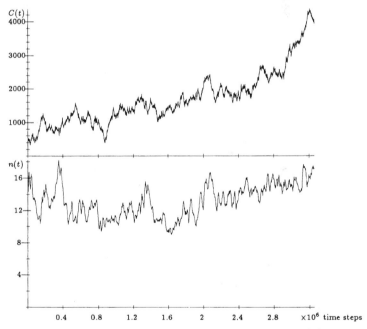

Figure 3.7 Total population size (top) and number of extant subpopulations (bottom, smoothed) of another run.

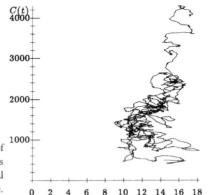

Figure 3.8 Number of extant subpopulations (horizontal) and total population size (vertical).

3,205,100 time steps), so that a period of further survival may be expected. Figure 3.7 shows the total size plotted against time and Figure 3.8 shows the individual subpopulations, the most successful of which (#18528) grew to 704 members at 3,154,000 time steps. No correlation is to be seen between the number of extant subpopulations and the total population size.

As in the run reported in the previous section, an analysis of the individual subpopulations shows that the viability of the subpopulations depends strongly on their productivity coefficient k_i. Of the 32 subpopulations that ever exceeded a size of 100 (of 158,582 subpopulations generated altogether), 17 have k_i's over 0.95 and another 11 have k_i's over 0.8. Again, the N_i's do not seem to have any effect on the survival time: only 10 of these 32 subpopulations have N_i above the mean. The saturation coefficients (a_{ii}) of the 32 subpopulations are somewhat lower than might have been expected: 19 of them are below and only 13 are above the mean of 0.15; 14 are below 0.1 and eight are below 0.05.

The time series of the overall population size is again ARIMA(0, 1, 0), at least for the first 100,000 time steps. Nevertheless, an explanation of part of what is obviously a random walk at the level of the whole population by means of an analysis at the level of the subpopulations can be attempted. At about 874,400 time steps, the total size of the population has a local minimum of only 389. From this point on, seven subpopulations will be considered, five of which are rapidly and jointly growing (see Table 3.4 and the frame in Fig. 3.9). After this phase of overall growth, the next local maximum is 1,462, at 971,000 time steps.

MODELLING EVOLUTION ON THE INDIVIDUAL LEVEL

Table 3.4 Size and coefficients of some selected subpopulations.

(a) Size at 880,000 and 960,000 steps

	Subpopulation						
	1669	18,356	18,528	22,541	28,025	33,061	42,550
880,000 steps	20	72	88	93	120	64	87
960,000 steps	14	23	177	233	294	154	281

(b) N_i and k_i parameters of the subpopulations

Parameter	Subpopulation						
	14	23	177	233	294	154	281
N_i	1.310	0.139	0.326	2.300	1.388	0.355	0.172
k_i	0.997	0.969	0.952	0.966	0.996	0.942	0.932

(c) a_{ij} parameters of the subpopulations

Subpopulation i	Subpopulation j						
	1669	18,356	18,528	22,541	28,025	33,061	42,550
1669	0.053	0.241	0.068	0.221	0.245	0.054	0.001
18,356	0.161	0.028	0.253	0.262	0.204	0.164	0.045
18,528	0.296	0.223	0.008	0.209	0.145	0.196	0.271
22,541	0.049	0.251	0.227	0.029	0.210	0.106	0.284
28,025	0.113	0.152	0.256	0.269	0.148	0.292	0.274
33,061	0.292	0.289	0.181	0.137	0.267	0.237	0.270
42,550	0.177	0.224	0.223	0.235	0.243	0.181	0.001

We again see that strong and growing subpopulations have high k_i's, that the N_i's do not seem to have any influence on the viability of the subpopulations, and that the coupling coefficients of the growing five populations are rather high, whereas the saturation coefficients (a_{ii}) are rather low. Although both coupling and saturation coefficients stem from the same uniform distribution on the interval [0, 0.3], four of the five saturation coefficients are lower than 0.150, while 17 of the 20 coupling coefficients of the five growing subpopulations are greater than 0.15 and eight are greater than 0.25.

From this observation we may conjecture that a strong coupling of the major subpopulations may become advantageous for the population as a whole because a random drift upwards is then amplified (compare the corresponding remark at the end of Sec. 3.6.1). The coupling coefficients in the last five positions of the first two lines in Table 3.4(c), which express the contributions of the growing to the decaying subpopulations (#1669 and #18356), are rather uniformly distributed, and this might be why the latter do not join the growth of the other five subpopulations.

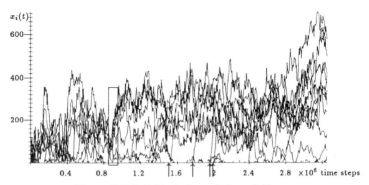

Figure 3.9 Individual subpopulations of this run.

In Figure 3.9 we can easily detect four subpopulations growing rapidly from zero at about 1,500,000, 1,800,000, 1,938,000, and 1,952,000 time steps (see the arrows in Fig. 3.9). It is interesting to see what is special about these subpopulations: that they can grow rapidly from zero to several hundred members. At about 1,500,000 time steps we have the five major subpopulations already described in Table 3.4 and which have continued their co-operation. All of the coefficients coupling the new subpopulation #64649 to the earlier major subpopulations are above the mean. The same is true for #86059 arising at about 1,800,000 time steps, for #94311 arising shortly before 1,938,000 time steps and growing to 303 members at 2,040,000 time steps, and for #95001 arising at 1,952,000 and growing to 183 members at 2,050,000. Of the 5+6+7+8=26 coefficients coupling these new four subpopulations to their respective predecessors, 24 are above the mean of 0.150, 12 are above 0.250, and 6 are above 0.290.

We may conjecture that the chance of an individual subpopulation growing rapidly and surviving for a long time is related to how well it is adapted to its predecessors. If it has high coupling coefficients with respect to them, it has a good chance of making a successful start.

3.7 Conclusions

The models developed here can be seen as functions from $W \times P$ (with W as the event space or the set of possible random number generator seeds, and P as the parameter space of the stochastic processes involved) to the space of possible realizations. In the macro-model case we saw that we must

CONCLUSIONS

make a counter-intuitive assumption, namely that new subpopulations have to start with a positive (if small) size since a subpopulation starting from zero will never grow. This leads to an implausible result: an overall population size that is a non-decreasing function of time. Consequently, the population can never become extinct. The micro model based on a stochastic birth-death process with discrete subpopulation sizes shows that the macro model is unrealistic because of its continuous subpopulation sizes. The macro model is also wrong since the deterministic (differential equation) algorithm used to calculate the subpopulation sizes *between* successive mutations does not yield the expected values of the stochastic birth–death process (see e.g. Weidlich & Haag 1983: 112–22). "Wrong" is meant in the sense that, when a micro and a macro model are inconsistent, we are always safer in discarding the macro model than the micro.

Of course, both are far from being realistic models of the historical process of technological evolution. To achieve a better correspondence with reality,

- new subpopulations (or at least the majority of them) should come into being as copies of existing subpopulations with the parameters describing their technology only slightly different from those of their parent subpopulations; this would reflect the deliberate development of technologies occurring much more often than would completely new inventions;
- each subpopulation should apply several technologies and subpopulations should share some of their technologies, since in reality the division of labour never goes so far that subpopulations produce only one kind of goods;
- in addition to birth and death, the education process should be modelled. In reality, people do not participate in production for several years after their birth and stop producing several years before their death. In addition, people do not necessarily enter the same profession as their parents and choose their profession not only according to the benefits a profession is expected to yield, but also according to their own perceived intellectual and technical capabilities. In contrast, in our micro model all members of a subpopulation are of equal skill during the whole of their lifetimes.

Nevertheless, the simplifications of our models seem to be necessary, at least for this first modelling step. The refinements suggested above might complicate our models to the point where understanding what goes on in a simulation run becomes impossible.

61

THE EVOLUTION OF TECHNOLOGIES

In any case, it is desirable to have an analytical solution for the probability function over the space of possible realizations. This requires the derivation of a master equation to describe the macro state in terms of a variable length vector (see e.g. Weidlich & Haag 1983: 58–62). Because no calculus for such an equation has been developed, we have to content ourselves with simulation experiments such as the ones reported above.

Our intermediate results may be paraphrased in the following manner:

- Contrary to the partly deterministic approach developed by P.M. Allen (1976) (see also Prigogine & Nicolis 1977: 455–8), it is possible to escape the infinite growth of the overall population despite using a stochastic approach, for an evolutionary process allows the possibility of total extinction.
- Only subpopulations with a high productivity have a chance of growing and surviving for long periods.
- Subpopulations strongly coupled to their predecessors have a good chance of making a successful start and surviving for a long time.
- High coupling coefficients between subpopulations seem to amplify a random drift either upwards or downwards, while low saturation coefficients seem to be useful for the success of subpopulations.

Much research remains to be done to investigate the complexity of our model. Future efforts will focus on the rôle of the coupling coefficients a_{ij} for the evolution of the whole system and the survival times of the individual subpopulations, taking the discussion beyond our remarks above about the fate of single subpopulations during periods of change.

Acknowledgements

Research for this chapter was done as part of a project on 'micro and multilevel modelling and simulation software environment (MIMOSE)' funded by the Deutsche Forschungsgemeinschaft, grants Tr 225/3–1 and Tr 225/3–2. Thanks go to the members of the MIMOSE working group for their readiness to discuss earlier versions of this chapter several times, and especially to Michael Möhring and Volker Strotmann who added some useful features to MIMOSE to make it run the model described here more efficiently. Further thanks go to Jim Doran for his comments on an earlier version of the chapter.

Chapter 4
Simulating the emergence of social order from individual behaviour

Andrzej Nowak & Bibb Latané

This chapter shows that computer simulations can model the change in attitudes in a population resulting from the interactive, reciprocal and recursive operation of Latané's (1981) Theory of Social Impact. This theory specifies principles underlying how individuals are affected by their social environment, in particular, how individuals are affected by the strength, immediacy and number of people holding alternative or similar viewpoints. Several group-level phenomena emerge from these individual processes. We describe how the simulations are implemented and some of the parameters that have been included.

4.1　Social influence as a central process

If one were to name the most important processes underlying social phenomena, social influence would undoubtedly be one of them. The influence of other persons and groups on individual attitudes and behaviour is one of the main factors to which we attribute social change. Even after more than eighty years of research and thousands of studies, however, there are surprisingly few well tested quantitative models of social influence suitable for computer simulation. Latané's Theory of Social Impact (Latané 1981) is one of the few.

Social impact is defined, almost as broadly as the field of social psychology itself, as "any change resulting from the real or imagined presence of others" (Latané 1981). The theory states with considerable empirical support that the impact of other people on a given individual is a multiplicative function of three classes of factors: the "strength" of the members of the group (how credible or persuasive they are), their "immediacy" (a decreas-

EMERGENCE OF SOCIAL ORDER FROM INDIVIDUAL BEHAVIOUR

ing function of their social distance from the individual) and their number. It has been shown that this general theory can predict the magnitude of impact in a wide variety of situations, regardless of the form in which influence takes place. The theory can make quantitative predictions about such diverse phenomena as crowding in animals (Latané et al. 1970), bystander intervention in emergencies (Latané & Darley 1970; Latané & Nida 1981), helping in elevators (Latané & Dabbs 1975), tipping in restaurants (Freeman et al. 1975), social loafing (Latané et al. 1979), interest in news events (Latané 1981), stage fright (Latané & Harkins 1976; Jackson & Latané 1981), conformity (Latané & Nida 1980; Wolf & Latané 1985) and, of course, attitude change where an individual is affected by his or her social environment (Latané & Wolf 1981; Wolf & Latané 1983).

The Theory of Social Impact has been built and tested as a theory of individual change. (A single individual is affected by or is affecting a group.) In our current work, we explore and test the emergent group-level consequences of this static theory to create a dynamic theory of social change, and we apply this dynamic theory to the development of public opinion from individual attitudes. We use computer simulation as a derivation-machine to see the results, on the group level, of assumptions we make about individual interactions.

In this chapter, we will describe how we use computer simulations to test the theoretical consequences of the dynamic application of the Theory of Social Impact to interacting populations. The consequences of our model for social groups have been described in more detail in Nowak et al. (1990), an analysis of the formal properties of our model is given in Lewenstein et al. (1992), and the measurement of group-level processes and comparisons between computer models and real social processes are discussed in Latané et al. (1992).

Here, let it suffice to say that several macro-level phenomena emerge from the simple operation of this micro-level theory, including an incomplete polarization of opinions reaching a stable equilibrium, with coherent clusters of people sharing similar attitudes emerging, often near the borders of the population, allowing minority opinions to remain viable. In other words, as people talk among themselves, public opinion develops a spatial organization, such that people's views become similar to those near to them, protecting them from exposure to those with opposing views.

These clusters of opinion (regional differences in attitudes) are a robust consequence of the theory, appearing under a wide range of specific assumptions and parameters. The necessary conditions for their emergence include the existence of individual differences in persuasiveness (clusters tend to form around powerful individuals, distinguishing these models from similar models in physics, e.g. Ising ferromagnets and cellular automata), a decrease in social influence with increases in physical distance (unlike most social network models, in which connections are either present or absent), and a nonlinear attitude change process (where attitude change is not simply an incremental response to pressure to change).

Simulation results can be compared with public opinion data from social surveys, sociometric and attitudinal data from middle-school classrooms and e-mail communications in computer networks, and preliminary data suggest that they provide a good description of such real-world phenomena (Latané & L'Herrou 1992).

4.2 The input to the simulation model

To simulate the interaction of individuals in social space, we need to find ways of representing that social space, the individuals, and the rules of interaction in a computer program.

4.2.1 Social space

According to the Theory of Social Impact, the distance between two individuals determines how much impact they exert on each other. A set of the distances between all pairs of individuals comprises the social space. If this set of distances can be reduced to locations in a space with a specified metric, we can talk about the geometry of this social space. Our formula for calculating impact does not make any assumptions about the geometry of social space, so if this is needed we can use any set of social distances for calculating social impact. Although many social network theorists might argue that social relations have too complex a structure to be represented by any simple geometry, there are reasons to believe that, not only may social space be characterized by a particular geometry, but this geometry is one of the most important factors determining the result of social processes (Latané & Nowak 1992; Lewenstein et al. 1992; Nowak & Latané 1993).

Our lives are lived in space, and spatial relations provide a major constraint for the operation of social influence processes. The earth's surface is a two-dimensional manifold, so a two-dimensional space may be used as a working approximation for the geometry of social space. The importance of physical distance for human social interaction is well documented: the probability that two people will marry strongly decreases with the distance between where they live; attendance even at elite universities is a function of the inverse square of distance from one's home town; and the volume of communication and transportation between two cities is the inverse square of the distance between them (Zipf 1949). Our own survey data show that the frequency of contacts between individuals can be fitted almost perfectly by the inverse square of the distance between the places where they live (Latané et al. 1992).

For the above reasons, we have decided to represent social space as a two-dimensional square matrix (grid), where each individual occupies one cell of the grid. Each individual in our simulations is characterized by the two coordinates of the matrix cell he or she occupies. The distance between each pair of individuals is calculated as a distance in Euclidian space. It is simply the square root of the sum of squared difference between their position on the row and column of the matrix. (The distance between an individual located at the fourth column of the sixth row and an individual at the first column of the second row is $[(4-1)^2+(6-2)^2]^{1/2}=5$.) The distance between individuals remains constant throughout the simulation, since they are not allowed to move in space.

Such a representation of social space is obviously a simplification with respect to the real world, with its walls and doors, elevators and telephones, interstate highways and airline hubs, and unequal housing densities. For some contexts, hierarchical, probabilistic or fractal geometries may describe social space more adequately than the Euclidian variety. Representing such geometries is no problem for our simulation approach, since any set of distances may be input to the social impact formula. In the most general case, we may simply use an $N \times N$ matrix representing the distances from each individual in an N-person group to each other. With such a representation, we can even handle asymmetric distances. The main disadvantage of such representations is that the results are very difficult to visualize.

4.2.2 Individuals

An individual is represented as a set of characteristics or attributes – specifically, a location in space, some strength parameters and one or more attitudes. As discussed above, locations are designated as coordinates in two-dimensional space (rows and columns) and are assigned such that one and only one individual is located at each node of the grid and is not allowed to

THE INPUT TO THE SIMULATION MODEL

move. Strength parameters represent the degree to which an individual can influence others to change their opinions (persuasiveness) or help them resist pressures to change (supportiveness). These parameters reflect the net effect of such social variables as credibility, social status, and motivation to influence others, and under some assumptions can change during the simulation. Finally, attitudes are represented simply as values between −1 and 1 that can be interpreted as positions on issues like abortion, rock and roll music or wearing ties. We most often use a dichotomous representation of attitude which can be seen as being for or against a proposal, or preferring one of two political candidates. An attitude can thus be used to classify the population into two different subgroups holding different opinions. Except in the special case of a 50/50 split, we can distinguish the majority (☺) from the minority (●) by their numbers – the computer knows nothing of the content of opinions.

Simulations start by assigning initial values of individual attributes for each member of the population, including their spatial location, strength and attitude. (These are usually assigned randomly within some distributional constraints.) As simulations progress, the attitude of each individual is recalculated according to a change rule based on social impact theory until such time as the system reaches equilibrium (there are no further changes) or a specified number of steps has been completed.

4.2.3 Rules of interaction

The computer program contains a set of assumptions and procedures for calculating changes in the attributes of members of the simulated group. On the most general level, we determine the net social impact of the total group on each individual by calculating both persuasive impact $(\hat{i}_p)$, i.e. the total force needed to change opinion coming from those with opposing positions, and supportive impact $(\hat{i}_s)$, coming from individuals sharing the same opinion, including oneself. The change rule is simple: if persuasive impact is greater than supportive impact, the individual changes opinion; if it is equal or smaller, the individual stays with the present opinion. In other words, an individual will change attitude if and only if $\hat{i}_p/\hat{i}_s > 1$.

To make these calculations, we need to make many specific assumptions concerning such issues as the formula for calculating impact, how to simulate parallel processes on a serial computer, whether to limit the distance over which individuals exert any impact, the nature and behaviour of strength parameters, whether to assume that the process is totally deterministic or has a random component, and so on.

In the simulation program we describe below, we can test the effect of changes in 20 different parameters or assumptions, with two to five alternatives for each. These parameters were chosen for one of five reasons: unresolved theoretical questions in social psychology, important rôles in similar dynamic systems in physics, capturing the effect of externally driven forces and events in the real world, determining the range of generality of the results, and seeing whether they depend on particular, perhaps idiosyncratic, features of the model. We think we have a pretty good representation of important variables, but others could, no doubt, be introduced.

Not only may these variables have direct effects, they may also interact. That is, the effect of a given formula may depend in part on other factors in the system, or a particular assumption about the coupling of strength parameters may have different effects depending on whether these parameters are reassigned after attitude change. Ideally, one would like to test the effect of all possible combinations of parameters and assumptions. Unfortunately, this is not feasible – a single complete test of all combinations of even our incomplete list of variables would require 0.2 trillion simulations, which, at the optimistic rate of one minute each on a single PC, would require some four million years. For us to report such data, we would have had to start before the first hominids walked the earth!

4.2.4   Randomness in a multi-determined system

To make matters even worse, a single replication would not be sufficient. Although the dynamic model of social impact is essentially deterministic in how it describes individual change, there are several sources of randomness – most notably, in the initial assignment of attributes to individuals. Randomness may also come in the sequence with which people change attitudes, in the form of reassignment rules for the strength variables, and as "temperature" or noise added to the attitude change rule. Therefore, successive runs under identical conditions may lead to different outcomes. As in other complex systems of the sort now receiving a great deal of attention (Gleick 1987), it may be that slight variations in the location of particular individuals may have large consequences for the system as a whole, with different examples of identically specified initial conditions resulting in very different outcomes.

To distinguish the genuine effects of changing assumptions from the effects of chance, we need to run several repetitions of each set of the conditions we are interested in. The tools of statistical analysis are very useful for determining the generic, robust outcomes of the model. In particular, the analysis of variance allows us to assess not only the main effects of variations in particular assumptions and parameters, but also how they interact.

4.3   SITSIM: a program for simulating dynamic social impact

Our method for simulating the dynamic effects to be expected from social impact theory has been implemented in a number of programs written in several different languages. The roots of our method date back to attempts to develop cellular automaton models of public opinion by Andrzej Nowak, Jacek Szamrej and Stanislaw Gasik at the University of Warsaw starting in 1986. The initial models implementing the rules of Latané's Theory of Social Impact were developed by Nowak and Szamrej, and the program was written in Fortran by Szamrej for implementation on a BASF mainframe computer in 1987. With advice from Richard Palmer on how to conduct simulations of collective phenomena, Latané, Nowak and Szamrej developed the present set of rules for simulating social processes in 1988. In writing a FORTRAN program for the IBM-PC, Szamrej developed the loop-within-loop structure and several parameters of the current model as well as many programming methods designed to speed execution of the program. The basic structure of the Pascal version of the current program was written by Gasik in 1989 and subsequently developed by Nowak and Andrzej Ziolkowski for use on DOS-based personal computers. As part of this enterprise, Gasik developed a special programming language (WSL) in 1989, which has unusual flexibility in allowing a wide variety of social processes to be simulated. This language, however, is somewhat restricted in important respects and tends to be quite slow.

The current program, revised extensively by Ziolkowski in 1991–2, is written in Turbo Pascal. The program consists of 12 subprograms which total over 2600 lines of code and require 103K of disk space. In compiled form, the executable file takes 58K of disk space and can be run on any DOS machine with 110K of free memory. The main subprograms serve the following functions:

(a)   The control routine allows us to set conditions and choose assumptions and parameter values from a control panel of options for running the simulations. This routine executes the main simulation repeatedly, us-

EMERGENCE OF SOCIAL ORDER FROM INDIVIDUAL BEHAVIOUR

ing a loop-within-loop structure to assign the chosen values for each of the control parameters in each run.

(b) Initialization routines randomly assign the initial values of attributes for each individual according to some specified distribution.

(c) Simulation routines implement another loop-within-loop structure to calculate the effect of the social environment on each individual in turn.

(d) Output routines which calculate and record group-level indices of social order for later analysis.

4.3.1   How the program works

The program can be called up simply by typing the command SITSIM at the DOS prompt. This will provide access to the control panel, which allows one to choose from a menu of alternatives and to start simulating.

4.3.2   The control panel

One of the best ways of explaining how to fly an aeroplane is to provide a guided tour of the cockpit, showing each instrument and control and explaining how it works. Figure 4.1 displays the "control panel" for our simulation program, which lists the various parameters that one might want to test, gives two to five values of each and allows the user to choose what combination of values and assumptions to explore. For each choice, there is a

```
╔═══════════════ SITSIM: Social Impact Theory Simulation ═══════════════╗
║ Formula             ΡΫͶΝ        √ΣΥ²                                   ║
║ Group Size          3 x 3       5 x 5       7 x 7     18 x 18  20 x 20 ║
║ Minority%           18          28          38        40       58      ║
║ Borders             No          Yes                                    ║
║ Window Size         1           4           8         Full             ║
║ Parallel Process    Synch       MC          KT                         ║
║ Persuasiveness      38          48          58        68       78      ║
║ Supportiveness      38          48          58        68       78      ║
║ ID Distribution     F(58)       N(58,18)    N(58,25)  U(8-188) B(18/98) ║
║ Coupling            Same        Random      Opposite                   ║
║ Reassignment        Same        Random      Opposite                   ║
║ Bias mean           -58         -25         0         25       58      ║
║ Bias sd             0           18          25        58       188     ║
║ Dist. Exponent      8           1           2         4        8       ║
║ Self Distance       .48         .71         .84       1        1888    ║
║ Pre-Clustering      .0          .2          .4        .6       .8      ║
║ Nonlinearity        1           5           18        58       ∞       ║
║ Multiattitudes      OneAtt.     Opindiff.   Allsame                    ║
║ Temperature         0           18          25        58       188     ║
╚═══════════════════════════════════════════════════════════════════════╝
Tag Untag   ↑↓←→ Home End   Esc= Quit   Enter= Accept        Version 5.92
```

Figure 4.1   The SITSIM control panel.

70

SITSIM: SIMULATING DYNAMIC SOCIAL IMPACT

default value (displayed on the screen in a different colour), which can be changed by moving the cursor (using the Home, End, $\uparrow$, $\downarrow$, $\leftarrow$ and $\rightarrow$ keys) to that position and pressing "U" to untag it. New choices can then be made by pressing "T" to tag them. The program can be set to run any combination of one or more choices for each parameter, but at least one entry on each line must be tagged.

4.3.3 Formulae

The program provides the choice of two different formulae for calculating social impact, each based on Latané (1981). Both formulae assume that the influence of a single individual (i) is directly proportional to the strength of that individual (S) and an inverse square function of his or her distance (d), so that $i = S/d^2$. In calculating the net influence in a particular direction $(\hat{\imath})$, the "accumulative impact" model simply takes the square root of the accumulated squared impacts of the individual members of the opposing or supporting group, so that $\hat{\imath} = \sqrt{\Sigma i^2}$. The "faction size" model, on the other hand, assumes that the net impact on an individual of those people who espouse a particular position can be estimated as their average weighted influence (μ_i) times the square root of their number $(\sqrt{N})$, so that $\hat{\imath} = \mu_i \sqrt{N}$. This formula requires the assumption that people know the size of their faction, since N is introduced explicitly into the equation.

Each model may be especially appropriate in different situations. For example, the accumulative impact formula may be more appropriate for most social influence situations, where the impact of other people accumulates as the person is exposed to their different opinions; while processes involving explicit group identification, where people are aware of the size of their faction, may be better captured with the faction size formula.

Under the default conditions, both models lead to qualitatively similar outcomes. We treat the accumulative impact formula as our default, because we believe that it applies under a wider range of situations and because it has somewhat more elegant mathematical properties. Details of these formulae and their results can be found in Nowak et al. (1990), Latané (1992), and Latané et al. (1992).

4.3.4 Group size

This parameter refers to the size of the simulation matrix, and thus the number of people in the simulated group. We use a square matrix, with the numbers in the menu referring to the sizes of the side of this square. The program allows for a choice from 3×3, 5×5, 7×7, 10×10 and 20×20 matrices, corresponding to group sizes of 9, 25, 49, 100 and 400 people. Having a range of matrix sizes allows us to check whether the emergent phenomena occur only in large groups such as neighbourhoods or also in small ones such as juries. Under the default conditions, we find that the size of the simulated group has surprisingly little effect on the outcome of simulations. Small groups unify more often than large ones, but they unify no more than comparably sized *areas* of larger matrixes.

The most noticeable effect of changing the group size parameter is on the speed with which simulations are run. Under default conditions, doubling the size of the matrix leads to quadrupling the number of people in it and to a 16-fold increase in the number of calculations and consequent running time. For this reason, it may be more efficient to do, say, 100 replications of the 10×10 matrix than 10 of the 20×20.

4.3.5 Minority percentage

The starting proportion of the minority can be set from 10 to 50 per cent, and is one of the most important control parameters in our simulations. The minority proportion helps determine the chances that enough minority neighbours will happen to be in the same neighbourhood to support each other and form a coherent cluster that can resist the pressure of the majority. Under default conditions, a 10 per cent initial minority will often be unable to survive, and the group will unify, while at the default value of 30 per cent minorities almost always survive. The size of the initial minority sets the base rate from which polarization can be calculated.

4.3.6 Borders

The simulation matrix is a square and thus has borders and corners. A location on the border and, even more, in the corner restricts the number of other persons who can influence you. Minority members located on the borders are thus better protected from the impact of the majority. To make all the locations in a matrix equal, eliminating the effect of borders, one can wrap the matrix around to form a torus or doughnut, so that a person on the left border is considered to be the neighbour of the corresponding person located on the right border and a person located on the top is considered to be the neighbour of the corresponding person on the bottom.

Borders allow for the simulation of social groups where locations in social space are uneven. How distortions in the evenness of social space affect social processes thus can be observed. Locations on the border correspond to people with marginal social positions and restricted access to other members of the society. We find that minority groups tend to locate themselves on the borders of the simulation matrix, although borders are not crucial for minorities to survive.

The ratio of the number of people located on the borders to the rest of the group depends on group size. A matrix without borders can be thought of as an approximation to a very large or even infinite matrix (the ratio of individuals on the borders goes to zero as the matrix grows) and for that reason is often used in simulating physical systems. It is our default.

4.3.7 Window size

This parameter sets the size of a "window" of influence around each individual. Only people within this window are considered when calculating their impact on an individual. In effect, this parameter sets a limit to the distance over which influence can take place.

This parameter may be interpreted as the broadness of one's psychological perspective. It may also be used as a way to speed up the simulation, since in our model the impact of individuals drops as a power of the distance and soon becomes negligibly small. Window size, however, may still influence the results in the faction size model, where the *number* of individuals sharing or opposing one's opinion is explicitly present in the formula, since the size of the window will influence this number.

The numbers on the menu refer to columns or rows. A window size of 1 means that only the closest neighbours will be included in the calculations, a window size of 4 that any individual further than four rows or columns will be excluded, and a "full" window (the default) that everybody in the group will be included.

4.3.8 Parallel process

There are three methods for simulating parallel processes on a serial computer with discrete time steps. The "Synchronous" method calculates the net social impact on all individuals before updating anybody's attributes, as if during the day they all listened to the talk in their neighbourhoods and only after later rumination decided whether to change their minds. This is achieved in practice by having two matrices to represent individual attributes. Attribute changes for each person are calculated on the basis of the first matrix and the results are entered into the second matrix. At the end of each simulation step, the second matrix replaces the first and the whole process is repeated. This method may lead to oscillations in which two individuals with opposite opinions each repeatedly succeed in persuading the other. Although the synchronous method is perhaps the closest to being truly parallel, in the real world things rarely happen in such a strongly synchronized way and people are likely to show some variation in when they decide to change.

In the "Monte Carlo" method, the net social impact on an individual chosen at random is calculated and his or her attributes updated before the next individual is selected. Physicists prefer this method for simulating parallel processes, since it avoids problems with the order in which individuals are chosen. One Monte Carlo time step is completed after N individuals have been exposed to influence, but, since some individuals may be chosen several times before others have an opportunity to respond to influence, not everybody is picked up in every step.

In the "Knight's tour" method, social impact is calculated and attributes updated for individuals selected sequentially, just as in the Monte Carlo technique, except that a systematic algorithm chooses non-adjacent individuals in such a way that everybody in the group will be chosen during a single step before anyone is repeated. Since the order of choosing individuals is the same in every step, it is important that succeeding individuals are not adjacent, so the choice of the previous individual will not have much systematic effect on the next individual. At present this is our preferred (default) way of simulating social processes.

In most cases, the choice of method seems to have little effect on outcomes, other than that the synchronous procedure leads to oscillations in some conditions, and the Monte Carlo procedure takes somewhat more steps to achieve the same outcome.

4.3.9 Persuasiveness

This sets the mean value of the persuasive strength parameter, the parameter used when calculating the pressure on an individual to change attitude. Persuasiveness represents the net sum of all the factors determining how much impact a person has when trying to influence others to change their opinions. It relates to such variables as credibility, motivation to influence others, trustworthiness, social status and perceived expertise. It is represented in the program as an attribute of an individual: a number between 0 and 100. The values of this parameter are meaningless in themselves, but assume great importance in relation to other parameters such as supportiveness, bias, temperature, etc. The default value is 50.

4.3.10 Supportiveness

This sets the mean value of the supportive strength parameter, the parameter used when calculating the influence of people sharing the same opinion. The ratio of mean persuasiveness to supportiveness represents the relative weight that people attach to arguments advocating the opposite point of view relative to arguments in agreement with their own opinion. One can choose many different ratios of supportiveness to persuasiveness ranging up to 2.3/1 by using different combinations of the persuasiveness and supportiveness parameters. Although there are reasons to believe that in reality this ratio may be less than one, we use a 1/1 ratio as our default. Smaller ratios slow down attitude change and decrease polarization and clustering. If persuasiveness is much higher than supportiveness, a strange process of oscillations may develop, where after each round people change opinions because they consistently find the arguments advocating the opposite viewpoint more persuasive.

4.3.11 Distribution of individual differences

Individual differences in strength help distinguish our model from models used in physics. This parameter sets the degree to which individuals vary in strength: "F(50)" sets everybody to the same fixed value of 50, so there is no variation in strength. "N(50,10)" and "N(50,25)" assume that strengths are distributed normally, with mean 50 and standard deviation 10 and 25, respectively. "U(0–100)" refers to a uniform or flat distribution between 0 and 100, such that equal numbers of people can be expected at any value of strength. Finally, "B(10/90)" creates a bimodal distribution where 10 per cent of the people are normally distributed around a mean of 90, and 90 per cent of the people are normally distributed around a mean of 10, with a standard deviation of 5 in each case. This choice may be interpreted as representing a society with few leaders and many followers.

Although it is not very important what rules govern individual differences, it seems to be critical that individual differences exist. Strong individuals anchor opinion clusters and help keep the system from sliding into uniformity.

4.3.12 Coupling

Coupling refers to the relationship between persuasiveness and supportiveness at the individual level. If strength is just a function of such objective characteristics as education or intelligence, it should be unaffected by whether someone agrees with you, and persuasiveness and supportiveness should be positively correlated. On the other hand, someone who is especially influential to one group of partisans may have become discredited by the other side, leading us to expect negative correlations. The choice of coupling parameters allows us to test the effect of such assumptions.

With "Random" coupling, the two parameters are treated as statistically independent random variables. In the "Opposite" case, values of the strength parameters are negatively correlated, so that people who are particularly credible to partisans of one side of an argument will be discounted by partisans of the other. The "Same" choice refers to a situation where the two parameters are positively correlated, so in fact we are dealing with only one strength parameter. Under most conditions, we do not find qualitatively different results with different assumptions concerning coupling, so we allow "Same" to be the default choice.

4.3.13 Reassignment

What happens to a person's credibility after the person changes his or her mind? This parameter determines whether and how the values of the strength parameters change after an attitude change. "Same" means that the strength parameters for a given individual remain constant throughout the simulation, "Random" that after each change of attitude they are reassigned randomly, and "Opposite" that after each attitude change the strength of an individual is reassigned to the opposite of what it used to be. (Since our strength parameters can range between 0 and 100, they are reassigned as 100 minus actual value.)

There are reasons to believe that each rule of reassignment is plausible. (See Nowak et al. 1990 for a discussion.) The decision whether to reassign strength parameters after a change in attitude is relevant to whether we treat strength as a parameter of a person, or of a held position. For example, if we see credibility as a function of social status, leaving it constant would be

SITSIM: SIMULATING DYNAMIC SOCIAL IMPACT

an appropriate choice. However, if it is a function of a held position, it is likely to change as the attitude changes. Given this uncertainty, "Random" is the theoretically neutral choice and was used by Nowak et al. (1990). Although the choice of reassignment rule is very important with respect to individual opinions, it does not seem to have much effect on group-level outcomes and so we use "Same" as the default.

4.3.14 Bias μ

In the real world, some attitude positions are more attractive or appealing than others, inherently better or more functional for the self. Our program represents this feature as "bias", a term that is added to $\hat{i}_p$ or $\hat{i}_s$, depending on which position an individual holds. Mean bias (bias μ) remains constant throughout a simulation, and can range from 0 (the default) to 100 and favour either the majority or the minority. Bias makes it easier to change in one direction than the other and may help the initial minority increase in number and eventually become the majority.

4.3.15 Bias *s*

Depending on the issue, people may have individual tastes, preferences and interests. Our program represents this feature as the standard deviation (s) of the bias term, which is regarded as being normally distributed across individuals but constant for a given individual throughout a simulation. Bias s can range from 0 (the default) to 50 and represents the degree to which individual differences in preference are important, relative to social influence.

4.3.16 Distance exponent

In our formulation, we assume that social influence decreases as a power of the distance between two people. The distance exponent sets the rate at which influence decreases. An exponent of 0 means that all distances are equal (any number to the power of 0 is equal to 1) so that impact is not affected by distance. The default exponent of 2 best corresponds to empirical data (Latané et al. 1992). An exponent of 8 effectively limits impact to the closest neighbours, making the simulation similar to a cellular automaton.

With exponents less than 2 and a two-dimensional matrix, the group will often unify, since the total influence of distant people grows faster from their increasing numbers than it drops from their increasing distance. As a general rule, the exponent representing decreasing influence has to be no smaller than the dimensionality of the social space for local ordering to emerge.

4.3.17 Self-distance

We assume that the self acts as a source of influence, helping to counteract external pressure. Self-distance determines the relative importance of the self relative to others with respect to social influence. In our present program we treat it as an independent variable, setting it to a default value of 0.84, resulting in the self being somewhat more influential than any other single individual in the group. We can, however, set self-distance to other levels, even extremely high ones which make self-influence negligibly small. As self-distance gets smaller, of course, susceptibility to social influence decreases. In previous simulations (Nowak et al. 1990) we assumed that the distance to self is $\sqrt{2}$, with distances to others calculated by adding 1 to the differences in position on each dimension. Thus, the self was the closest person in the matrix.

4.3.18 Preclustering

In the real world, attitudes may already be clustered even before people start discussing issues, because they may be related to other issues or affected by local conditions. Under the "0" default value of the preclustering parameter, the simulation starts from a random configuration. If a positive value of preclustering is chosen, the program will randomly select two individuals with different opinions and exchange their locations. If this exchange leads to increased clustering, it will be retained; if not, it is abandoned. This iterative algorithm is repeated until the chosen degree of preclustering is attained. Preclustering protects minority opinions from the beginning, decreasing polarization.

4.3.19 Nonlinearity

Although we have described attitudes as being bipolar, the simulation program provides for an attitude change model in which attitudes can be represented as points on a continuum from -1 to 1. In this general form of the model, the starting distribution of attitudes is a uniform random distribu-

SITSIM: SIMULATING DYNAMIC SOCIAL IMPACT

tion. The impact of each person is computed as the product of that person's strength and position on the attitude scale, divided by the square of his or her distance.

For a variety of theoretical and empirical reasons detailed in Nowak et al. (1990) and Latané & Nowak (1992), we believe that a critical element of dynamic social impact is that attitudes are, if not bipolar, at least nonlinear – that is, the amount of change is some nonlinear function of the pressure to change, rather than being strictly proportionate to it. Latané & Nowak (1993) present evidence that attitudes, especially when they are important, do indeed behave this way.

Each person's attitude is computed as the average of other people's attitudes weighted by the person's own strength divided by the chosen power of his or her distance. To vary the degree of nonlinearity, the resulting attitude is multiplied by k, a nonlinearity parameter which can range between 1 and ∞. With $k = 1$ attitudes follow a linear rule, changing directly in proportion to the weighted distribution of attitudes in the social environment. Greater values of k represent successively greater degrees of nonlinearity until k reaches ∞, at which point the attitude is dichotomous.

The resultant values are normalized by resetting all values higher than 1 to 1 and all values lower than -1 to -1. If the nonlinearity parameter is 1, the attitude behaves as a linear function. If k is high, any divergence from 0 is likely to exceed the absolute value of 1 and in these cases the value is reset to either -1 or 1; the system then operates as if attitudes were binary.

4.3.20 Multi-attitudes

Our program provides for comparing the evolution of different attitudes in the same social network. The multi-attitude menu item selects whether and how the option of an individual having more than one attitude is implemented. "One attitude" refers to our default choice of dealing with only one attitude. "Opinions different" means that the individuals retain the same strength parameters for as many different issues as you desire, but the starting configuration of opinions is reinitialized and therefore different for each issue. With the "All same" choice, both the strength variables and the starting distribution of attitudes are kept the same for all issues. Thus, the only difference in the outcome of simulations is due to the effects of whatever randomness is present in the simulation (and thus provides a way of testing the magnitude of these effects).

Since we do not assume that attitudes have any influence on each other,

EMERGENCE OF SOCIAL ORDER FROM INDIVIDUAL BEHAVIOUR

the multi-attitude option is implemented by running the program in a loop several times, keeping the desired parameters constant for all of the individuals for different simulations.

4.3.21 Temperature

The basic model of dynamic social impact is deterministic, with the total impact on a given individual being completely controlled by the relative strength, immediacy and number of people opposing and supporting that individual's attitude. In the real world, of course, factors other than social impact can have an effect. Your attitudes about the criminal justice system may be affected one way by being mugged and another way by having your son falsely arrested. From the point of view of our model, such changes represent random variance, not caused by social impact. We can describe the joint impact of all these random factors as "noise" which is to be added to the deterministic rules of attitude change. We refer to this noise as "temperature", because this is how it is interpreted in physics.

Non-zero temperatures makes our change rules stochastic, so that people may change in a direction opposite to the social force field. In the program, temperature is introduced as a random variable drawn anew for each individual on every step with a mean of 0 and a standard deviation corresponding to the temperature level. The temperature is added to the net persuasive impact.

Temperature turns out to have important and counter-intuitive effects. Although zero-temperature systems reach stable equilibria, at moderate temperatures the systems reach dynamic equilibria with a great deal of individual change but with stable and even increased degrees of order. At extremely high temperatures, of course, noise prevails and attitude change is mostly random, with only a reduced and degraded degree of order remaining.

4.3.22 Using the model

Once you have chosen which assumptions and parameter values you wish to explore by tagging and untagging the appropriate items on the control panel, you can proceed with the simulation. At this time, you can decide how to name your output files, what information to save, how many replications to conduct and what kinds of statistical analyses are to be performed.

4.4 Output

As the simulation progresses, the program displays the attitudes of each individual as either an open ☺ or closed ● face (ASCII characters 1 and 2), enabling one to observe their evolution (Figure 4.2).

In addition, it calculates group-level measures, which are displayed on the screen as the simulation proceeds. Three collective variables – polarization, dynamism and clustering – capture the most important aspects of the emergent group-level phenomena and can be considered order parameters (see Lewenstein et al. 1992). Polarization represents the degree to which the initial minority is reduced during the course of discussion; dynamism describes the frequency with which an average individual changes opinion; and clustering describes the extent of local ordering, or the degree to which individuals end up holding similar opinions to their neighbours. Each of these variables can be represented by indices normalized to a range between 0 (chance values) and 1 (maximal values) and is discussed in more detail in Latané et al. (1992).

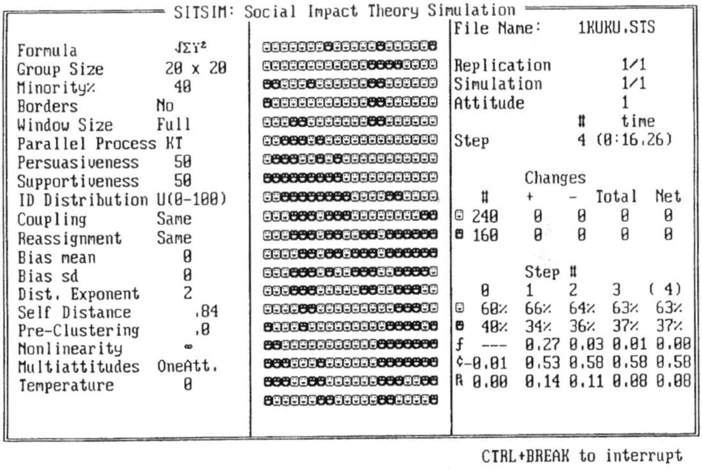

```
══════ SITSIM: Social Impact Theory Simulation ══════
                                    File Name:      1KUKU.STS
Formula          √Σⱼ̄Υ²    ▓▓▓▓▓▓▓▓▓▓▓▓▓▓▓▓▓▓▓▓
Group Size       20 x 20   ▓▓▓▓▓▓▓▓▓▓▓▓▓▓▓▓▓▓▓▓  Replication         1/1
Minority%        40        ▓▓▓▓▓▓▓▓▓▓▓▓▓▓▓▓▓▓▓▓  Simulation          1/1
Borders          No        ▓▓▓▓▓▓▓▓▓▓▓▓▓▓▓▓▓▓▓▓  Attitude            1
Window Size      Full      ▓▓▓▓▓▓▓▓▓▓▓▓▓▓▓▓▓▓▓▓                   ‖  time
Parallel Process KT        ▓▓▓▓▓▓▓▓▓▓▓▓▓▓▓▓▓▓▓▓  Step      4 (0:16,26)
Persuasiveness   50        ▓▓▓▓▓▓▓▓▓▓▓▓▓▓▓▓▓▓▓▓
Supportiveness   50        ▓▓▓▓▓▓▓▓▓▓▓▓▓▓▓▓▓▓▓▓        Changes
ID Distribution  U(0-100)  ▓▓▓▓▓▓▓▓▓▓▓▓▓▓▓▓▓▓▓▓   ‖    +    -   Total  Net
Coupling         Same      ▓▓▓▓▓▓▓▓▓▓▓▓▓▓▓▓▓▓▓▓  ☺ 240  0    0    0    0
Reassignment     Same      ▓▓▓▓▓▓▓▓▓▓▓▓▓▓▓▓▓▓▓▓  ● 160  0    0    0    0
Bias mean        0         ▓▓▓▓▓▓▓▓▓▓▓▓▓▓▓▓▓▓▓▓
Bias sd          0         ▓▓▓▓▓▓▓▓▓▓▓▓▓▓▓▓▓▓▓▓       Step ‖
Dist. Exponent   2         ▓▓▓▓▓▓▓▓▓▓▓▓▓▓▓▓▓▓▓▓      0    1    2    3   ( 4)
Self Distance    .84       ▓▓▓▓▓▓▓▓▓▓▓▓▓▓▓▓▓▓▓▓  ☺ 60% 66% 64% 63%  63%
Pre-Clustering   .0        ▓▓▓▓▓▓▓▓▓▓▓▓▓▓▓▓▓▓▓▓  ● 40% 34% 36% 37%  37%
Nonlinearity     ∞         ▓▓▓▓▓▓▓▓▓▓▓▓▓▓▓▓▓▓▓▓  ƒ  ---  0.27 0.03 0.01 0.00
Multiattitudes   OneAtt.   ▓▓▓▓▓▓▓▓▓▓▓▓▓▓▓▓▓▓▓▓  ¢-0.01 0.53 0.58 0.58 0.58
Temperature      0         ▓▓▓▓▓▓▓▓▓▓▓▓▓▓▓▓▓▓▓▓  R 0.00 0.14 0.11 0.00 0.00
                           ▓▓▓▓▓▓▓▓▓▓▓▓▓▓▓▓▓▓▓▓

                                     CTRL+BREAK to interrupt
```

Figure 4.2 View of an output screen. The left panel shows the parameter values for the present simulation, the centre panel, the distribution of attitudes, and the right panel, group-level statistics.

4.4.1 Statistical analyses

After all the simulations have been run, SITSIM calls another module to conduct statistical analyses on the simulation output. The first of two basic options computes correlations between attitudes on different issues, if the multi-attitudes option is in effect (i.e. if more than one attitude is simulated). This analysis is performed by a module written in Turbo Pascal.

The second and most often requested option provides descriptive analyses and analyses of variance to test the significance of differences in the statistics characterizing simulations run under different assumptions and parameters. SITSIM writes a batch file requesting the appropriate analyses and calls the SPSS statistical package to conduct them. If all the simulations have been run under the same assumptions and parameters, only the descriptive statistics will be reported. If only one parameter varies, a one-way analysis of variance will be computed along with the descriptive statistics. If more than one parameter varies, a multi-factor analysis of variance will be conducted. Automating the statistical analyses makes it quite easy to work with the program.

4.5 Discussion

4.5.1 Evaluating the model

All too many computer simulations stop once they have achieved a set of more or less plausible outcomes. The present program can be (and is being) evaluated in at least four different ways, the last three corresponding to the differing levels of detail that can be found in the simulations:

1. Specific assumptions identified as necessary by the simulations (i.e. the nonlinearity of attitude change, the nature of social space) are directly tested with new empirical studies.
2. Qualitative aspects of group-level phenomena are checked for correspondence with real-world phenomena. For example, the simulations show that, under a wide range of assumptions and parameter values, we obtain stable equilibria with incomplete polarization and substantial degrees of clustering. This finding is consistent with what we know about the historical distribution of attitudes about religion, for example.
3. Quantitative aspects of group-level phenomena can be derived through statistical analysis of the simulation results and tested with experimental

DISCUSSION

social groups. Most parameters make a difference and the results lead to testable predictions.

4. Individual-level predictions can be tested. We hope to use the model in conjunction with longitudinal sociometric and attitudinal data from an actual social system (we are now conducting studies in a school) to see whether we can estimate parameter values with sufficient precision to predict, for example, Harry's opinion at time 2 from knowing Tom and Dick's strength parameters at time 1.

4.5.2   The domain of the model: internal dynamics of social change

Our goal as social scientists is to understand the *internally* driven dynamics of social processes. When explaining social change, social scientists most often point to external events as causal agents. It is easy to see the social consequences of such events as the invention of the telephone and the aeroplane, the discovery of oil, and how wars and economic depression bring social change. In our models we usually treat those factors as independent variables driving social change. We will call this kind of change *externally* driven.

An important source of social change is, however, the internal dynamics of society. Many social situations are intrinsically unstable. Even in the absence of external factors, the society will evolve until it reaches some point of equilibrium. For example, if a new social problem arises people may have some initial opinions about how to solve it. They will, however, discuss this problem with each other, trying to arrive at a more widely agreed opinion. As a result of this discussion, some people will change their attitudes. The introduction of the new social problem may be seen as an external event to the social group. The resulting drift of opinion as a result of a discussion within the group is an internally driven social change. Forces from within the group are causing the evolution.

Our model is a model of internally driven social change. This change is caused by people exerting influence on each other. Our model belongs to the class of models of collective phenomena and is in many aspects similar to such models from physics as spin-glasses, ferromagnets or cellular automata. Within this model we can represent the social forces present in a real society and the factors affecting it. Within our program we have tried to represent those factors that are likely to be most important for the simulation of internally driven social changes.

83

4.5.3 Scope of the model

Attitudes are central to many social phenomena. The state of the economy is determined by consumer confidence. International relations, including issues of war and peace, are shaped by leaders' concerns for the electorate back home. The availability of planetary resources for the future are being determined now by people's attitudes toward such things as family planning, environmental degradation and transportation preferences. Thus, this model carves out a large and socially important domain for investigation.

However, social impact theory deals not only with attitudes, but also with all the other ways in which people affect each other. Presumably, it can be applied to a variety of other problems, such as the contagion of rudeness leading to regional differences in social style, the spread of values such as the work ethic, the emergence of social networks from individual friendship choices and the development of ideology and social identity.

We think we have taken just the first step towards the heart of a very specific problem: understanding the inner dynamics of society. In a recent review of sociological work on the problem of the micro–macro interface, Barbara Entwisle concluded that: "Theoretical weaknesses pose an even more fundamental threat. The area that needs work most urgently involves theories about micro–macro linkages, especially the development of theories about change, and even more especially, theories about change at the micro level affecting the macro level" (1991: 286). The present program addresses itself specifically to those needs.

Acknowledgements

Preparation of this chapter was made possible by Grant 1–1113–91–02 from the Polish Science Foundation to Andrzej Nowak and by National Science Foundation grant BNS9009198 to Bibb Latané.

Chapter 5
The architecture of society:
stochastic simulation of urban movement

Alan Penn & Nick Dalton

A fundamental problem in the simulation of systems of discrete interacting entities is how to represent the environments they inhabit. However we think about it, if individuals move in space and social interaction takes place through meeting, space patterns that constrain movement may intervene in the construction of social behaviour. This chapter investigates the spatial patterns that human societies construct – the forms of their towns and cities – and argues that they are far more than just a background to, or expressions of, social action, but are instrumental in the formation and reproduction of patterns of social behaviour that make meaningful personal and social action possible.

The problem is of more than just theoretical interest. If we are to answer the practical questions architects and planners ask about the relative merits of different physical design options in terms of their implications for social function, we need to understand *how* the space patterns constructed by physical design can be social in the first place. This requires new knowledge, since little exists in the way of a principled understanding of the relationship between space and society. The research reported in this chapter results from work founded by Professor Hillier and his research group in the Unit for Architectural Studies, Bartlett School of Architecture and Planning, University College London, which has concentrated its efforts on the development of just such a theory. The main reference text for this work is *The social logic of space* (Hillier & Hanson 1984).

Our argument is in four parts and proceeds through a combination of simulation experiments and empirical and analytic studies. First we show that urban space patterns and their evolution may be subject to lawful constraints that give rise to regularities. We do this though simulated growth processes that give rise to a recognizable class of settlement types, Hillier's

THE ARCHITECTURE OF SOCIETY

"beady ring" villages. Next we introduce the analysis of patterns in urban space by looking at a series of larger "organic" towns, and show that these also exhibit regular and describable underlying structures. Then we look at the observable effects of space patterns on patterns of social behaviour in a case study. Again, we show that regularities arise which relate behaviour and spatial patterns, and which suggest a lawful evolution of spatial patterns and land uses in a way that makes urban systems intelligible and so open to individual as well as social interpretation. Finally, we use simulations of movement in real systems to begin to isolate the nature of the rules that might operate at the level of the individual that would give rise to the observed social regularities. We end by suggesting that part of the "memory" people need in order to understand, move through and use urban systems in a purposive way resides in the regularities of the urban system itself. In this sense it may be that urban space patterns play a fundamental rôle in the reproduction of social structures through time as well as in their evolution, and so forms a fertile area for social research using simulation techniques.

5.1 The problem of urban intelligibility

For designers and urban theorists alike, a fundamental problem is how we understand and find our way around towns and cities. The problem is of a kind both difficult and familiar. Since we live in and use urban space every day, our knowledge of the rules we use to interpret it – like the knowledge of grammar we use in speech – is exercised largely unconsciously. For most of the time we find our way around town without giving it conscious thought, even in areas that are relatively unfamiliar. Where we do have to make conscious decisions, we often rely more on hunch than explicit criteria.

The problem becomes still more complex when we consider the wider social issues of how people "understand" their urban environment. These problems have become a central concern of recent attempts to question the failures of modern architecture. Some of the theories concerning these issues that have had most influence on recent design were put forward in the 1960s by Kevin Lynch, who, using psychological methods and cognitive mapping in particular, investigated the way that people conceptualize the urban environment. He surmises:

> In the process of way-finding, the strategic link is the environmental image, the generalized mental picture of the exterior physical world that is held by an individual. This image is the product of

86

THE PROBLEM OF URBAN INTELLIGIBILITY

both immediate sensation and of the memory of past experience, and it is used to interpret information and to guide action. The need to recognize and pattern our surroundings is so crucial, and has such long roots in the past, that this image has wide practical and emotional importance to the individual.   (Lynch 1960: 4)

He goes on to suggest that this image depends on three components:

A workable image requires first the identification of an object, which implies its distinction from other things, its recognition as a separable entity. This is called identity, not in the sense of equality with something else, but with the meaning of individuality or oneness. Second, the image must include the spatial or pattern relation of the object to the observer and to other objects. Finally, the object must have some meaning for the observer, whether practical or emotional. Meaning is also a relation, but quite a separate one from spatial or pattern relation.   (Lynch 1960: 8)

Thus, for Lynch the key lies in the mental image that we each possess of the city, that is, an image in which the city is decomposed into identifiable elements in some relation to one another. The identity – and identifiability – of objects in the urban landscape, whether these are landmarks, identifiable places or even the edges between areas, and the way these are related with one another through the path structure of the city determine urban "imageability" and therefore the strength of the mental map we hold that allows us to relate to and interpret our environment. Lynch argues that when the city loses its imageability problems occur at both the practical and the emotional level.

The argument is compelling and seems to make sense of many of the problems, aesthetic and social, that we recognize in modern urban environments. Indeed, during the past thirty years these ideas have been highly influential in the design field. But there is a problem. Lynch's psychological explanation of the relationship between the environment and aspects of social function in cities gives no account of how the historical city, with the characteristics he so much admires, should have gained its imageability in the first place. Perhaps more importantly, many of the most recent schemes, which apparently adhere to Lynch's criteria for imageability, with identifiable landmarks, edges and pathways, signally seem to fail the final test and provide some of the worst examples we have of socially problematic housing. It seems that there is actually more to imageability and intelligibility than just the kinds of local visual phenomena that Lynch proposes.

In response to these more recent failures, there is a widely voiced feeling

THE ARCHITECTURE OF SOCIETY

that modern society has lost the ability to design that people used to have in the days before it was a subject of conscious study. In those days people seemed to be at one with their environment and somehow got it right. Cities were immediately understandable because they were the product of the collective unconscious. Modern society is thought to have lost innocence in this. The argument is again familiar and essentially anti-rational, with "scientific" knowledge, and the functionalist architectural theories that are seen to have stemmed from it, considered the main culprits.

Is there a rational response? We believe there is, but that it requires an understanding of how the characteristics of intelligibility and understandability can have arisen as a natural product of the way cities are formed and the ways they grow and change and are used from day to day. An adequate response also requires an understanding of the reverse: the ways in which social processes themselves may respond to the form and layout of cities. First we must generate a testable definition of intelligibility. We believe one of the simplest ways of defining the term is in the relationship between local and global properties of space. A system is intelligible to the degree that what you see immediately around you gives a good guide to where you are in the whole system. This is both a dynamic and a relational concept – as you move through a city, what you see locally is constantly changing, even though the whole city remains almost completely unchanged. In an intelligible area your global location is essentially predictable from local information. In a maze, the structure of space is designed to break the part–whole relationship as far as possible.

In the first stage of the argument we investigate one aspect of the part–whole relationship. This is the relationship of the parts to the whole in the construction of settlements. Undesigned or "organic" settlements have the property that they are both seemingly the product of discrete individual actions – for example, the construction of individual houses – and at the same time often gain a remarkable degree of coherence and intelligibility at the level of the whole settlement. It seems possible that intelligibility and the "local to global" process of construction of organic settlements may be related.

5.2   Lawfulness in unplanned settlements

Figure 5.1 shows the plans of a series of hamlets and villages in the south of France. This kind of settlement may be familiar to us from a number of

LAWFULNESS IN UNPLANNED SETTLEMENTS

Figure 5.1 Beady ring settlements from the Vaucluse region of France (reproduced from Hillier & Hanson 1984).

other places in the world. At first sight they seem to be haphazard and unplanned, but a more careful study reveals a number of regularities in the way they are laid out. Hillier & Hanson describe the villages as follows:

> In plan the settlement appears irregular because it lacks the formal geometric properties we normally associate with spatial order. Yet as a place to walk about and experience, it seems to possess order of another, more subtle, more intricate kind. The very irregularity of the ways in which the buildings aggregate appears to give the hamlet a certain recognizability and suggests a certain underlying order. (Hillier & Hanson 1984: 57).

They go on to note individual features of the settlements that appear regularly: each individual building opens directly on to the open space structure of the village; the open space structure is like beads on a string, in that there are wide and narrow parts but each is linked together directly; the open space forms at least one major ring around an inner clump of buildings; outer clumps of buildings define the beady ring of space and the outer boundary to the village; the beady ring structure coupled to the immediate adjacency of building entrances creates a high degree of permeability and mutual accessibility of dwellings; there are by definition at least two ways from any building to any other. These features appear to be almost invariant from settlement to settlement although the geometry of each settlement is entirely individual.

How could such genotypical features arise? Hillier & Hanson propose an answer. They construct a computer experiment in which there are two kinds of object, closed cells and open cells, joined to one another facewise with an "entrance" linking them:

> Allow these doublets to aggregate randomly, requiring only that each new object added to the surface joins its open cell full facewise

THE ARCHITECTURE OF SOCIETY

onto at least one other open cell. The location of the closed cell is randomized, one closed cell joining another full facewise, but not vertex to vertex.   (Hillier & Hanson 1984: 60)

Figure 5.2 shows the result of a run of their experiment as a settlement grows from a single dyad (a). The genotypical similarities to the real settlements are striking. However, when we look at larger towns in the same region (Fig. 5.3a for example), and compare these to the results of a more extended growth process in the simple model (Fig. 5.3b), it is clear that something else is going on.

The open space structure still maintains certain characteristics of the beady ring settlements: it is formed by blocks of outward facing buildings; it is characterized by fatter and thinner spaces; and on the whole there is a continuous relationship maintained between entrances to buildings and pieces of urban space. However, the structure of the open space is now recognizable as a "deformed grid" of more or less linear streets which are considerably longer than would result from the beady ring process. It seems as though as a settlement grows larger the rules change to create a more globalized form.

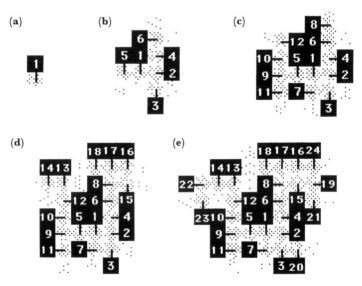

Figure 5.2 The random cell aggregation process resulting in 'beady ring' like clusters (after Hillier & Hanson 1984).

LAWFULNESS IN UNPLANNED SETTLEMENTS

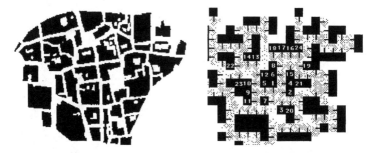

Figure 5.3 The town of Apt in the Vaucluse shows a deformed grid street structure which is more linearized than the product of a random growth process on the simple "beady ring" model.

We can be quite precise about what we mean by this tendency towards a more global form. Figure 5.4 shows a map of Apt, this time representing open space in black since this is the object of interest. We can see that there are a number of large, more or less convex, "squares" in the town. Urban squares are often thought of as relatively enclosed, but if we look at these in detail we find that they are characterized more by the length of lines of sight that pass into and through them (Fig. 5.5). In fact, the lines of sight from each square intersect one another and provide a more or less continuous route structure in which it is never more than one or two changes of direction from one square to the next.

The properties of convexity, lines of sight and changes of direction turn out to be particularly relevant in the analysis of urban spatial configuration.

Figure 5.4 The deformed grid of open space in Apt coloured in black.

Figure 5.5 The main square like spaces in Apt and their 'isovists', the zone of all space that can be seen from some part of the square.

This is by no means trivial. All three notions carry with them social, or at least functional, potential. People see and usually move in straight lines; when a group of people stop to talk they usually define a convex space so that if two people can see each other a third can see, and be seen by, both

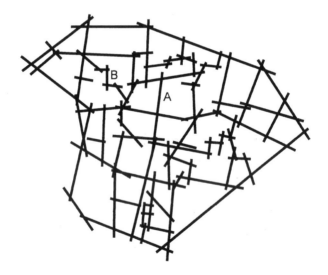

Figure 5.6 The line map of Apt.

LAWFULNESS IN UNPLANNED SETTLEMENTS

(this would be a mathematical definition of convexity were we to talk of points instead of people); and changes of direction are about breaking convexity since you can't see around corners.

An important representation of spatial layout in the analysis that follows takes the "line of sight and access" as its basic element. By breaking up continuous open space – everything that is black in Figure 5.4 – into the fewest and longest lines of sight and access that make all rings of circulation in the system (Fig. 5.6), we simplify a complex geometry into a form that can be represented as a binary matrix of connections between each line and those that intersect it.

This simplified line map can then be easily represented by computer in the form of a graph in which line elements are considered as nodes and intersections between lines as links. This allows representations of the pattern of space in real urban forms to be analyzed or experimented on. Various local properties of space in the line map can be quantified straight away. The simplest of these are line length and the "connectivity" of lines, that is, the number of other lines a particular line intersects with directly. However, the most interesting properties for our purpose here – and as it turns out for empirical studies of urban function – are those that measure the more global properties of the configuration. From starting line A the rest of the system is shallow, from B it is deep.

One of the most important global measures is based on the mean depth of the graph from any particular line. Figure 5.7 shows graphically how the

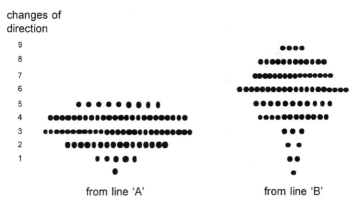

Figure 5.7 The distribution of lines by numbers of changes of direction or steps of depth.

town of Apt appears from the point of view of two different lines, marked A and B in Figure 5.6. Line A is directly connected to five other lines; these are at depth 1 and can be reached by changing direction once. These lines in turn are connected to 16 other lines, which are thus at depth 2 or two changes of direction from A. There are 27 lines at depth 3; and so on. From line B the picture is quite different: there are only 7 lines within three steps, and the bulk of the system is over 5 steps away. We call a normalized measure of the depth of a system from the point of view of a line its "integration" value. Shallow spaces have high integration values and deep spaces have low values, indicating their relative spatial segregation.

Can this kind of analysis tell us anything about the way larger towns take on a more globalized form? We believe they can. Figure 5.8 plots the degree of integration calculated for each line in the town back on to the line map as a grey scale from darkest for the most integrated – shallowest – through to lightest for the most segregated lines. The pattern of dark lines takes on a form that we find is characteristic of a large number of towns and urban

Figure 5.8 The integration map for Apt with dark lines the most integrating through to light lines for the most segregated.

LAWFULNESS IN UNPLANNED SETTLEMENTS

areas and which we call the "deformed wheel" integration core. It consists of some of the peripheral "rim" of the town, some main radial "spokes" and a central deformation forming a "hub".

The more segregated lines cluster between the spokes of the wheel. The shape of this core of shallow space appears to be more than just a matter of chance, for two reasons. First, there are functional correlates of the spatial pattern; that is, the core of dark lines picks out pretty well what we understand intuitively to be the main road structure of the town, and this goes with the location of the market square and main shopping streets, while the more private residential streets are relatively segregated. Secondly, we have found the same deformed-wheel shape across a wide range of towns and urban areas throughout the world. Figure 5.9 shows a slightly smaller town from the same area of France, which although more elongated has the same type of deformed- wheel core. Figure 5.10 shows an apparently completely different form of hutted compound settlement from southern Africa in which the shape of the integration core is again a deformed wheel.

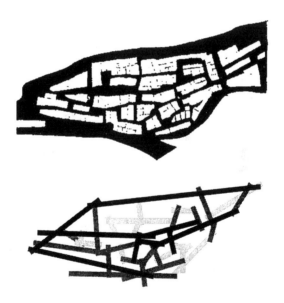

Figure 5.9 The town of Gassin in southern France and its deformed-wheel integration core (after Hillier & Hanson 1984).

THE ARCHITECTURE OF SOCIETY

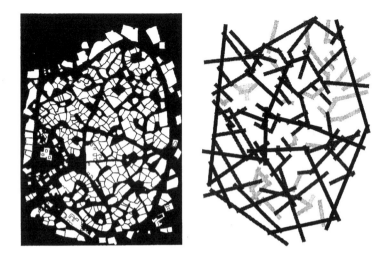

Figure 5.10 The village of Serowe in southern Africa and its integration core.

What could account for this regularity across such a range of settlement forms? We believe the answer lies in the need for the town to structure movement, and in particular the movement of strangers from the exterior, past the shops and markets in the town centre and then back out again, while keeping the main residential areas relatively private but not structurally isolated.

Of course this bears directly on Lynch's problems of way finding and imageability, but instead of invoking the psychological and emotional need for urban intelligibility, it suggests that a social and functional mechanism is at work in which the form of the town is directly implicated in the construction of the interfaces between people necessary for transactions to occur. We suggest that Jane Jacob's aphorism, that "towns are mechanisms for generating contact" may provide the underlying mechanism through which urban intelligibility arises. If this is so, we would expect the relationship between social function and space to be detectable through observations of social behaviour.

5.3 The urban movement economy

Empirical research has begun to provide evidence for a direct relationship between social function and space patterns in urban areas. One recent study entailed the development of a detailed set of simultaneous observations of movement by wheeled and pedestrian traffic in each street segment of a compact urban area. Although the study was aimed at investigating the relationship between vehicular and pedestrian movement in residential urban neighbourhoods (an interface that is currently regarded as problematic), its findings are of broader theoretical interest.

A case study area of just under 1 square kilometre was selected in Barnsbury, north London, bounded in the first instance by the Caledonian Road, Liverpool Road, Offord Road and Copenhagen Street (Fig. 5.11). The area is a relatively homogeneous residential neighbourhood dating mainly from the nineteenth century. Peripheral streets such as the Caledonian Road are the major through routes in the area and have substantial retail land uses, and the area to the east and south-east has a further concentration of retail establishments around the Chapel Market. There are a few convenience shops and public houses within the area itself. The area has been the subject of various traffic management and calming measures intended to stop "rat running". During the latter part of the project the observation area was extended to cover Upper Street and Essex Road which are major north-south routes in the area, though in this case observations were made of only a sample of street segments in the extended area.

Within the main study area 116 street segments (between road intersections) were observed. Observations were made during five time periods: 8–10am, 10–12am, 12–2pm, 2–4:30pm and 4:30–6:30pm. The observation technique used a stationary observer counting all the persons and vehicles crossing a notional "gate" across the segment. At least two five-minute observations were made during each period in each street segment, giving more than 50 minutes of coverage through the day.

Figure 5.12 shows the mean all-day flow rates in movements per hour for motor vehicles (part a) and adult pedestrians (part b) in all observed street segments in the main case study area. Over 40,000 motor vehicles and 10,000 pedestrians were counted in total. The database is therefore highly detailed and robust, both in terms of its spatial coverage – almost every street segment of the area – and in terms of its coverage of times of the day and of modes of space use.

The characteristic time profiles shown in Figure 5.13 suggest that the

THE ARCHITECTURE OF SOCIETY

area behaves very much as one would expect for an urban residential neighbourhood. However, the coefficient of variation through the day, a measure of the degree to which flow rates vary as a function of time for each mode, shows that there are spatial structures in the way space is used over time. It is notable that adult pedestrians and private cars have relatively low coefficients of variation, between 7 and 13 (compared with bicycles and chil-

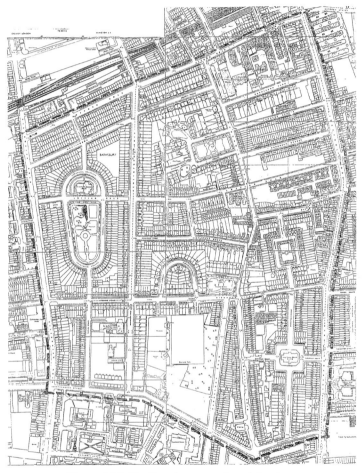

Figure 5.11 The Barnsbury area of north London.

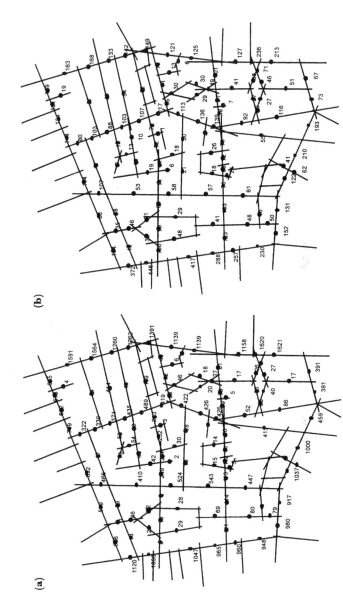

Figure 5.12 (a) Daily mean flow rates per hour for all categories of motor vehicles; (b) daily mean flow rates per hour for adult pedestrians.

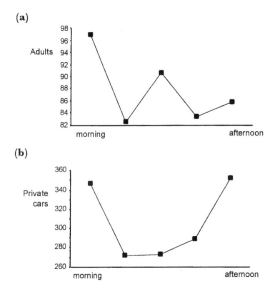

Figure 5.13 (a) Adult space use shows distinct morning and lunchtime peaks, with mid-morning and mid-afternoon troughs. (b) Private cars show clear morning and afternoon peaks with a midday trough.

dren, at 47 and 64 respectively). Across both modes, the variability for internal spaces is higher than for peripheral spaces. This suggests that variability of flow rates through time may be related to the degree to which a space acts as a carrier of through movement from a large number of origins and destinations. A space that is cut off from the urban fabric will be used mainly for trips starting or ending in it. In a residential locality these trips will show marked morning and afternoon peaks coinciding with journeys to and from work. Spaces that are more strategically located in the grid will gather a higher proportion of through movement and so will figure in trips other than just the journey to work, with the consequent effect of smoothing out rush-hour peaks. It is also possible that these spaces will in turn gain non-residential land uses, such as retail, and that these will generate space use out of the normal rush-hour peaks, again helping to reduce variation through time.

A preliminary inspection of the spatial distribution of movement shown in Figures 5.14 and 5.15 suggests that broad divisions into internal and

Table 5.1 Mean pedestrian and vehicular flow rates and ratio for internal, peripheral and internal through routes.

Spaces	All vehicles except buses	Adults	Ratio of vehicles/adults
All	355.9	87.6	4.1
Periphery	983.5	181.7	5.4
Internal (average)	129.4	55.7	2.3
Main internal through routes	377.0	83.3	4.5
Remaining internal spaces	41.3	46.2	0.9

peripheral spaces can be supplemented in this study area by the main internal through movement spaces (streets such as Hemingford Road, Thornhill Road, Barnsbury Road and Bewdley Street). Table 5.1 shows the all-day mean flow rates per hour for internal, peripheral and internal through routes for adult pedestrians and for all categories of motor traffic excepting buses. It also gives the vehicle pedestrian ratio (the number of vehicles, excluding buses, per adult pedestrian) for the same sets of spaces.

The vehicle/pedestrian ratio for internal spaces is about 0.9, rising to about 4.5 for through routes and to about 5.4 for the peripheral spaces. Although the vehicle/pedestrian ratio for internal through routes is similar to that for peripheral spaces, the flow rates are only about half as high.

The spatial variation of flows for the key vehicular and adult pedestrian categories can be examined more closely by inspecting relative flow rates, segment by segment, for the whole dataset, including the additional data collected to the east of the main study area. Figure 5.14 is a scattergram

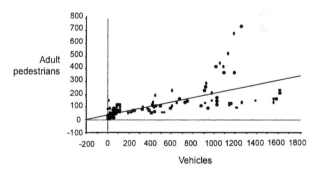

Figure 5.14 The relationship between adult pedestrian flows vertically, and vehicular flows horizontally.

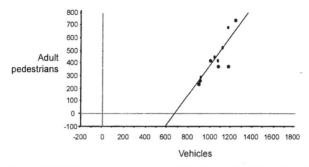

Figure 5.15 The observed segments of Caledonian Road, Essex Road and Upper Street plotted on the same scale.

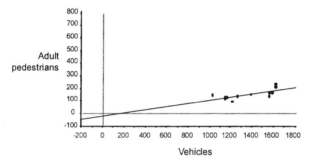

Figure 5.16 The high vehicular flow rates on the Liverpool Road are not matched by equivalent pedestrian flows.

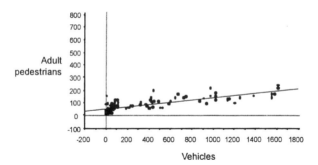

Figure 5.17 The remaining observations in the internal streets of the area continue the alignment of the Liverpool Road regression line.

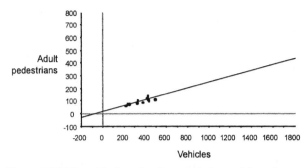

Figure 5.18 The vehicular pedestrian ratio for internal through-route segments.

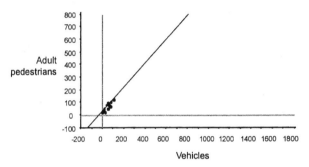

Figure 5.19 The vehicular pedestrian ratio for internal one-way route segments.

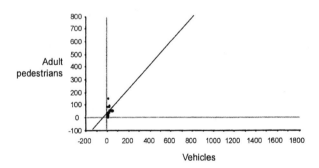

Figure 5.20 For cul-de-sac spaces the regression line is meaningless since there is no correlation between the two flows.

THE ARCHITECTURE OF SOCIETY

showing the relationship between the two categories of movement. The distribution shows a clear bifurcation at the higher vehicular flow rates (above 800 per hour). This bifurcation is resolved by considering street segments belonging to the main grid of primary routes (the "supergrid") separately (Figs. 5.15–5.17). The upper limb belongs exclusively to observations on segments of the Caledonian Road, Essex Road and Upper Street, the principal retail streets in the area. The right-hand lower limb belongs exclusively to observations of the Liverpool Road. This is historically the "back street" and has few retail premises, but it does create a strategic link from Chapel Market to the Holloway Road, bypassing the congestion of Highbury corner, and is used as a vehicular through route.

The underlying trend indicated by the shallow angle of the regression line in Figure 5.17 shows that, for all the street segments that do not form part of the main retail foci of the area, higher vehicular flows outstrip any corresponding growth in pedestrian flows by a factor of about 8 to 1.

It seems at first that it is only through major retail land uses, such as those on the Caledonian Road, Upper Street and Essex Road, that a steeper regression line can be attained, and so a more favourable vehicular pedestrian ratio. Figure 5.15 indicates roughly even growth in each mode for these retail streets. However, a more detailed inspection of the internal street segments within the study area reveals further distinct structures to the vehicular pedestrian ratio.

Figures 5.18 and 5.19 show that steeper regression lines hold for the internal through route segments and for internal one-way street segments. The latter approach equality in the rates of growth of the two types of movement. However, Figure 5.20 shows that, where traffic calming has created culs-de-sac which virtually eliminate vehicular movement, vehicular and pedestrian movement rates are unrelated.

It seems clear from this analysis that the processes relating vehicular and pedestrian movement rates in individual segments of the case study area depend on a number of factors. First, there is an implication that there is a hierarchy of routes, at least at the level of the peripheral supergrid, internal through routes and the remaining internal spaces. Secondly, it seems that the major retail foci depend on a historically accessible location – translated today into a relatively high vehicular movement rate (800 per hour and upwards). It also seems clear that there is a multiplier effect that increases pedestrian space use in line with the retail land use. While this holds for the Caledonian Road, Essex Road and Upper Street, the Liverpool Road, which also in present-day terms seems to be a potential candidate for this

THE URBAN MOVEMENT ECONOMY

type of retail focus, seems to have failed to gain pedestrian use but has become a vehicular through route instead.

The configuration of the street grid was analyzed using line maps and integration analysis. Figure 5.21 shows the line map of the largest model, area 4, with the central study area circled. Figure 5.22 is a greyscale integration core map with black for most integrated, through to light grey for

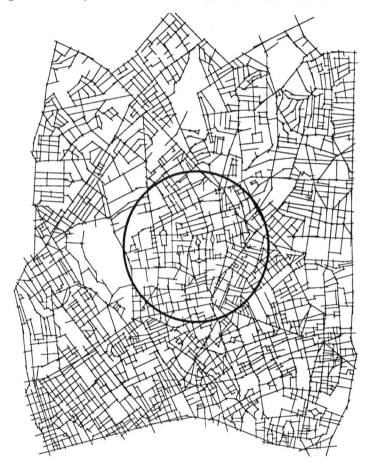

Figure 5.21 The line map of the largest model area.

least integrated (most segregated and deepest on average). The map clearly shows the main structure of integrated lines and picks out the Euston Road–Pentonville Road–City Road arc as the main focus of integration in the area. The main structure of integration makes intuitive sense of the area towards the centre of the picture, but towards the periphery of the area it

Figure 5.22 A greyscale integration core map with black for most integrated through to light grey for least integrated.

THE URBAN MOVEMENT ECONOMY

is clear that the colours are not so representative, fading into the light grey end of the spectrum. This is because a global measure (which takes account of the whole system) is of necessity sensitive to the chosen boundary. Lines on the boundary such as the Kingsland Road on the eastern edge would be major integrators in a system in which they were central.

A second measure seeks to overcome this limitation. This is the measure

Figure 5.23 A radius 3 "local integration" map of the same area.

THE ARCHITECTURE OF SOCIETY

of integration in which a limited "radius" is taken. By convention, a radius or "girth" in the graph of three steps of depth is assumed, and the mean depth of the graph within that radius is computed for each line in turn. This effectively creates a moving boundary while maintaining some degree of globality. Figure 5.23 is a radius 3 "local integration" map of the same area using the same colouring convention. The dark lines in this map pick out what we might intuitively think of as the main route structure for this part of London and seem to overcome the effect of the boundary on segregating the edges of the model.

The value of these and other measures for configurational analysis is not just their ability to give a good intuitive picture of the relative priority of different street alignments in the structure of the urban grid, but also their ability to quantify the pattern properties of a complex urban spatial configuration and so allow searching for empirical relationships between urban structure and urban function. In this case, it makes it possible to control for variations in spatial configuration (which is essentially what is open to urban designers and traffic engineers to manipulate), in studies of the empirical relationships between vehicular and pedestrian movement rates and the ratios described above.

When studying the different effects of spatial configuration on patterns of pedestrian and vehicular movement, it is necessary to construct different line maps, since the effective space structure is different for the two types of movement – culs-de-sac for cars may be through-spaces for pedestrians, and certainly the ground-level space structure of most modern housing estates presents a radically different configuration for a pedestrian than for a driver. It also seems likely that vehicular and pedestrian trips are on different spatial scales, and this may be reflected in differences in the performance of local or global measures of the configuration and in differences between different-sized systems in modelling patterns of movement.

In general, for all types of movement the best correlations are given by the radius 3 measure of integration. Figure 5.24 shows the correlation between the basic vehicular movement pattern and this local measure of integration for the complete sample of observed segments, including the additional observations on the Essex Road and Upper Street supergrid. The correlation coefficient of 0.854 is strong, highly significant at $p < 0.001$, and larger than the equivalent correlation coefficient of 0.601 for the relationship between vehicular flows and the radius infinity global measure of integration, shown in Figure 5.25. It should be noted that the vehicular flows are plotted on a logarithmic scale.

108

THE URBAN MOVEMENT ECONOMY

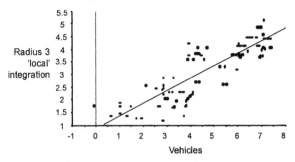

Figure 5.24 A scattergram of the relationship between radius 3 'local integration' and vehicular flows on a logarithmic scale in all segments, for the largest system.

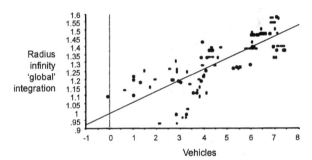

Figure 5.25 A scattergram of the relationship between radius infinity 'global integration' and vehicular flows on a logarithmic scale in all segments.

This finding is somewhat surprising, since the pattern of vehicular movement is composed in the main of large-scale trips and might have been expected to be more strongly related to the global than to the local measure of integration. Inspection of Figure 5.25 shows that the reason for the lower correlation with global integration is the rather odd bifurcated distribution of vehicular movement. However, this plot also indicates that there is an interesting structure to the global pattern of vehicular movement in the area. Figure 5.26, for instance, shows only the segments observed on the super-grid and peripheral spaces (Upper Street, Essex Road, Caledonian Road, Copenhagen Street, Offord Road, and the internal through routes in the

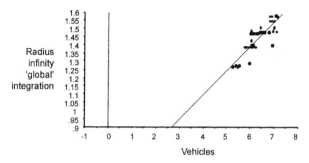

Figure 5.26 The same relationship for supergrid and peripheral segments and the internal through routes in the main study area, all plotted on the same scale.

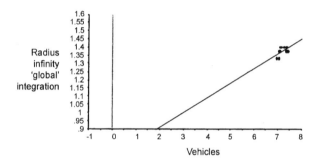

Figure 5.27 The same relationship for the Liverpool Road segments alone.

main study area, Hemingford, Barnsbury, Thornhill and Lofting Roads, and Bewdley Street). The correlation considering these areas only is somewhat higher (0.827) than for all the segments together.

Figure 5.27 shows the Liverpool Road segments, which clearly over-perform in terms of the degree of vehicular movement they attract for their degree of global integration. It is possible that this reflects the historical status of this route as a "back street" to the main route through Upper Street. Figure 5.28 plots only one-way segments, culs-de-sac and "trivial rings" formed by traffic-calming measures around the residential squares in the study area. The five points to the bottom of the scatter are the street seg-

THE URBAN MOVEMENT ECONOMY

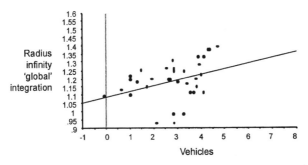

Figure 5.28 Only one-way segments, culs-de-sac and 'trivial rings'.

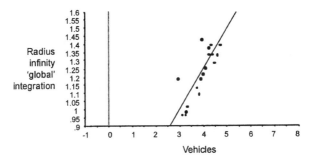

Figure 5.29 Non-cul-de-sac, two-way, non-trivial rings.

ments around Cloudsley Square and on Bridgeman Road through Thornhill Square that are used for parking for Chapel Market and Caledonian Road respectively. It is clear that the vehicular use levels in these segments depend on their strategic location in a pedestrian model of the area. The main lower arm of the bifurcation turns out to be composed of non cul-de-sac, two-way, and non-"trivial ring" segments (Fig. 5.29). The outlier on the left of the strong regression line is segment 17, the south side of Barnsbury Square, which is effectively turned into a trivial ring bypassed by the Bewdley Street–Islington Park Street line to the North and the cutting off of Brooksby Street to vehicular traffic.

The measure of global integration thus gives a very good account of the pattern of vehicular movement in the area, though the story is different for each category of street space. To uncover the effective structure of vehicu-

THE ARCHITECTURE OF SOCIETY

lar space use in the area, a division is necessary into through-route and supergrid spaces, spaces that are subject to traffic management by the creation of cul-de-sacs, trivial rings and one-way segments, and spaces where no such restrictions apply.

The dependence of vehicular movement rates on the global structure of the grid is further confirmed by applying the same selection criteria to street segments under the more localized radius 3 measure of integration. Although this gives a better prediction of movement rates overall, it is not so good for subsets. For example, Figure 5.30, which uses the radius 3 measure, shows a similar scatter to Figure 5.29, which is based on the radius infinity measure, but with a much reduced correlation.

The local measure performs better, however, for the subset of cul-de-sacs, trivial rings and one-way street segments (excluding those used for parking), giving a correlation coefficient of 0.719 as opposed to 0.517, and bringing them close to the overall regression line. This suggests that for these spaces levels of use depend more on the local properties of the configuration than on the global. In fact, it seems that the better performance of the radius 3 measure overall is due mainly to the preponderance of the local and traffic-managed street segments in the area sampled.

Patterns of pedestrian movement in the area also relate strongly overall to the pattern of radius 3 integration, though the best correlations are obtained in a model using a relatively small boundary to the model area (Fig. 5.31). This finding confirms the local scale of pedestrian trips. However, there is again an effect that is best interpreted as one of a hierarchy of glo-

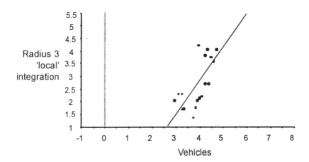

Figure 5.30 The equivalent scatter to Figure 5.29 for non-cul-de-sac, two-way and non-trivial-ring segments against the local radius 3 measure of integration.

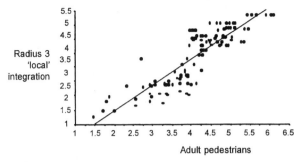

Figure 5.31 The correlation between adult pedestrian space use and radius 3 integration in system 2 (omitting segment 93 a cul-de-sac that was virtually never used): $r = .872$; $p < .0001$.

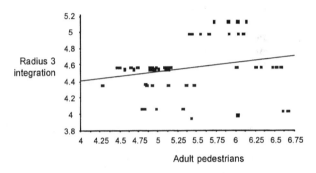

Figure 5.32 Pedestrian movement rates in supergrid spaces in the extended case study area show virtually no relation to local integration.

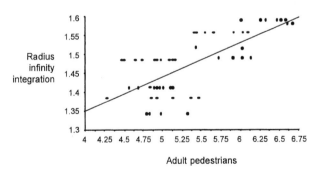

Figure 5.33 Pedestrian movement in the same set of supergrid spaces as shown in Figure 5.32 correlates strongly with global integration in the larger area.

THE ARCHITECTURE OF SOCIETY

Table 5.2 Multiple regression Beta Coefficient table of the vehicle/pedestrian ratio against local and global integration measures showing that both play a strong role in determining the ratio.

Parameter	Value	Std. Error	β	t	Probability
Global integration	72.98	23.03	.341	3.17	.002
Local integration	11.90	3.84	.334	3.10	.003

bal and local routes. If we look only at the main supergrid spaces in the extended case study area, the correlation with radius 3 integration virtually disappears (Fig. 5.32). It is replaced, however, by a strong correlation with global integration in the largest boundary area (Fig. 5.33).

What this suggests is that for both vehicular and pedestrian movement patterns the most useful modelling parameter will depend on the place of the spaces in the street grid hierarchy. For major supergrid spaces the larger radius global measures will predict the longer trips. Within the more localized streets of urban neighbourhoods, and for more local modes of movement, smaller radius measures are better.

Table 5.2 shows the result of a multiple regression analysis in which local and global integration measures are used as predictor variables of the ratio of vehicles to pedestrians. We find almost equal effects from the local variable that produces pedestrian movement rates and the global variable that produces vehicular movement rates. This suggests that it is the dynamics of the interaction of these two variables in the urban network that is at the root of how vehicular and pedestrian movement patterns come together.

When we look at the vehicle pedestrian ratio and set it against the product of local and global integration in the area, a general trend emerges relating increased integration to increased predominance of vehicular over pedestrian traffic (Fig. 5.34). However, if we look just at the supergrid spaces (Essex Road, Upper Street, Liverpool Road, Caledonian Road and Offord Road), a very strong negative trend emerges (Fig. 5.35). This shows that within these supergrid spaces an increase in local and global importance leads to a reduction in the vehicular predominance through increased pedestrian movement.

The Liverpool Road is the supergrid space that has the lowest product of local and global integration, and so the highest vehicle/pedestrian ratio. This suggests the possible historical process which might have led to the strong retail foci in the area being on the other supergrid spaces but not the Liverpool Road. In order for a retail focus to be successful, it must relate to

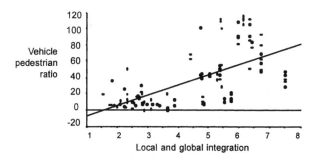

Figure 5.34 The vehicle pedestrian ratio and the product of local and global integration in the area.

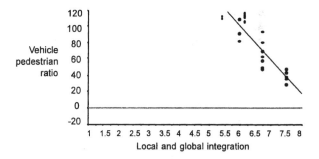

Figure 5.35 The same correlation for just the supergrid spaces plotted on the same scale.

both a wide pedestrian community in its local surroundings, and a wide catchment area of through movement traffic. Spaces in the urban grid will attract retail use in proportion to their success in bringing these two — local and global — configurational properties together. At this point a multiplier effect takes over, bringing additional, mainly pedestrian, movement to spaces with high levels of retail. The effects of configurational differences are thus reflected not only in the patterns of land uses and relative vehicular and pedestrian movement rates, but also perhaps in the dynamics of the evolution of the city.

This begins to resolve a long-standing question in urban design: which comes first, the people or the shops? It seems clear that, as every shop owner

THE ARCHITECTURE OF SOCIETY

will tell you, the shops locate themselves to take advantage of the passing trade and may then attract additional people. (See Hillier & Penn 1993 for a more complete discussion of this effect.) The pattern of movement created by the structure of the street grid gives rise to a by-product in the form of the economics of urban land use that we have called the "movement economy" (Hillier & Penn 1992).

However, when it comes to the intelligibility of urban systems we can go one stage further. The effect of this set of dynamic and economic processes in urban evolution leads to a series of correlations between different factors that can be observed in the urban environment. Patterns of movement go with configurational properties of the grid, patterns of land use follow both, different scales of movement follow differently scaled properties of the grid, and so on. It does not seem too far-fetched to propose that what we read as urban intelligibility and understandability are precisely these correlations: that the human mind is in effect a correlation detector in so far as it tries to retrieve and construct viable ways of making sense of perceptual data. If the mind has problems with making sense of these data, it is because the correlations have broken down – for instance, the shops are in the wrong place, or the patterns of movement do not relate to the spatial configuration.

This marks a clear distinction between Lynch's conception of imageability and our own of intelligibility. Where Lynch looked for the ability consciously to recall the map of an area and to be able to transcribe it more or less correctly, we suggest that an essentially unconscious process is at work: the search for correlations between factors as we move through space. The most important of these factors are the relations between local spatial properties, such as the connectivity of a space (the number of other spaces it links to), and the integration value of those spaces that are global in their extent. The correlation between the two tells us how well we can predict from local perceptual inputs our position in the global system. We call this the "intelligibility" of a system. It is also possible to look at other correlations. One such is the degree to which local movement patterns, predicted by radius 3 integration, and global movement patterns, predicted by larger radius measures of integration, are correlated. We suggest that this is a measure of the local to global interface in a system, a property that we have found necessary to support major retail streets.

The properties of intelligibility and interface are both commonly found in naturally evolving urban systems. They are also often absent in many modern and socially problematic urban areas. As one moves into recent planned housing estates, the relationship between local and global spatial

THE URBAN MOVEMENT ECONOMY

properties is all too often found to break down. With it other relationships break down as well: shops are located in the segregated interior of the estate to attract people – which history shows they fail to do; patterns of movement are found to be biased towards the edges regardless of spatial configuration, and therefore are essentially unpredictable from local spatial information; and the social networks on which residents rely for support are often said to be weakened.

These findings are of practical importance in the design and planning of cities and urban areas, since they suggest that physical design and the spatial patterns it produces are indeed of social relevance. However, we believe that the findings are also of theoretical importance in that they lend strong empirical support to one side of a long-running debate within the social sciences. The debate is over the relative priority of behaviour and action in the construction of social phenomena (Doyal & Gough 1991). The distinction between behaviour and action turns on the fact that, although we can often tell how someone is behaving – running down the road for instance – we do not have a full understanding of their actions unless we know their reasons for running – to escape a mugger, to catch a bus, or perhaps just for fun. It is this distinction that forms the basis for much of social science's interest in "goals" and "purposes" in action. One camp in the debate holds that individual goals are what relates the individual to his or her social actions. The other camp holds that for someone to act as an individual with purpose does not require that the person know other people's purposes, just that she is able to predict others' behaviour with some degree of certainty, and therefore to make a real choice in her own actions. Thus, in so far as goals are truly subjective, we cannot use them for prediction and they are therefore not social; in so far as they are predictable, they are also open to purposive reaction by others and so become social, but at the expense of subjectivity. Their predictability makes them objective.

The replacement of purpose by predictability as the main prerequisite for social action allows us to take a theoretical stance in which behaviour is predicted and used as the basis for purposive action, while the purposes of others are merely inferred from the sum of evidence. In the context of "way-finding", however, this seems to raise a problem. How is it possible to talk of people finding their way through a city without invoking knowledge at the level of purposes and goals? Surely we need to know at least what they are aiming for? One approach to the question of the degree to which we need to invoke destinations and goals in way-finding is to use computer simulations of individual entities moving through a configurational model of a street grid.

117

5.4 Simulating "intelligent rats" in intelligible systems

Our approach to this has been to perform a series of simulations of random movement, versions of which were first described by Hillier (Hillier & Hanson 1987). The model for this simulation consists of a simulated "pedestrian" that chooses its direction of movement randomly. The randomness removes any possibility of making a decision based on global information. The outcome is dictated only by the probabilities inherent in the configuration itself.

The central elements of the simulation were the urban system represented as a configurational model and the simulated pedestrians. The pedestrians are simple rule-based automata. No attempt was made to try to simulate a human being in this experiment, and there is no implication that the automata's rules are the actual rules humans might use; they are, rather, a simulation of possible rules in a large-scale system. In order to convey this, we refer to the automata as "rats".

The simulation consists of a rat performing journeys though a model of the Barnsbury urban environment. Configurational analysis is normally based on a graph formed by the intersection of the line elements (Fig. 5.36). However, the heuristics in the simulations use information such as distance and angle. The graph was therefore preprocessed to form a set of nodes and links (Fig. 5.37). In this, a node has a link to the set of nodes that share the same axial line (Fig. 5.38). Where axial lines intersect to give coincident nodes (i.e. three lines intersecting at the same point), a "fuzziness factor" was applied to ensure that only one node would be created. This copes with some of the approximations inevitable in digitizing a map of the real world.

The rats had a heuristic which they applied to the current state (the current location and possible directions of movement) to choose the next node to move to. The simulation was performed by repeating a large number of trips from random origins to random destinations. The paths were collected

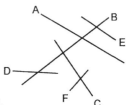

Figure 5.36 Line set [*A,B,C,D,E,F*] as digitized.

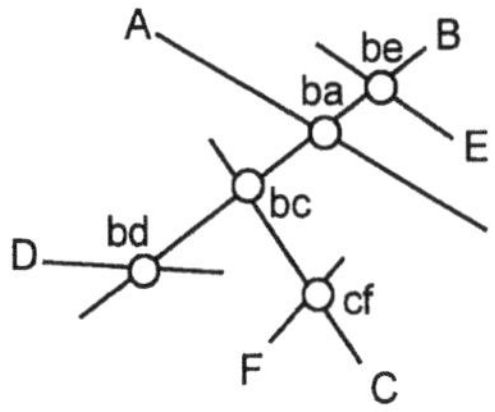

SIMULATING "INTELLIGENT RATS" IN INTELLIGIBLE SYSTEMS

Figure 5.37 Node set [*bd,bc,ba,be,cf*] created by intersecting the lines in the map.

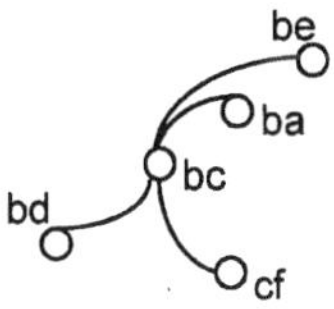

Figure 5.38 The neighbours for node *bc*. Notice that since *be* shares a parent axial line with *bc* it is also a neighbour. For all node maps created in this chapter it is true that connection[x,y] → connection[y,x].

and summed, line by line. This is analogous to the "observation gate" method used to observe movements in Barnsbury itself. In this way, the simulated observations could be compared with the real data and with the results of configurational analysis.

The simulation defined the location in the urban system that a rat wished to get to, and a rule to use to decide how to reach this target. A run of the simulation consisted of giving the rat an origin in the set of nodes and letting the rat roam over the node map until it either reached its target or used up a large quantity of system resources (which in practice never happened). When the rat successfully reached its target, those lines along which it had travelled at least one segment had their observational gate counts incremented. This gave a stochastic sample of urban movements. It was assumed that any part of the urban system is equally likely to be an origin or a destination of a journey. Journeys though Barnsbury starting or ending outside the site were modelled by embedding the site within a larger surrounding system, but counting only those parts of the trips through the site itself.

5.4.1 The simulation

At each node the rat has available its location and other information about the current node, and a list of nodes that the current node is linked to by virtue of sharing one of the same lines of sight. The rat returns a list of nodes

THE ARCHITECTURE OF SOCIETY

sorted in order of preference determined by the heuristic under investigation. The rat then tries to go to nodes in order of preference.

Simple rules seemed liable to give rise to failures to reach the goal. Intuitively, it seems likely that people use many different rules, replacing failing rules with other rules as needed. In the simulation, however, it is the product of the rule and the configuration of the system that defines the area of investigation. Creating complicated multi-part rules would obscure the effect of any individual heuristic.

Simple rat heuristics, for instance, require no memory and so always produce the same result given the same state. The rats are finite-state machines with the current node representing its state. A rat that selected as its next node one that it had already visited would walk round in circles for ever, because it would be doomed to repeat exactly the same choices it previously made. To cope with this, a single meta-heuristic monitored the rat's path to ensure that the rat was not allowed to visit the same node twice in the same journey. If a previously visited node were selected, the rat would be sent to its next preferred node instead. In effect, this gave the rat a limited temporary memory of its journey. This form of memory seems quite lifelike: we have all experienced the feeling of having "been there before" when we are lost and selecting a different way out.

One of the problems faced by analysis of urban areas is in the selection of a system boundary. The rule of thumb was to create a system that extended to about the equivalent of a 10-minute walk around the site of interest. Figures 5.39 and 5.40 show the line maps used in the analysis.

The first simulation experiment used a random heuristic to select the next node. The results show that, for 5,000 completely random journeys with random origins and destinations, rat counts on lines tracing the journeys correlate with line connectivity as well as with the integration radius 3 and integration radius infinity measures, giving correlations of 0.903, 0.877 and 0.790 respectively (see Table 5.3). Clearly, all other things being equal, random movement is largely determined by the local connectivity of a node. This is different from what has been found for real people – pedestrians' flow rates correlate with radius 3 integration and drivers' flow rates with radius infinity integration better than with connectivity.

The paths the rats take to find their goals are often long and inefficient. In order to replicate more nearly what a real person would do, it was clear that some form of more global knowledge would be required. It seemed possible that this is what gives rise to the better correlations with more global measures found for real-world populations.

SIMULATING "INTELLIGENT RATS" IN INTELLIGIBLE SYSTEMS

Figure 5.39 Small area line map for Barnsbury.

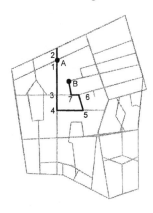

Figure 5.40 A journey from node A to node B. In this case node 2 has the smallest rounding error and therefore comes higher in the priority list.

THE ARCHITECTURE OF SOCIETY

Table 5.3 Correlations between configurational measures and the results of the three simulation experiments for the Barnsbury area.

Heuristic	Connectivity	Local integration	Global integration	Observations of Barnsbury
random	0.903	0.887	0.790	0.688
angle 40	0.898	0.869	0.856	0.693
longest line	0.848	0.747	0.759	0.781

This was investigated using two more elaborate heuristics, one based on orientation and the other on distance. Because people usually know the general direction they want to go in, the rules that govern people's movements seem likely to involve a clear direction towards their goals rather than away from them. It is possible to build this type of rule into the urban movement simulation. The rat in this case has a notion of where the target is in relation to its current position. This is stored as a vector pointing in the direction of the target. The rat is located on a node where it has to make a decision about which new node to move to. It knows the direction of each line passing through its current node and therefore the direction of each node that it can reach directly. The rat then compares the angle of the node with the angle of the target. After sorting by angle, the rat then sorts any nodes with the same angle (e.g. the nodes on the same axial line) by the distance it would have to travel to get to them, choosing the closest node in preference to more distant nodes. This allows it to construct a preference list, and the same rules are used as before in working through that list.

Because this heuristic involves sorting nodes by their angle, and nodes on the same axial line are associated with the same angle, there is a danger that such nodes will be ranked merely on minute inaccuracies arising from rounding errors in angle calculations. This can give rise to problems such as those shown in Figure 5.40. To avoid this, the comparison used for sorting was made deliberately "fuzzy", and all nodes with angles differing by less than 40 degrees were treated as having identical angles (see Fig. 5.40) At 40 degrees the notion of direction is clearly very fuzzy, but our experiments found it to work best in selecting sensible routes. A fuzzy view of angle thus appears to provide a more powerful route-finding algorithm than a deterministic one.

The correlations of the angle rat simulation counts with connectivity was 0.898, with integration radius 3, 0.869, and with radius infinity, 0.856. Clearly, the larger-scale orientation rule does promote the importance of the more global measures, although connectivity remains the best correlated.

SIMULATING "INTELLIGENT RATS" IN INTELLIGIBLE SYSTEMS

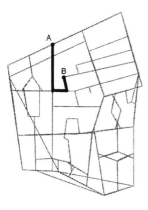

Figure 5.41 Given a coarser rounding factor, the rat selects a more obvious route.

The correlation with observations of flows in Barnsbury is somewhat lower at 0.693 (see Table 5.3).

When moving through the system, the angle-based rats move in a very local way and often produce a complicated path involving many changes of direction (Fig. 5.42). This does not resemble what we find real people doing. When faced with an alternative of a complex, albeit shorter, path through a housing estate and a simpler but longer path around the outside, observations show that most people use the longer simpler path. One method of simulating this is to use a heuristic which, from a given origin, chooses the node on one of its current axial lines that is closest to the target as the next to visit. This provides a useful partner to the angle-based rat

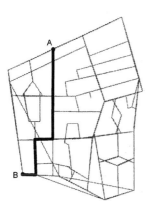

Figure 5.42 Path of an angle-based rat showing the tendency for shorter more complicated routes.

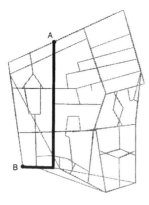

Figure 5.43 The path of a longest-line-based rat showing the preference for longer simpler routes though a system.

heuristic in which the rat moves on the longest line of sight in the correct direction from its current node. It can be seen that rats that use this longest-line heuristic favour longer simpler routes with fewer changes of direction (Fig. 5.43).

The heuristic performs reasonably well against connectivity with a correlation of 0.848, but less well for radius 3 integration (0.747) and radius infinity (0.574). The correlation with observations is somewhat stronger than for the other heuristics (0.781). The results for the longest line heuristic show that it is picking up elements of the movement in the Barnsbury system that are different from those for the random and angle-based heuristics.

5.4.2 Architecture as the memory store

The results at first seem baffling. Real-world observations have been found to correlate better with the more global measures of integration than with connectivity. However, in the simulations the heuristics (including those that are goal-based) correlate best with connectivity. Although goal-oriented heuristics that incorporate some degree of global knowledge do result in improved correlations with the more global measures of integration which predict real movement, the correlation with connectivity remains greater than the correlation with these global measures. It seems that the rats may require a more extensive form of global knowledge than either of the heuristics used to date. Although the results of these simulations confirm the importance of global knowledge in producing the patterns of movement we find among real human populations, they also stress the importance of the

SIMULATING "INTELLIGENT RATS" IN INTELLIGIBLE SYSTEMS

effects of the configuration alone. This produces a pattern of movement related to the connectivity of the lines in the system which persists in out-performing the goal-directed movement of the angle-based and longest-line rats.

Of course, this places at a premium the intelligibility and interface potential of a system, since these are the means by which the local spatial configuration of an urban area can give us information about its global structure and its likely use patterns. In effect, the configuration of the grid may itself be the storage medium of cultural knowledge, and use patterns themselves may give us global knowledge of the sort used in both way-finding and in understanding a culture.

It is tempting to go further. We suggest that in systems of discrete interacting individuals, such as those that characterize human societies, the regularities in behaviour that allow us to predict, and so react in a purposive way, are dependent in part on a mathematics of random movement constrained by global spatial configuration. The finding that global spatial patterns can emerge as a result of rule-restricted random aggregations of buildings suggests a possible mechanism for storage of patterns of interface between social groups in a kind of spatial memory. Movement through the spatial system actively retrieves the memory itself, in such a way that through daily use we not only understand the society but reproduce it. In this sense we would replace individual goals needed to understand actions as the prime movers of social systems, with an exosomatic genetic code, in the form of architectural and urban spatial configurations that constrain the behaviour and meeting of moving populations. This formulation is robust because it is non-deterministic. Clearly, individual goals and preferences (in all their subjectivity) determine individuals' actions, but configuration affects the dynamics of the population as a whole in which the sum of many different individuals moving with their own goals approximate randomness.

Chapter 6
Multi-agent simulation as a tool for studying emergent processes in societies

Alexis Drogoul & Jacques Ferber

This chapter presents a general model of multi-agent simulation based on the definition of computational agents that represent individual organisms (or groups of organisms) in a one-to-one correspondence. As an illustration of this general model, we describe both a generic multi-agent simulation tool called EMF and its first instantiation, the simulation of an ant colony.

Understanding the process of evolution is important in the study of ecological and sociological systems. We are interested in the simulation of the evolution of complex systems where interactions between several individuals at the micro level are responsible of measurable general situations observed at the macro level. When the situation is too complex to be studied analytically, it is important to be able to be able to recreate an artificial universe in which experiments can be done in a reduced and simulated laboratory where all parameters can be controlled precisely.

In this chapter we describe a general model of the simulation of societies which is based on the simulation of the behaviour of their individuals. We present an example of application of this model, called the MANTA (Modelling an Anthill Activity) Project, managed in association with the Laboratory of Ethology of Paris XIII University. This project, previously described in Drogoul et al. (1991) and Drogoul & Ferber (1992), is an application of the EthoModelling Framework (EMF) to the modelling and simulation of the social organization of an ant colony.

We will first introduce some principles of multi-agent simulation, then describe EMF as a particular instance of these principles and show how to program agents in this system. Finally, some early experimental results obtained within MANTA will be described.

6.1 Simulation

Simulation usually consists in artificially reproducing natural phenomena and can be described by the following quintuplet:

<system, model, representation link, tool, evaluation procedure>

where *system* is the natural system to be studied, *model* is an abstract definition of the system according to a theory, *representation link* is an abstract function which maps individuals and/or properties of individuals to elements of the model, *tool* is a computational device (usually a computer), and *evaluation procedure is* a methodology for evaluating the results and comparing them to the real system. Figure 6.1 illustrates the simulation process.

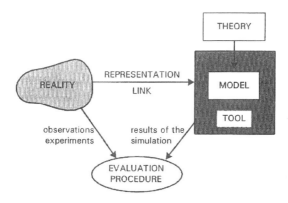

Figure 6.1 The simulation process.

Traditional techniques of simulation are based on mathematical or stochastic models, usually in the form of differential equations, that relate various parameters and describe the system's dynamics. They examine cause-and-effect relationships during the simulation by relating output variables to input ones. For instance, ecological simulations can relate the population size of specific species to the growth of other species and the number of predations. The following simple differential equations show the well known formulas defined by Lotka and Volterra (Volterra 1926) which express the rate of growth of predator and prey populations:

$$\frac{dN_1}{dt} = r_1 N_1 - P N_1 N_2$$

SIMULATION

$$\frac{dN_2}{dt} = aPN_1N_2 - d_2N_2$$

where P is the coefficient of predation, N_1 and N_2 are the prey and predator populations, a represents the efficiency with which predators convert food into offspring, r_1 is the birth rate of prey and d_2 is the death rate of predators. Although differential equations have been used for simulating societies, they have severe limitations:

(a) *Micro to macro relationship*   Input and output parameters are defined at the same level; i.e. they do not relate global parameters to local ones. For instance, it is not possible to relate a global parameter such as the population size to local parameters such as the decision processes of the individuals. Individual behaviours, i.e. decisions made at the individual or group level, cannot be incorporated into these simulations.

(b) *Complexity and realism of parameters*   Complexity in models leads to the definition of new parameters whose relation to reality is not obvious. For instance, although the above equations are very simple, the parameter a, which relates the food obtained to the number of offspring, does not model reality in a very accurate way, for offspring are the result of many complex processes and behaviours (mating, nesting, foraging, etc.) where the group structure is of primary importance. Detailed simulations require complex differential equations and the definition of many parameters that are difficult to interpret.

(c) *Taking behaviours into account*   Differential equations, and numerical methods in general, do not represent actions, i.e. activities that result in modifications of the world. Actions are seen only in terms of their measurable achievement and the probability of their occurrence.

(d) *Multi-task behaviours and conditional task switching*   In numerical modelling, actions cannot be considered as proceeding from evaluative decisions whose outcomes depend on perceived situations and stimuli. For instance, in numerical modelling, a feeding and hunting process can be described by an equation that relates the number of prey to the probability of a predator finding a prey and the number of predators. This type of equation does not show the different kinds of strategy by which a predator can find and hunt a prey. It does not describe the behaviour of the predator but only the relation between the number of predators and the number of prey.

(e) *Qualitative information*   Numerical simulations cannot cope with qualitative data such as the relation between a stimulus and the behaviour

129

STUDYING EMERGENT PROCESSES IN SOCIETIES

of an individual. These relations, which are typical of ethological models, are beyond the scope of analytical equations and numerical simulations. They require new computing models and tools that can capture the local interactions from which the global behaviour of the population emerges.

6.2 Multi-agent simulation

The life of an individual can be characterized by its behaviour, where the term behaviour means the set of actions an agent performs in response to its environmental conditions, its internal states and its drives. Multi-agent simulations are based on the idea that programs exhibit behaviours that can be entirely described by their internal mechanisms, namely the program instructions. By relating an individual to a program, it is possible to simulate an artificial world populated with interacting processes. Simulation can be achieved by transposing the population of a real biosystem to its artificial counterpart. Each organism of the population is separately represented as a computing process, an agent. The behaviour of an agent during all its stages of life (e.g., birth, feeding, mating, reproduction and death) is programmed with all the required details (Doran et al., Ch. 9 below; Hogeweg & Hesper 1985). The simulations are based on the construction of microworlds, where particular hypotheses can be explored by controlling and repeating experiments in the same way as real experiments are performed in a real laboratory.

Multi-agent simulations are used primarily to represent situations in which there are many individuals, each with complex and different behaviours, and to analyze the global structures that emerge as a result of the individuals' interactions. The purpose of such simulations is to take into account both quantitative and qualitative properties of the situation, as opposed to traditional simulations which only link properties to quantitative parameters. Multi-agent simulation is also called *microanalytic* simulation, meaning that each individual's behaviour and the environmental conditions are represented (Collins & Jefferson 1991).

In a multi-agent simulation, each biological and sociological individual (or a group of individuals) is represented as a computational agent, i.e. an autonomous computational process capable of performing local actions in response to various stimuli and communications with other agents. The behaviour of an agent is a consequence of its observation and interactions with

MULTI-AGENT SIMULATION

other agents, where "interaction" includes communication with other agents, the influences of environmental stimuli and the direct actions of other agents. There is therefore a one-to-one correspondence between individuals (or groups) in the world to be described and agents.

In a multi-agent simulation, the model is not a set of equations as in mathematical models, but a set of entities that can be described by the quadruplet:

<agents, objects, environment, communications>

where *agents* is the set of all the simulated individuals; *objects is* the set of all represented passive entities that do not react to stimuli (e.g. furniture); *environment* is the topological space where agents and objects are located, where they can move and act, and where signals (sounds, smells, etc.) propagate; and *communications* is the set of all communication categories, such as voice, written materials, signs, etc.

Agents are defined by their ability to perceive specific kinds of communications, by their skills, i.e. their ability to perform various actions, by their decision model, if any, and by their control structures, i.e. their ability to relate perception to action.

6.2.1 Goals of multi-agent simulation

Multi-agent simulation can be used for several different purposes. The first is to *test hypotheses* about the emergence of social structures from the behaviours of each individual and its interactions. This can be done by experimenting to discover the minimal conditions at the micro level that are necessary to observe phenomena at the macro level.

The second is to *build theories* that contribute towards the development of a general understanding of ethological, sociological and psycho-sociological systems, by relating behaviours to structural and organizational properties.

The third is to *integrate different partial theories* from disciplines such as sociology, ethology, ethnology and cognitive psychology into a general framework, by providing tools that allow for integration of disparate studies.

6.2.2 Cognitive and reactive multi-agent worlds

The field of distributed artificial intelligence distinguishes between cognitive and reactive multi-agent systems (Werner & Demazeau 1992). Cognitive agents have a symbolic and explicit representation of their environment on which they can reason and from which they can predict future events. Cognitive agents are driven by intentions, i.e. by explicit goals that affect their behaviour and make them able to choose between possible actions. Examples of this approach are Doran et al. (Ch. 9), who use cognitive agents to model social changes in Palaeolithic societies, and Conte & Castelfranchi (Ch. 12), who build a theory of cognitive emergence by virtue of cognitive dependence using the formal apparatus of Cohen & Levesque (1990a).

As we will see below in the presentation of the EMF model, reactive agents do not have a representation of their environment and act according to stimulus–response rules. The MANTA project is an example of the use of reactive agents to simulate insect societies. Although the remaining part of this chapter will be concerned only with reactive multi-agent systems, most of what will be said can be transposed directly to cognitive multi-agent simulation.

6.2.3 The importance of topological structures

The structure of the space where agents live is of a great importance for organizing a society, because spatial differences are transformed into organizational structures and the social differentiation of agents. As Nowak & Latané (Chapter 4) have pointed out, spatial relations provide a major constraint for the operation of social organizations. Because a stimulus's propagation and reciprocal influence decrease as a function of the distance between agents, behaviours of agents are strongly influenced by their relative positions in a topological structure.

Figure 6.2 exemplifies this process. Let us assume that we are in a reactive multi-agent system, and that a stimulus s produced by a source S_o is

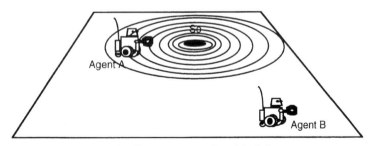

Figure 6.2 The importance of spatial relations.

capable of triggering a behaviour P in agents A and B. Let us suppose also that agent A is closer to the source S_o than agent B. Because stimulus intensity decreases as an inverse function (either linear or square root) of the distance between the source and its receiver, the stimulus level of s is such that level$_s$(A) > level$_s$(B). Then the impact of s will be stronger on A than on B, and the behaviour P will be triggered more easily in A than in B. If reinforcement takes place, as in the EMF model described below, A will tend to be more specialized than B in dealing with actions triggered by the stimulus s, thus providing social differentiation of the agents' rôles in the society.

6.2.4 Feedback

> The situation itself is the controlling agency. Each accomplished
> job creates a new situation which in itself is a stimulus and guide
> for the activities to be done next.   (Lindauer 1986)

Emergence of functionalities and stable states are produced by the combined forces of different feedback mechanisms. Positive feedback tends to create diversity among agents whereas negative feedback regulates societies, imposing a conservative force upon their social structures.

In multi-agent systems, feedback can be classified into two categories: local feedbacks, which are built by the agent designer and are part of the primitive constructs of agents, and global feedbacks, which are the results of interactions between agents and whose action is not explicitly described at the agent level.

For instance, a reinforcement process that makes an already specialized agent more inclined to perform the same tasks is a kind of positive feedback that can be implemented at the agent level. Its effect is to strengthen any differentiation and create disparities among agents. A regularity such as the distribution of rôles in a society is an example of a negative feedback that can be observed as emerging from agents' interaction, as we shall see below. While local feedbacks are deterministic because they have been designed as such by a programmer, global feedbacks are not always deterministically predictable. They often result from the autocatalytic processes that arise from interactions in open systems (Prigogine & Stengers 1984).

6.2.5 Multi-agent simulation and statistical analysis

Multi-agent simulation and numerical analysis are not contradictory, but they are intended to be used at different levels. Multi-agent models are used

Classical stochastic simulation

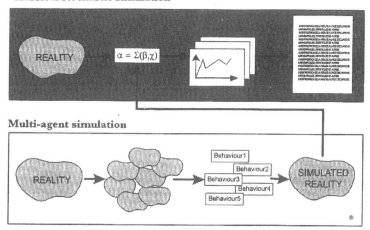

Figure 6.3 Multi-agent simulation versus stochastic simulation.

at a local level as analogical mappings of a real system. From the simulation, one can derive global parameters that can be studied and incorporated into a mathematical model, as suggested in Figure 6.3, which illustrates the differences between the two approaches.

In multi-agent simulations, numerical data and statistics are not eliminated, but are used as evaluation procedures to compare the results coming from the simulation tool with the observed data coming from the "real" world. Thus mathematical models are used at the macro level, whereas multi-agent simulation models are used to cross the micro–macro bridge by letting global configuration emerge from the local agent interactions.

6.3 A reactive multi-agent simulation system

Although the characteristics of our agents have already been fully described in Drogoul et al. (1991) and Drogoul & Ferber (1992), this section provides a brief digest of their key features. EMF is implemented using an actor language in Smalltalk–80. Agents are viewed as actor-objects, i.e. objects embodied within actors that allow them to work asynchronously. EMF provides the programmer with a domain-independent kernel that drives the internal functioning of the agents and the interactions between them and the environment. Its main component is a class named Etho Behaviour. The model entities are defined as instances of classes that inherit from Etho Behaviour. Each class represents a species of agents, each instance an individual in this species.

The environment is defined as a set of squares of the same size, called *places*, which know about the agents that are located on them and about their neighbouring places. Places can also act as obstacles, refusing agents and failing to distribute stimuli. Agents are able to disperse individual pheromone-like signals, called *stimuli*, into the environment. A stimulus is a doublet, <name, strength>, *name* being the identifier of the stimulus and *strength*, the value that is propagated. Stimuli are used as triggers for the behaviours of the other agents.

An agent is seen as consisting of a set of behaviours called *tasks*, only one of which can be active at a time. The selection and the suspension of tasks are entirely stimuli-oriented. This means that an agent's behaviour is a stereotyped response to a stimulus, and the selection and duration of its responses are entirely governed by the intensity of the stimuli it receives. The term "task" refers to a set of behavioural sequences rather than to the low-level actions (moving, and so on) which called *primitives*. The behaviour of an agent is defined by a set of tasks, each related to a particular stimulus name and encapsulating a sequence of primitives. Each task is provided with:

- a *name*, usually the name of the stimulus that triggers it;
- a *weight*, which specifies the importance of the task for the agent;
- a *threshold*, below which the task will not be triggered by a stimulus;
- a *level of activity* computed when the task becomes active.

There are two sequences of primitives, one executed when the task becomes active and the other, when it becomes inactive.

An agent always knows the current task in which it is involved. When this task executes one of its primitives, the agent performs the *task selection process*, to determine if another task is not more appropriate to its environment than the current one (Fig. 6.4). This process is made up of three steps:

(a) *Sensing* The agent collects stimuli and eliminates those that do not match with a task.

(b) *Selection* The agent computes each activation level by multiplying the strength of the stimulus and the weight of the related task; those tasks whose activation levels surpass both the threshold and the activity level of the current task are selected.

(c) *Selection* If some tasks can be activated, the agent chooses the one with

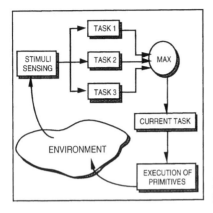

Figure 6.4 The task selection process.

the greatest activation level. It then stops the current task and activates the new one. When no task can be selected, the current task is continued and its activity level is decremented.

When a task is selected, it becomes the current task of the agent and its activity level is initialized to the value of its activation level. The agent then performs its *activation behaviour*. When a task is stopped, the agent performs its *deactivation behaviour* and zeroes its activity level.

Agents must be provided with a task called *default*. This task is always activated, with an activation level equal to 1. It is chosen when no other tasks can be selected and when the activity level of the current task becomes nil. This task specifies the default behaviour of the agent when its environment is not particularly attractive.

"Real" creatures, although they are often provided with preprogrammed behaviours, exhibit flexible mechanisms of behaviour selection and can often take account of former experiences of interactions with their environment in choosing their next behaviour. Numerous types of plasticity mechanisms (Beer 1990) have been studied in animals; in EMF we have implemented only a simple one: *behaviour reinforcement*. Behaviour reinforcement has been observed in many animal species and has been particularly well studied in social insects as a mechanism of social organization (Theraulaz et al. 1991). With behavioural reinforcement, the more an agent performs a task, the more likely it is to perform it again. The *reinforcement process* takes place after the current task has been deselected and increases the task's weight proportionally to its duration.

6.4 MANTA agents and their behaviour

6.4.1 Environmental agents

Each environmental agent represents an environmental factor, such as light or humidity, that can be placed anywhere and can propagate its particular stimuli. For example, light agents are used to create the difference between the outside and the inside of a nest. Light agents are also intended for simulating the alternation between day and night (by changing the strengths of their stimuli). These agents propagate stimuli named #light and #humidity, respectively. Another class of agents that can be included in this category is FoodAgent, which is intended to model any kind of food that can be eaten either by the ants or by the larvae. Eggs and larvae (see Sec. 6.4.3) can become food agents. Food agents propagate a stimulus called #food, the strength of which is dependent on their nutritive value.

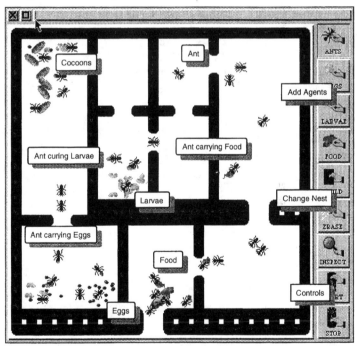

Figure 6.5 The MANTA nest: a snapshot of the simulation in progress showing the ants, eggs, larvae and cocoons in a simulated laboratory nest.

6.4.2 Spy agents

Spy agents extract information from the simulation and translate them into statistical, numerical or textual data. These agents can be added or removed at any time during the progress of a simulation. They can manage special windows displaying text or graphs, save their data on files or perform complex data analysis. Spy agents do not propagate any stimuli.

6.4.3 Brood agents

The agents that compose the brood are the eggs, the larvae and the cocoons. They represent the three steps leading to the adult stage of an ant. According to ethological and biological data (Corbara 1991), these agents just have to be fed (only in the case of larvae), cared and carried by other agents to be satisfied. The propagated stimuli are named, respectively, #egg, #larva and #cocoon. Because of the inheritance of classes that implement implicit stimuli (see Drogoul & Ferber 1992), the agents also propagate stimuli named #cureEgg, #cureLarva, #cureCocoon, #maturingLarva and #hungryLarva. The strengths of these stimuli are related to the agent's state variables (e.g. foodLevel, cureLevel). The #maturingEgg, #maturingLarva and #maturingCocoon stimuli, the strength of which depend on the age of the agent, are used to trigger the tasks that allow an egg, a larva or a cocoon to become, respectively, a larva, a cocoon or an ant, assuming that it does not lack appropriate care. If it does, this task leads eggs and larvae to become FoodAgents, and cocoons to die.

6.4.4 Ants and queens

These are the most complex agents in the simulation. We have provided them with almost all the behaviours described by Corbara (1991) (see Table 6.1). The stimuli that could be present in the environment are shown in the left-hand column, while the tasks directly related to them are in the right-hand column. The one stimulus that is internal and is not propagated to the environment is italicized. Internal stimuli can just trigger the tasks of the emitter.

The ant and queen agents are provided with a lot of primitives (almost twenty), including all the moving, feeding, caring and sensing primitives. The two classes AntAgent and QueenAgent share the same basic properties (QueenAgent is a subclass of AntAgent), but queens live much longer than workers and, above all, can lay eggs. In the model, this involves pro-

MANTA AGENTS AND THEIR BEHAVIOUR

Table 6.1 Links between the stimuli and the tasks of the ants.

Stimulus	Propagated By	Related Task
careAnt	AntAgent, QueenAgent	Take Care of Ants
careEgg	EggAgent	Take Care of Egg
careLarva	LarvaAgent	Take Care of Larvae
maturingLarva	LarvaAgent	Take Care of Larvae
careCocoon	CocoonAgent	Take Care of Cocoons
maturingCocoon	CocoonAgent	Take Care of Cocoons
hungryAnt	AntAgent, QueenAgent	Feed Ant
hungryLarva	LarvaAgent	Feed Larva
maturingAnt	AntAgent, QueenAgent	Die
ant	AntAgent	No Task
egg	EggAgent	Carry and Aggregate Eggs
larva Larvae	LarvaAgent	Carry and Aggregate
coocon Cocoon	CocoonAgent	Carry and Aggregate
food	FoodAgent	Carry Food
light	LightAgent	Flee Light
humidity	HumidityAgent	No Task

viding queens with a longer expectation of life (a domain-dependent item of knowledge) and a new task, called layEggs, which consists in creating and putting down an instance of EggAgent. layEggs is triggered by an internal stimulus possessed only by the queen, the strength of which depends on the time. (According to biological data, a queen can lay between two and three eggs a day, which means about one egg every 10 hours on average.)

Before presenting the experimental results obtained with simpler agents, we will describe how tasks are constructed. Although there are no strict rules for building the sequences of primitives that make up tasks, most follow these guidelines:

– Be as short as possible. Otherwise, try to split the task into two smaller ones. For instance, tasks in MANTA never exceed four primitives.

– Try to implement "consumption" behaviour, that is, behaviour that eventually decreases the stimulus that triggers the task. For example, feeding the larvae when they are hungry reduces the intensity of the hungryLarvae stimulus.

– Avoid primitives that test a condition. The strengths of stimuli can be computed using a combination of state variables, and the behaviour selection process should be a sufficient filter. For example, the layEggs

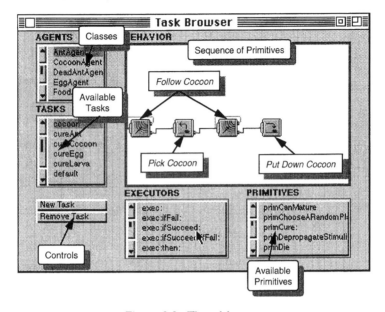

Figure 6.6 The task browser.

task does not test whether it is time for the queen to lay eggs: it just assumes that its selection has taken the time parameter into account. In this way, a typical task (for example, the carryCocoon task) can be formulated with only four primitives: follow the gradient emitted by the cocoon; pick up the cocoon that needs to be carried; follow the gradient emitted by other cocoons if there are any; and put down the cocoon.

Using the visual programming tool called the Task Browser, the task can be written very simply (see Fig. 6.6).

6.5 An example of experimentation

As a simple example, we will consider a model of ants provided with three tasks (#egg, #larva, #food). These tasks are similar to carryCocoon described in the previous section. The case study is composed of 30 identical ants (all with the same initial weights and thresholds), 50 larvae, 50 eggs and

AN EXAMPLE OF EXPERIMENTATION

50 pieces of food randomly distributed throughout the nest. The amounts of time spent on each task by each ant during the simulation are measured. The simulation ends when the eggs, larvae and pieces of food are completely sorted into three separate clusters.

Although this example is not intended to simulate a real nest, because the ants are not provided with all their behaviours, two lessons can be drawn from it:

(a) The average partition of the overall working time between the three tasks matches the initial partition between eggs, larvae and pieces of food (33% each). A similar result is obtained in other examples (Drogoul et al. 1991).

(b) A division of labour appears within the nest, characterized by five functional groups (see Fig. 6.7, which plots the observed distribution of groups within the population):

(i) egg nurses (group 1: 8 ants), distinguished by a high level of care of eggs and a low level of inactivity;

(ii) specialized (group 2: 8 ants), distinguished by a high level of inactivity; the ants nevertheless contribute to the other activities in the nest;

(iii) feeders (group 3: 7 ants), distinguished by a high level of feeding activities; the members of this group are also often inactive;

(iv) inactive larvae nurses (group 4: 3 ants), distinguished by a high level of care of larvae, a high level of inactivity and a very low level of care of the eggs;

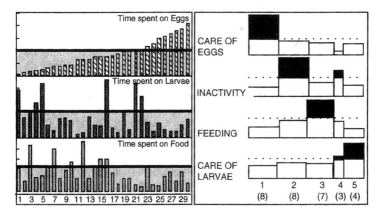

Figure 6.7 The division of labour of a simulated population.

STUDYING EMERGENT PROCESSES IN SOCIETIES

(v) larvae nurses (group 5: 4 ants), distinguished by a high level of care of larvae and a low level for the other activities.

This division of labour appears to be simpler than those observed in reality. As mentioned above, the reason is that we provided the ants with a relatively small set of behavioural capacities. However, the structure of the division of labour appears to be a consistent feature of the many simulations we have run, and this helps to confirm the validity of our approach. It suggests that we can look forward in the near future to modelling anthills that are much closer to reality than in this example.

Our current work consists of experimenting with the full set of ants' behaviours depicted in Table 6.1. The experiments can be classified into three categories: sociogenesis, division of labour and sociotomy.

Sociogenesis is intended to simulate a basic process observed in the natural counterpart of MANTA's ants, when the queen has to take care of the whole brood alone as well as finding food. In this way, we hope both to validate the individual behaviour we have given the simulated ants (and the queen) and to obtain truly artificial ant societies.

The *division of labour* will then be studied by comparing the clustering of our ants into functional groups in these artificial societies with the sociograms obtained for natural societies.

Finally, we hope to show the stability of this division of labour through experiments on artificial *sociotomies*, consisting of cutting an adult society into two smaller societies in order to observe the individual readjustments. An experimental "natural" sociotomy usually separates a group of highly specialized individuals from the rest of the colony, providing each sub-society with the same number of eggs, larvae and cocoons, and the same amount of food. Then, a phenomenon comparable with homeostasis makes each sub-society recover its division of labour to allow it to survive.

Results from these experiments should soon be available and we will then be able to explore more precisely the relationships between the ants' behaviour and the behaviour of the colony as a whole. This should contribute to studies on the links between the micro and macro levels of any society.

Chapter 7
Simulating fishermen's society

F. Bousquet, C. Cambier, C. Mullon,
P. Morand & J. Quensiere

The management of natural environments exploited by man, especially aquatic environments, has been considered from an ecological point of view for many years. Ecological studies have led to a better understanding of the natural environment and have indicated how acceptable exploitation may be achieved by imposing catch limits consistent with fish resource dynamics. Social scientists, especially economists, have been increasingly involved in assessing these optimum catches. Also, researchers in sociology and anthropology have recently been studying how societies adapt to the exploitation of resources through modifying the social structures that define access to space and to the resources. Thus, in research on small-scale fishing, a new theme – society – has come to the forefront. For example, the TURF concept (Territorial Use Rights in Fisheries) is a current focus of research (Berkes 1989).

It is now time to go beyond this bipolar approach in order to embark upon research on the links between society and environment, analyzing the relation between the types of exploitation and the dynamics of fishery resources, rather than considering either in isolation.

The interaction between people and environmental resources varies in space – there are different locations with different characteristics among which fish can move – and in time, for the environmental conditions (climate, hydrology, etc.) change with the seasons, leading to variation in the behaviour of fish populations. And the processes that constitute the inherent dynamics of the resource (growth, reproduction and mortality) differ considerably between populations. Together, these space–time and biological variabilities lead the resource subsystem to follow specific trajectories.

This variability in the resource affects fishermen. It is taken into account both at the individual level by each fisherman's choice of strategy, and also collectively by the fishermen's society, which adapts to the variable environment and its dynamics. The adaptations lead to a social organization of activities and to a division of space between the different users of the same resource. Thus, spatial and other variations in the resource contribute to the structure of society.

We have been considering fish stocks in terms of variability: variability of the environment and variability of the people subjected to this environment. At a higher level, we can describe a society in terms of changes through time and a diversity in the occupation of space. Simulation can be used to study the transition between the individual behaviour of the fishermen's households and the general behaviour of a group of households, in order to see whether the variability of the individuals and the variability of their environment can be linked to the variability that is characteristic of the society.

7.1 Case study: the central delta of Niger

The central delta of Niger in Mali covers several thousand square kilometres in the Sahelian zone (Fig. 7.1). The river, whose water level varies considerably in the course of the year, flows into a very flat zone. During the flood period, water rises from the flooded plains into channels; when the water recedes, ponds remain until the plain is nearly completely dry. This creates a highly productive ecosystem in which fish ascend streams to reproduce in the plains during the flood and descend again during the recession. The delta territory is inhabited by various ethnic groups including fishermen, farmers and stock breeders. The zone yields nearly 100,000 tonnes of fish per year but has been severely affected by various factors, including the great Sahelian drought, which have led to a decrease in fish catches. A multidisciplinary research team from ORSTOM and IER (Institute of Rural Economy, Mali) is trying to identify the causes of this crisis (Quensiere 1990). The team includes demographers, anthropologists, micro- and macroeconomists, biologists, fish biologists and ecologists.

Researchers in ecology and biology are studying the adaptation of the fish populations to space heterogeneity and to hydrological variation. They are investigating the interaction between people and resources on a local level (studying fish catches in given place, at given moment, with given equipment), and also on a general level, in villages and in fishermen's groups (studying the time and space distribution of the activities of the fishermen's households).

144

At the same time, researchers in anthropology and microeconomics are studying social structures and their history. They have shown that in the 1940s access to water and the distribution of land between ethnic groups or families was highly organized. However, the State then introduced free access and fishing licences, and more productive equipment from Europe and Asia became available (Fay 1990; Kassibo 1990). These new opportunities for exploitation of the fish stock gave rise to economically rational individual

Figure 7.1 The central delta of Niger.

SIMULATING FISHERMEN'S SOCIETY

behaviours. The crisis that currently affects this area results both from conflicts between fishermen who claim different rights, and from a severe drought which has shrunk the resource.

In short, the zone includes various types of households of fishermen, differing according to ethnic group, number of people, origin, etc., and subjected to a fluctuating hydrological and ecological environment. A number of theories, points of view and models are available to explain the

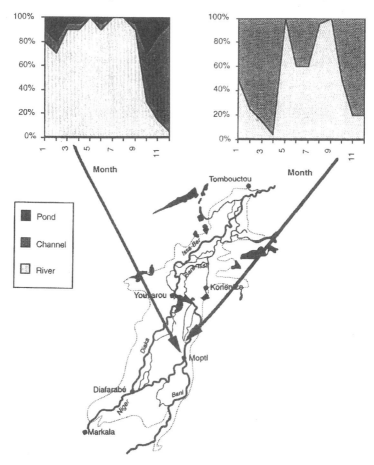

Figure 7.2 The space occupation of two groups of fishermen. (*Source*: Laë 1990.)

production strategies, the fishermen's decisions, the space occupation and the organization of the activities carried out by these groups of fishermen. Figure 7.2 (Laë 1990) gives some results observed in the field. We have created a model to simulate different types of individual behaviour and to address the following questions:

— By subjecting a population of fishermen to hydro-ecological variability, is it possible to go from individual behaviour to the distribution of activities and space occupation observed within the group?

— What is the interaction between the different types of decision-making and the resource dynamics?

Investigators typically represent the behaviour of the fishermen's society by the occupation of space (Fig. 7.2). Consequently, this measure is the main output of the simulation. In the following sections, the structure of the simulation model is presented, followed by examples of experiments demonstrating its use.

7.2 Building a simulator

The model simulates the decisions made by households in a fluctuating environment. We will first introduce the knowledge representation techniques used, secondly describe the basic module which simulates the dynamics of the fish populations in a heterogeneous area and thirdly explain the process of decision-making in fishermen's households.

7.2.1 Representation of knowledge

Modelling of ecological processes traditionally uses mathematical representations (differential equations, matrix analyses) to capture the relationships between concepts and those variables, such as stocks, biomass and population density, for which measurements are available. In contrast, we propose that the modelling of knowledge should be based on the principles of distributed artificial intelligence (Hewitt 1976; Lesser & Corkill 1987; Ferber 1989). A number of techniques and methods are used and developed as part of our application (Fig. 7.3) (Bousquet & Cambier 1990). We selected object-oriented design (Pave 1989) as our basic approach to the construction of the model. Object-oriented design consists in modelling the world by representing its different constituent objects. It translates the observed elements of the world (fish, fishermen, biotopes, etc.) into computer objects

SIMULATING FISHERMEN'S SOCIETY

Object oriented representation

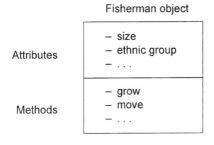

The simulator organization

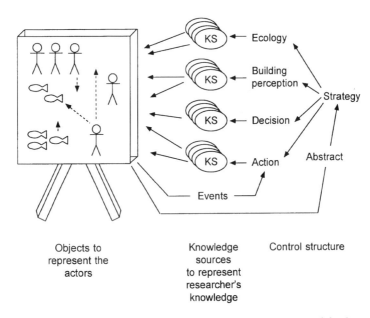

Figure 7.3 The representation of knowledge and the organization of the simulation.

which include a description of the real object expressed in terms of its attributes (for instance, a fish object will have size and weight attributes) and its behaviours (for instance, growth and movement).

Object-oriented design is well adapted to our study and its multi-disciplinary basis. Researchers can make use of different concepts (biomass, price, migration flows) while observing the same design discipline. Object-oriented design and its associated use of inheritance permits different points of view on the same object. For instance, an anthropologist might consider the household object through its ethnic group, household size and origin attributes, while the fishing specialist might consider it through the various types of equipment available to it and its members' technical ability.

Researchers have different types of knowledge about the dynamics of objects in the world and their interactions. This knowledge can refer to complementary disciplines (for instance, there are, on the one hand, rules on the dynamics of fish populations and, on the other hand, rules on the social relations between fishermen) or even opposed disciplines (for instance, an economist will not describe the dynamics of fishermen's decisions using the same rules as an anthropologist). Regardless of its origin, the knowledge can be described in the form of a set of symbolic rules (a "knowledge source") which expresses a distinctive evaluation of the dynamics of the objects in the world.

We selected a "blackboard system" to organize this knowledge and to enable different evaluations and points of view to co-operate. The blackboard system controls the dynamics of the simulation and makes use of the different types of knowledge when they are necessary. For example, the system will invoke a knowledge source embodying ecological rules in order to specify fish growth and a knowledge source embodying the rules of the fishing specialist in order to determine fish catches.

The simulation model has been implemented in the Smalltalk language on a SUN workstation. It is divided into two major parts: one concerned with ecological dynamics and the other with fishing dynamics. We will first give a simple description of the ecological dynamics and then turn to the simulation of the activities carried out by the groups of fishermen.

7.2.2 Hydro-ecological modelling

In the delta, four main types of biotope can be distinguished: the river which is supplied with water all the year round, channels which are supplied with water at the time of the flood, flooded plains which are supplied with wa-

SIMULATING FISHERMEN'S SOCIETY

ter at the height of the flood, and ponds. During the recession period, plains and channels are no longer supplied with water and the ponds gradually dry up. These four main types of biotope, with, in addition, agricultural fields, represent the areas common to both fish and fishermen and the locations where they interact. We simulated the dynamics of fish populations within these areas by defining fish groups in terms of objects that reproduce, grow bigger, die, migrate and enter into competition.

This simulation is used as a basis for the simulation of fishermen's decisions and also as a basis of comparison for the different production strategies to be tested. We observe how different strategies change the characteristics of the fish populations (e.g. the evolution of the biomass, weight and age structure).

7.2.3 Modelling the fishermen's decision-making

We can add "household objects" to the hydro-ecological simulation. These formal objects are given attributes corresponding to the ethnic group they represent, the numbers of individuals they contain, etc. The simulation model permits the creation of fishermen populations according to the distributions observed in the field. (For instance, 80 per cent of the households belong to the Bozo ethnic group, and the number of individuals per household approximates a normal distribution with a mean of 7 and a standard deviation of 2.) Once these household objects have been entered into the simulation, they take decisions about their activities and act accordingly.

Our decision-making model is divided into four phases: building, perception, decision (selection) and action. Thus we remain close to classical modelling of decision making (P. A. Allen 1984; Simon 1981). Some decision-making models yet to be tested are expressed in a stimulus-reaction form and do not require these four phases.

The *building* phase records all the activities likely to be carried out in the environmental conditions. Possible fishing activities are composed of combinations of biotope and equipment (e.g. pond-cast net, river-cast net, river-gill net) called *technotopes*. Agriculture is considered as another possible activity in order to study the relation between it and fishing. Each fisherman (object) defines an object called an *agenda* for each of the possible activities and stores information on these agendas in the course of the following perception phase.

The *perception* phase for a fisherman object consists of getting information about each of the potential activities. The environmental conditions of

BUILDING A SIMULATOR

the fishermen have been assessed by researchers who have provided the data that are stored on the agenda objects. This information must be transcribed in a common syntax so that it can be compared. We selected two types of representation. The first is quantitative and the second is qualitative.

Quantitative transcription Financial data are transcribed into an economists' decision-making theory. For example, given a household x and a flood y, the following rule indicates that the activity of fishing will yield 1000 monetary units:

$$\text{IF } y \text{ height} = \text{high THEN } x \text{ fishing river} = 1000$$

As mentioned before, the environment fluctuates and fishermen will therefore gain by foreseeing future environmental conditions. The fishermen acquire beliefs about the results of their possible activities and the variability of their environment. For instance, in order to calculate the receipts from an activity (a site–equipment combination), the resulting fish catch must be estimated. A fisherman has knowledge of the fish caught in the past at this location with this equipment. Each of the fishermen can use this experience either riskily, by estimating that catches will be maximal, or cautiously, by estimating that they will be minimal or moderate. Therefore, utility calculations must capture fishermen's varying attitudes towards uncertainty about the results of interaction with the resource.

Qualitative transcription When analyzing the knowledge produced by the researchers, it was observed that there is information that cannot be transcribed into this quantitative form. Therefore, we also employed a more qualitative representation, derived from poll theory. An activity can be favourable, unfavourable, impossible or compulsory. Each researcher, each point of view and each model can express an opinion on the possible activities using these four modalities.

The *selection* phase consists of making a choice among the various possibilities. For this purpose, different models are available. Some of them impose a decision, and then there is no choice. Others, for example decision-making based on economic considerations, compare the potential activities. Again, there are several possibilities: selection of the most profitable activity, selection of the activity that receives the most favourable opinions, selection of the activity that receives the least unfavourable opinions, etc.

When making a decision, the fisherman's household is involved in not only an ecological but also a social environment. The study of this environment is the first objective of this simulation. The social situation in which the fisherman is involved can be considered according to either of two ap-

151

SIMULATING FISHERMEN'S SOCIETY

proaches. The top-down approach consists of associating a set of constraints with the fisherman's household. The anthropologists supply knowledge which describes the structure of the fishermen's society and the distribution of their activities; for example:

IF x household AND x ethnic-group $=$ Bozo THEN A compulsory-activity

The bottom-up approach, in contrast, consists of associating with the fisherman other households with which he can have interactions and specifying the principles that govern these interactions. For instance, each household might have four neighbours and might copy the behaviour of the best one, the activity most common within the group or that least common. Each possibility leads to different social organizations. Simulation is important in that it can test these different models in the same artificial universe in order to compare them and to observe how closely they accord with reality.

The *action* phase After deciding on its activity, the household goes to fish. According to the activity selected, it selects equipment and goes to a site, the biotope. There, the fish catch depends on the amount of fish in the biotope, which is variable. The fisherman does not catch exactly the same amount of fish each time in the same biotope with the same equipment. A record of the amount of fish caught is added to the fisherman's stored experience (an attribute of the corresponding object). This experience records details of all the fishing operations of the fisherman's household for different sites, equipment and seasons, and is a source of new information for future decisions. For each fishing operation, the corresponding amount of fish is removed from the associated biotope. The environment is therefore modified for all fishermen. The construction–perception–selection–action cycle is now complete.

This simulator thus enables the testing of different models of decision-making for households living in a variable environment. We have described the principles of the simulator, the computer techniques and the simulation structure. Next, we will give examples of simulations based on different decision-making models in order to provide a general outline of the use of this system.

7.3 Simulations

We have already presented the data we are working with:
– statistical distributions, which define the populations of fishermen, the

SIMULATIONS

variability of the environment and the variability of the fish catches: these describe our artificial universe and its variability;
- output data on the fishermen's activities and their occupation of space (Fig. 7.2).

The empirical data available derive from 36 different villages in different areas and environments. To conduct simulation studies based on these data requires that they should be fully analyzed to yield reliable estimates of statistical distributions of variables such as the size of households, ethnic distributions, etc., to complement the output data already available. Unfortunately, these analyzes are not yet complete. Therefore we cannot yet report simulations that are grounded in the empirical data.

However, complementing these empirical data about the agents of the artificial world and their space occupation, there are models of decision-making that can be tested and discussed in relation to their ability to represent the observed variability.

We shall therefore present examples of simulations which show the potential of our simulation model and which test different decision-making models. The results of these simulations will be compared by analyzing how individual behaviour determines the areas that fishermen's groups occupy through the year.

7.3.1 The models

We have demonstrated the potential of the simulator by experimenting with several different decision-making models. The first simulation we shall report endows the fishermen with economically rational behaviour. Their aim is to maximize profit. We show how this rational behaviour relates to environmental variability. Alternatively, the households may be endowed with different attitudes towards risk, for example bold, cautious or average. Also, anthropologists have studied the behaviour of the fishermen's society and described the relations between fishermen's groups. We give a schematic representation of this organization in order to observe its consequences. Finally, various possible interactions between fishermen, such as copying, are tested and reported.

7.3.2 The resource without fishing

Preliminary work addressed the dynamics of the resource in the absence of fishing. We simulated an environment composed of a river biotope, a chan-

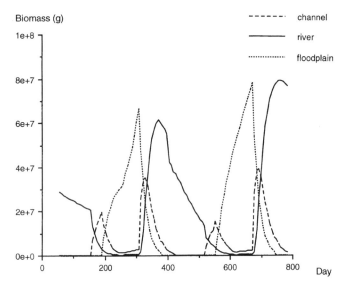

Figure 7.4 The dynamics of the fish resource in the absence of fishing.

nel biotope, a flooded plain biotope and a pond biotope. The hydrological cycle was as follows. At the beginning of the flood, water rises from the river to the channel and from the channel to the floodplain. The three biotopes are connected, allowing fish to migrate from the river to the plain. When the flood recedes, water withdraws progressively from the plain and the channel, and fish gather in the river. The pond is a special biotope for it is isolated from the others. Schematically, the resource cycle is as follows. At the flood period, fish reproduce, ascend to the channels or the plains, and find conditions that are very favourable to their growth. At the recession period, fish descend to the river where they become overcrowded. This slows their rate of growth. These results are represented schematically in Figure 7.4, where the change through time of the biomass is shown. Dynamic modelling of the resource in this way enabled us to incorporate in the fishing model a reliable environmental base for modification by fishing.

7.3.3 Model of economic rationality

We defined an initial population of fishermen that was identical for all the simulations to be presented, made up of 50 fishermen households, half of whom are Bozo and half, Somono. The number of individuals in a family is approximately normally distributed with mean 7 and standard deviation 2. We present results for simulations of two-year periods.

The first simulation is based on economic rationality. It does not address variation in fishing success. Any fisherman who goes to the same location with the same equipment makes the same catch. In each time interval, a household selects the most profitable activity. Figure 7.5 shows that all the fishermen simultaneously make the same choice. The only time when the fishermen occupy different areas at the same time is the low-water period, for then catches are similar in the pond and in the river. All the fishermen change their activity together at the same moment, so rapid changes in the space occupation are observed. These results indicated that a model based upon economic rationality, not including environmental variability and human variability, was too simple to be useful.

We needed to consider economic rationality in relation to human and environmental variability. Therefore, our second simulation included variability of catch. The catch of a particular fishing activity in a particular biotope was determined by selection from a normal distribution with mean and standard deviation set by reference to the fishing equipment used

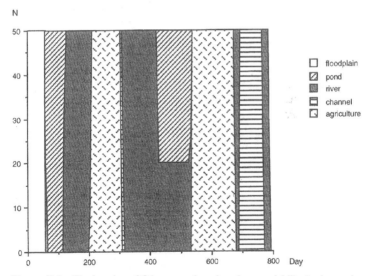

Figure 7.5 The location of fishermen when there is no variability in the catch.

SIMULATING FISHERMEN'S SOCIETY

and to the amount of fish existing in the biotope. Results are shown in Figure 7.6. Again, all the fishermen tend to do the same thing at the same time. However, activities are beginning to diversify and the changes in phase are less immediate than in the previous simulation.

In our third simulation we went further by giving the fishermen's households differing attitudes towards risk. We simulated a population comprising:
- one-third households which selected an activity by the average of their experience;
- one-third households which selected an activity by reference to their best achievement in the two previous weeks;
- one-third households which selected an activity by reference to their worst achievement in the two previous weeks.

The results are shown in Figure 7.7. Even more diversity is now observed in space occupancy. Fishermen select different activities and changes in space occupancy are more spread out over time. Our simulation shows that, subject to our assumptions, different attitudes towards risk may change the use of space.

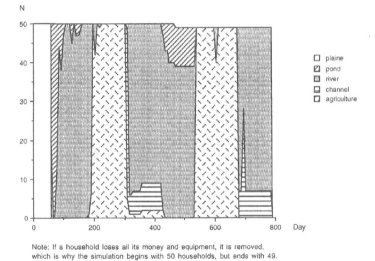

Note: If a household loses all its money and equipment, it is removed, which is why the simulation begins with 50 households, but ends with 49.

Figure 7.6 The location of fishermen when there is variability in the catch. *Note*: If a household loses all its money and equipment, it is removed, which is why the simulation begins with 50 households, but ends with 49.

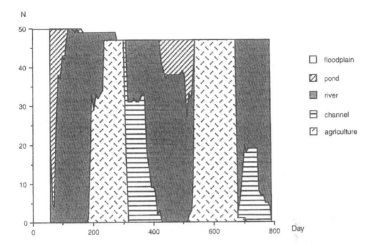

Figure 7.7 The effect of simulating diversity in attitudes to risk.

7.3.4 Social interaction

We have been discussing simulations of essentially individual decision-making. Interaction between households is only very indirectly addressed via the dependence of the amount of fish observed in a biotope on the collective exploitation of it. However, microeconomists and anthropologists have shown, by studying the history of populations and their use of space, that perception and decision-making are not only individual but also collective. Fay (1990) and Kassibo (1990) describe how different groups of fishermen share access to the resource and how their society adapts to environmental and other variability. Our simulation model must therefore allow us to represent different social relations. There are two possible approaches: bottom-up and top-down.

First we describe the *bottom-up* approach. In the literature there are many discussions and reports of how macro-level behaviour derives from the micro level. Many simulation studies, notably those using genetic algorithms (see Ch. 10), have addressed the evolution of groups over long periods of time and have sought to understand the learning process of their members by observing the circumstances in which groups do or do not survive.

Our team is considering relatively short time periods of about one to five years and is focusing on the rules of interaction between agents involved in

SIMULATING FISHERMEN'S SOCIETY

an already organized society (see the "top-down" approach described below). However, rules of interaction for the micro level that are able to account for the macro-level organization are not yet available. We plan to experiment with simulations in which several households negotiate the distribution of their activity in order to maximize a collective result. The formalization of this type of anthropological knowledge is proceeding. We plan to capture in our simulation representations of the negotiations conducted between the persons involved.

We have demonstrated the potential use of our simulator beyond the study of individual decision-making by testing the impact of communication and of information-sharing in these societies of fishermen. In the simulations reported earlier we considered no sharing of information. The fishermen decided only in the light of their own experience. But in reality fishermen are likely to get access to at least a part of the results obtained by others. We therefore simulated different ways in which information might be shared between fishermen.

To illustrate, we report two simulations involving households with first two and then five social relations. The results are shown in Figures 7.8 and 7.9. Comparison of these results with those shown in Figure 7.7 shows that the size of the communication network may change the use of space.

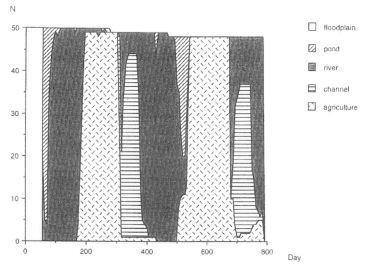

Figure 7.8 The effect of communication between pairs of households.

SIMULATIONS

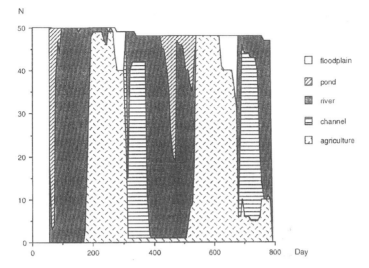

Figure 7.9 The effect of communication among groups of five households.

We have also tested the influence of spatial interactions between the households. We assumed that part of the population is composed of individuals who make "rational economic" decisions and the remainder of individuals who decide by copying or refusing to copy neighbours. We could thus study whether homogeneous groups do better or worse than heterogeneous ones.

For example, we have simulated 10 groups of five households. Each group includes one household that makes decisions of the "rational economic" variety, and four households that either consistently copy this decision or consistently do not. Figure 7.10 shows that after one year of simulated time the groups dominated by two, three or four households that do not copy the economic decision have bad results. The best results are obtained by groups that include just one non-copying household, rather than fully copying groups. From this simulation, we conclude that a good strategy for groups of households faced with environmental heterogeneity is to diversify the occupation of space.

In discussion with anthropologists, we can try to see if these collective strategies of information-sharing and spatial interaction can be observed in reality, and if so how they are expressed. Do the rules by which the society behaves achieve a global economic optimum?

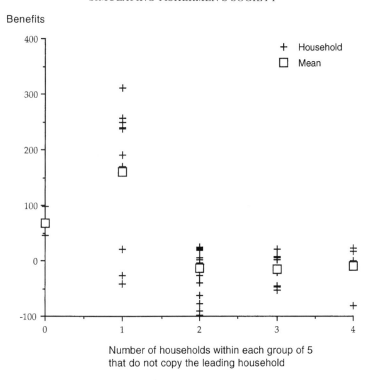

Figure 7.10 The influence of spatial interaction within groups of five households.

Next we consider the *top-down* approach to simulating social interaction. Anthropological observation reveals organization in the fishermen's society. In our simulations, this social organization partly determines the fishermen's activity, in that the social environment acts as a constraint on a fisherman's household. Our simulation makes it easy to represent this type of constraint. As with the simulations described earlier, anthropological knowledge is very schematically represented, but we feel we have demonstrated that it is possible to represent social constraints in this way. For instance, in the Niger delta the fishermen belonging to the Somono and Bozo ethnic groups share space and resources. Before the changes observed in the past thirty years, in some regions of the delta the Bozo people occupied flooded plains and ponds, while the Somono people concentrated on the river. We have repro-

SIMULATIONS

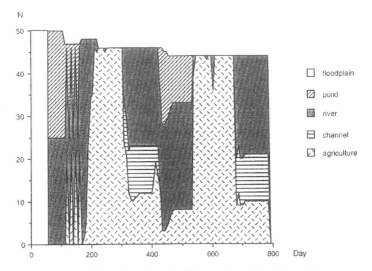

Figure 7.11 The effect of adding anthropological knowledge.

duced this situation merely by entering the following rule:
GIVEN x Household
IF x ethnic group = Somono THEN x fishingPond: veto.

The use of space is specified by this rule. The results observed in Figure 7.11 are therefore not surprising. Bozo and Somono fishermen are distributed on an equal basis by the ponds and by the river at the low-water period. However, it is particularly interesting to compare these results with those obtained for the other models and with field observation. Although the society was well organized before the 1940s, important changes (fishing licences which gave free access to all territories, highly profitable equipment, drought and population growth which led to reduced areas) have occurred since then that have led to less constrained individual behaviour. However, the details of these changes and their consequences are poorly known. We suggest applying different simulations to the 36 villages for which data are available to see just how far these models account for the observed use of space.

Moreover, the consequences for the resource of different uses of space may be studied. With the same assumption of economic rationality as before, the same evolution of the fish populations was observed as measured by their number and biomass (Fig. 7.12). The resource did not depend on

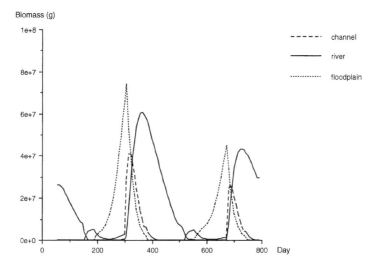

Figure 7.12 The dynamics of the fish resource with fishing based on the model of economic rationality.

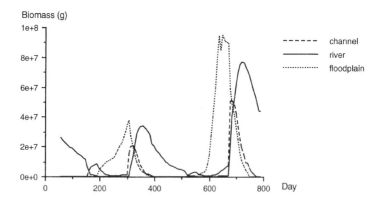

Figure 7.13 The dynamics of the fish resource with fishing based on the model of economic rationality and anthropological knowledge.

fishing. The resource dynamics were modified only by forcing fishermen to follow the collective model of exploitation (Fig. 7.13). Although the fishermen caught nearly the same amount of fish in all the simulations, the evo-

CONCLUSION

lutionary curves of the resource are different. These results, while obtained with highly simplified models, demonstrate the potential of such simulations. We underline the interaction between the decision-making of fishermen and fish population dynamics, and so provoke discussion involving both social and ecological scientists.

7.4 Conclusion

The simulation study presented here is an integral part of research being conducted by a multidisciplinary research team. We have designed a simulation model which includes the different types of knowledge of the members of the research team and which is intended to simulate a society organized around the use of a renewable resource. There are several theories that try to account for the activities selected by fishermen, and we make use of the simulation model to observe the impact of these theories on the dynamics of the resource and to compare them with one another and with the field data.

We are particularly interested in links between the individual behaviour of fishermen and the organization of the fishermen's society, especially as concerns use of space and exploitation of the resource. The techniques we use are derived from distributed artificial intelligence and have allowed us to build a highly modularized simulator which makes it easy to test very different hypotheses about the functioning of fishermen's households and their overall organization. For instance, we have shown that subjecting fishermen to environmental variability may induce different space usage.

By our simulation work we aim to show other research workers the consequences of their knowledge, to inform them of the dependence of their models on environmental variability, and to help them relate their different models one to another. For instance, we have shown here that simulating an individual's behaviour according to an economist's rather than an anthropologist's view of it changes the resulting society's use of space and hence, in turn, the dynamics of the resource.

Chapter 8
Simulating prehistoric hunter–gatherer societies

Steven Mithen

One of the first uses of computer simulation in archaeology was to test a model for the subsistence activities of prehistoric hunter–gatherers in the Great Basin of North America (Thomas 1972). Since then, simulation has been used to examine many archaeological problems and past societies (e.g. Hodder 1978; Renfrew & Cooke 1979; Sabloff 1978), but the main focus of computer simulation in archaeology has remained with hunter–gatherer societies. This chapter makes a selective review of prehistoric hunter–gatherer simulations by focusing on four: those by Thomas (1972, 1973), Aldenderfer (1978), Reynolds (1986) and Mithen (1990). It compares and contrasts these studies, using them to examine trends in simulation work and, from this basis, identify the most promising directions for future studies. Since many readers may be unfamiliar with the discipline of archaeology and the nature of hunter–gatherer societies, I will provide a brief introduction to the archaeology of hunter–gatherers to place the simulation work in context. This background is critical, since an important issue is the extent to which the character of simulation models of prehistoric hunter–gatherers has been, and should be, conditioned by the particular nature of the archaeological database.

8.1 Archaeology and prehistoric hunter–gatherers

The archaeological record stretches from the first appearance of stone tools at about c. 2.5 million years ago to the present. It consists of the material remains from the activities of modern humans, appearing in the fossil record around 100,000 years ago, and a range of hominid ancestors (e.g. *Paranthropus* spp., *Homo erectus*, Neanderthals). The bulk of this archaeological

SIMULATING PREHISTORIC HUNTER–GATHERER SOCIETIES

record relates to hunter–gatherer societies – farming appeared only about 10,000 years ago, and in many areas of the world a hunting and gathering way of life continued until very recently.

Archaeologists take upon themselves three tasks. First, they attempt to reconstruct what happened in the past. Secondly, they attempt to explain why it happened. Thirdly, they attempt to use this understanding to contribute to broader, multi-disciplinary questions concerning human and cultural evolution. The material remains of past societies is often sparse, poorly preserved and ambiguous in its implications. To move from the statics of the archaeological record, such as excavated stone tools, bones, and hearths, to the dynamics of past societies, archaeologists have a battery of methodological techniques, frequently drawing upon the knowledge and skills of other disciplines, such as zoology, botany and chemistry. Similarly, when they are attempting to explain the nature of past societies and the processes of culture change through time, they have often looked to other disciplines for inspiration and guidance. Evolutionary ecology, social anthropology, history and sociology have all been drawn upon in recent studies. In both of these areas of research, reconstruction and explanation, computer simulation has a rôle to play. However, the exact nature of that rôle has never been clearly defined.

The archaeological record of hunter–gatherer societies consists of a restricted set of data types; for instance, their there are no metal artefacts, town plans or written documents. Stone artefacts (including tools such as projectile points, knife blades and scraping tools, and the debris from their manufacture) constitute the largest class of surviving data, not being as susceptible to the many processes that destroy organic materials. Second to stone artefacts are faunal remains, indicative of the animals that hunter–gatherers exploited or with whom they shared their environment, but these survive only in exceptional circumstances. Other types of data archaeologists may recover deriving from prehistoric hunter–gatherers include botanical remains, evidence for structures such as post-holes, hearths, burials, carved bone and antler objects, and paintings on cave walls.

In addition to the information that can be acquired from these objects in themselves (including absolute dates from radiocarbon or thermo-luminescence dating), archaeologists draw inferences from the horizontal and vertical (i.e. stratigraphic) relationships between artefacts. Spatial patterning can be detected and interpreted at many different scales. These range from the distribution of artefacts within a site, perhaps reflecting different activity areas, to the distribution of settlements across continental areas, which

ARCHAEOLOGY AND PREHISTORIC HUNTER–GATHERERS

may relate to processes of colonization and adaptation to environmental variability. Similarly, the examination of the vertical distribution of archaeological data varies from the microscopic examination of sediments from cave floors to the interpretation of geological sections containing sequences of artefacts from millennia of hominid activity.

A further set of data which is critical for the interpretation of archaeological remains concerns past environments. Pollen, plant, insect and faunal remains, together with sediments, are used to reconstruct past environments and explore the relationship between prehistoric hunter–gatherers and the plant and animal communities they exploited. In this respect the study of prehistoric hunter–gatherers is very much a multi-disciplinary exercise integrating the results of work by many specialists.

The archaeological record of hunter–gatherers varies dramatically in terms of preservation and chronological resolution. At the poor end of the scale are records in which only stone artefacts survive, in contexts that have been markedly disturbed (destroying any original spatial patterning and stratigraphy) and which can be dated only to perhaps the nearest 100,000 years. The earliest archaeological records in many parts of the world are of this type, making the reconstruction of behaviour extremely problematic (e.g. that from the Middle Pleistocene of Europe: Villa 1991). At the other end of the scale are those archaeological records in which organic remains have been preserved along with stone artefacts and features, in undisturbed contexts, at many sites across an ancient landscape. The Mesolithic period (early post-glacial) of southern Scandinavia provides such a record where peat bogs have preserved many sites with an extensive range of wooden and bone artefacts. Detailed chronologies have been derived from these sites and spatial patterning in artefact distributions recorded. Interpretation of these has led to sophisticated models for hunter–gatherer societies of this period (e.g. Rowley-Conwy 1983; Price 1985).

Archaeologists are concerned with reconstructing the way of life of prehistoric hunter–gatherers, explaining the particular character of each society and why this varied across space and time. By "way of life" we mean a whole constellation of features including the nature of social organization, ideology, settlement patterns, subsistence behaviour and technology. A systems approach became popular during the 1970s in which each of these features was seen as a separate sub-system and notions of positive and negative feedback between them explored. Largely as a result of the predominance of stone artefacts and faunal material in the archaeological record, the subsistence–settlement system of prehistoric hunter–gatherers has been a prime focus of concern (e.g. Bailey 1983). Another prominent goal of hunter–gatherer research in archaeology has been the attempt to understand the relationship between the character of prehistoric societies and the nature of their physical environment.

The essence of these tasks lies in explaining the variability and patterning in the archaeological data. Why, for instance, are projectile points made in different shapes in different "cultures"? Why are faunal assemblages dominated by certain species rather than others? Why is there variability in the distribution of prehistoric hunter–gatherer settlements through time and space?

This process of explanation often involves a hierarchy of interpretations. For instance, to explain why a certain archaeological site has a large spatial area (as defined by the spread of artefacts or features), one might propose that this is because large numbers of people had occupied it. To then explain why there were large numbers of people, one might refer to a particular form of social organization in which people aggregated at certain times of the year. One must then, in turn, explain why this social organization was found, perhaps by reference to the need to maintain links between individuals and groups in order to survive in highly fluctuating environments. The critical feature of this hierarchy is that each level of explanation depends upon the assumption that a correct inference has been made at the preceding one . Simulation models are often built to tackle issues at a high level in this hierarchy and are therefore valuable only if the archaeological data have been interpreted correctly at the lower levels. In this example, the large spatial area may also have been due to a single occupation of long duration, or many repeated occupations, by a small group.

The task of reconstructing prehistoric hunter–gatherer societies, involving the explanation of variability and patterning in the archaeological record, contributes to some of the major questions concerning the development of the human species and human society. The archaeological record provides a database to trace the development of the human mind, the appearance of symbolic capacities, language and creative thought. Similarly, it provides a database to trace the development of human society in terms of the appearance of complex technology, social differentiation, big-game hunting and art. All of these occurred while people were living by hunting and gathering. To explore such issues, archaeologists need to work with a very particular type of database, dominated by stone artefacts and faunal remains, and to adopt a diverse array of techniques, including computer simulation.

8.2 Hunter-gatherer societies in the modern world

The study of living and historically documented hunter–gatherers is essential for the reconstruction and explanation of prehistoric hunter–gatherers. However, the contribution that the anthropological database can make is not necessarily straightforward. One must be vigilant against simply writing modern patterns of behaviour into the past and assuming that all possible patterns of hunter–gatherer life-style are represented in the modern world. As Wobst (1978) noted, one must guard against the tyranny of the ethnographic record.

A critical event in the study of living, or historically documented, hunter–gatherers was the "Man the Hunter" conference of 1966 (Lee & DeVore 1968). From this developed a generalized and universal model for hunter–gatherer societies based on just three critical features: group size was small (25–50 members); societies were highly mobile; there was a sexual division of labour, i.e. men hunting and women plant-gathering. From these factors other characteristics of hunter–gatherer societies were thought to derive, such as a lack of material possessions, absence of land ownership, flexible band membership, egalitarian social relations and various demographic factors such as child spacing. This model for hunter–gatherer societies drew heavily on the detailed ethnographic research by Richard Lee among the !Kung and rapidly became viewed as a universal model for all hunter–gatherers. It had a considerable influence on the interpretation of the archaeological record (e.g. Isaac 1978).

During the 1970s it became apparent that the "Man the Hunter" model was not appropriate for many hunter–gatherer societies. Ethnographic cases such as Indians of the Pacific coast were noted, where hunter–gatherers lived in very large villages and were sedentary for much of the year or perhaps for several years (Koyama & Thomas 1981). These communities exhibited storage, accumulation of wealth and social differentiation. Similarly, various archaeological cases from the Mesolithic societies of Europe and the Near East were described in which the material remains appeared to reflect societies closer to these ethnographic examples, rather than the !Kung, owing to the presence of rich burials, evidence for storage and large aggregation sites (e.g. Rowley-Conwy 1983).

This led to a polarization of hunter–gatherer societies as either "simple" or "complex" with archaeologists attempting to fit prehistoric hunter–gatherers into one or other of these categories (e.g. Price & Brown 1985). Other dualistic classifications were made, such as between "immediate" and "delayed" consumption (Woodburn 1982), or between "foragers" and "collectors" (Binford 1980), which broadly followed the simple–complex distinction with different emphases on the amount of storage and degree of residential mobility respectively.

More recently, the problems with such dualistic classifications have been realized. It has become apparent that features such as storage, sedentism and social differentiation do not necessarily come as a package and may vary independently from each other. Similarly, hunter–gatherer societies show a continuous, rather than bipolar, range of variability. Recent research has become concerned with describing and explaining the variability in modern hunter–gatherer societies and understanding the relationships between social, economic and environmental features, rather than attempting to fit societies into *a priori* defined categories (e.g. Whitelaw 1989).

Archaeologists have also become increasingly aware that we should expect an even wider range of variability among prehistoric hunter–gatherer societies. The majority of historically documented hunter–gatherers have inhabited marginal environments and been heavily influenced by neighbouring state societies. In prehistory we are often concerned with "pristine" hunter–gatherers (i.e. those without contact with other social forms) in very rich and diverse environments. Since the social and physical environment influence the character of social organization and economy, we should expect that forms of hunter–gatherer society existed in the past for which there are no historically documented analogies. This provides one simple rationale for the use of computer simulation: to build models for hunter–gatherer societies which have no analogue in the modern world.

8.3 Simulation studies of prehistoric hunter-gatherers

As we have now had more than twenty years of computer simulation studies of prehistoric hunter–gatherer societies, we are in a position to identify which themes have played, and are likely to continue to play, the central rôles in such models – although the number of studies remains pitifully small. In the following I use four models published between 1970 and 1990 to consider six themes: aims, time scales, social units, subsistence, environment and decision-making. These themes are arbitrarily chosen, and there are many others that could equally be discussed, including processes of validation and verification, software and hardware used, and "success" of

SIMULATION STUDIES OF PREHISTORIC HUNTER-GATHERERS

the model (however that might be defined). The models I will consider are those by Thomas (1972, 1973), Aldenderfer (1978), Reynolds (1986) and Mithen (1990), and initially I will give a brief summary of each.

8.3.1 Thomas (1972,1973): the "BASIN I" model

This simulation was designed to test whether a model developed during the 1930s by Steward of Shoshonean subsistence–settlement patterns was applicable to the prehistoric foragers of the Resse river area of central Nevada, part of the Great Basin where Steward had done his fieldwork. Steward studied the few remaining Shoshonean families and characterized their foraging behaviour as a multiple subsistence pattern, exploiting contiguous but dissimilar environments. Their diet was based on plant foods, notably pinon nuts and hard-shelled seeds. Thomas (1973) provides a succinct summary of Steward's model:

> A well defined seasonal round permitted the Shoshoneans to co-ordinate plants ripening in different seasons into an overall subsistence–settlement network. This demographic pattern centred about a semi-permanent winter village encampment, often located on the ecotone between the sagebrush flats and the pino–juniper belt flanking the mountains. Necessary conditions for winter encampments were "accessibility to stored seeds, especially pine nuts, water, sufficient wood for house building and fuel, and absence of extremely low winter temperatures" . . . Winter villages accommodated about 15 to 20 families. During these periods of maximal aggregation, co-operative hunting of jack rabbits and antelope was often attempted. Families left the winter village in the summer to establish habitation closer to the ripening herbaceous plants. Although families would occasionally travel up to 30 or 40 miles for an exceptionally abundant crop, most remained within a few miles of the winter village in order to reoccupy the site, provided that the local pinon crop was satisfactory.
>
> (Thomas 1973: 137)

Thomas was not concerned with testing whether this model was an accurate reconstruction for the families that Steward observed, but with whether it was an applicable model for the prehistoric foragers in that region. Other archaeologists, such as Flannery and McNeish, had already taken Steward's model and applied it to the archaeological remains in other regions.

171

SIMULATING PREHISTORIC HUNTER-GATHERER SOCIETIES

Thomas took Steward's model, simplified it and translated it into a systems theory framework. In each season the simulated prehistoric foragers undertook a sequence of subsistence activities, such as gathering nuts or deer hunting. Thomas specified the type of environmental zone in which these took place and the nature of the artefact assemblages created. Consequently he simulated the same year with a stochastic model 5000 times and was able to produce a statistical description of an average sequence of seasonal activities. From this, Thomas created an archaeological record of artefact distributions which compared favourably with that derived from fieldwork. This suggested that Steward's model was appropriate for the prehistoric foragers of the Resse river.

8.3.2 Aldenderfer (1978): the "ABSIM" model

The ABSIM (Aboriginal simulation) model contrasts with others in this review in that it did not aim to simulate a specific hunter–gatherer society, but to develop a generalized model of foraging behaviour to evaluate the use of statistical methods for inferring tool kits from artefact assemblages. The model Aldenderfer developed was, however, based on the Western Desert Aborigines and was probably as detailed and realistic as simulations designed to be models for specific hunter–gatherer groups. ABSIM was designed to simulate the creation of an archaeological record of stone artefact assemblages, varying in their location in the landscape and frequency of artefact types. To this end, it modelled a group of five foragers moving together between a series of settlements. At the start of each simulated day the model tests whether they need to move to another settlement by examining whether they have exhausted the food supply at their current settlement. If they have, then the group moves to the site within a 25km radius which has greatest amount of available food. If movement occurs, then no other activities take place on that simulated day. Otherwise the group engages in a sequence of activities which may result in the loss or discard of lithics, that is, stone tools and the waste from their manufacture.

ABSIM simulated five possible types of activity that can occur at a site: wood carving, spear sharpening, wood procurement, stone procurement and stone flaking. The model involved a decision tree to test which of these activities will be undertaken by which forager on each day. Essentially, this depends upon a series of probabilistic tests concerning the state of the tools possessed by each forager. Aldenderfer used six groups of variables to simulate technological behaviour:

172

SIMULATION STUDIES OF PREHISTORIC HUNTER–GATHERERS

- types: the current tool kit of the group;
- use life: the probable use life of each tool type until breakage;
- mapping relations: the probability that tool X will be used for activity Y;
- loss rate: frequency of loss of a particular tool type;
- recycling: the frequency with which a tool, having ended its useful life, will be shifted to a new function;
- scavenging: the re-use of already exhausted artefacts as *ad hoc* tools, after they had entered the archaeological record.

It is not entirely clear from Aldenderfer's text how these various probabilities and relationships were derived. He appears to have drawn heavily on Gould's ethno-archaeological work among the Western Desert Aborigines. The data generated by the model was of two types. On the one hand, there was a distribution of lithic assemblages across a landscape. On the other, there was a detailed record of all the activities that occurred which led to the creation of these assemblages. This included a complete list of all activities at each site, the tools that were used in each activity, a record of tool discard for each individual in the model and the number of site re-occupations.

8.3.3 Reynolds (1986): Guila Naquitz simulation

Reynolds's simulation model was designed to explore the origins of agriculture and was developed in the context of a research programme directed by Flannery (1986). Between 9000 and 6500 BC people living in central Mexico began to cultivate plants, gradually giving up the hunter–gatherer way of life that had existed since the region was first colonized. This phase of incipient agriculture was followed by the production of high-yielding strains and eventually, around 1500 BC, by sedentary agricultural communities. The transition from hunting and gathering to incipient agriculture was represented in the successive archaeological levels at the site of Guila Naquitz, a small cave in the Oaxaca valley of central Mexico. This remarkable site was excavated in four months during 1966 by Flannery, producing a well preserved sample of botanical remains deriving from the wild and cultivated plants exploited during its occupation. These had sufficient spatial and stratigraphic resolution to draw inferences about economic change through time and the spatial organization of activities. Along with the plant remains, there were assemblages of chipped and ground stone tools, artefacts made from antler and plant materials such as basketry.

SIMULATING PREHISTORIC HUNTER–GATHERER SOCIETIES

The data from Guila Naquitz were analyzed during 15 years following the excavation. The site was then interpreted as a shelter used by a group of four or five foragers on an annual basis, principally during August–November. It was argued that there was cultural continuity between the foragers who were represented by remains in the lower levels of the site, and who had lived a purely hunting and gathering existence, and those represented in the upper levels, who were also manipulating the distribution of certain plant species, notably beans. To aid in the interpretation of this dataset, Reynolds constructed a computer simulation to model the plant-gathering activities of the prehistoric hunter–gatherers and their adoption of incipient agriculture. This simulation drew heavily on the model for agricultural origins proposed by Flannery (1968) which emphasized the problems of scheduling plant-gathering activities. Flannery (1986) provides a succinct summary of simulation model:

> a hypothetical microband of foragers, starting from a position of ignorance, "learns" how to schedule its collection of the major 11 plant foods of the Guila Naquitz environment by trial and error over a very long period of time. They do this by attempting to improve the efficiency of their recovery of calories and protein per area searched during each cycle, or time step, of the simulation. They are confronted with an unpredictable sequence of wet, dry and average years that change the productivity of the plants; and information on their past performance gradually builds up in the memory of the system, informing their decisions on whether or not to modify their strategy when a similar year comes up again. Each strategy considers the vegetational zone searched, the rank order in which the plants are searched for in each zone, and the size of the harvest area for each. By evaluating *sets* of changes . . . the group arrives at what would be called "Co-adapted sets of decisions" in Holland's . . . framework. As time goes on increasing amounts of experience are available to inform the microband's decisions, until their performance is sufficient that no new modification has much probability of being an improvement . . . At this point, Reynolds compares the model group's strategy to the remains from Zone D of Guila Naquitz, our last largely preagricultural level. (Flannery 1986: 435)

SIMULATION STUDIES OF PREHISTORIC HUNTER–GATHERERS

8.3.4   Mithen (1990): the "MESO-SIM" model

Mithen used simulation to help explain the variability in faunal assemblages from the Mesolithic of southern Scandinavia, which in turn was used to propose a model for social differentiation in these early post-glacial communities. The faunal assemblages came from a variety of sites in southern Sweden and southwest Germany and principally varied in terms of the frequency of three large game species: red deer, roe deer and wild pig. Some assemblages were dominated by deer, others by roe deer, while others showed an approximate balance between these species. Mithen acknowledged that many factors are likely to influence such variability. These include inter-site variability in preservation and excavation methods employed. He used his simulation to explore hunters' choice of which game to hunt, the factor likely to create inter-site variability in faunal remains. He argued that these game animals had been hunted by an "encounter" foraging method; i.e., hunters had searched the forests for tracks and trails and chose to pursue some of these, and not others. The critical choice facing the prehistoric foragers that Mithen explored was the decision whether or not to follow the tracks of a particular animal type once encountered. Mithen defined nine animal types: adult male, adult female and juvenile for red deer, roe deer and wild pig.

This simulation modelled the formation of a faunal assemblage at a single settlement. It modelled a group of foragers who hunted individually during the day and then shared food and information concerning their experiences during that day. They occupied a site for a fixed number of days during which the game abundance decreased in response to their killing of animals and the disturbance the hunters caused. By monitoring the time they spent searching and the number and utility of kills they made, the foragers tracked this environmental change and modified their hunting decisions accordingly. It was assumed that each kill made by each hunter was represented in one accumulating midden at the settlement. The foragers were modelled as returning to the settlement after the game densities had replenished. The kills made on such later occupations were added to the earlier faunal assemblage. The simulation had facilities to vary the group size, length and number of occupations, and various parameters controlling environmental variables, such as the gross abundance of game. It explored the effect of these variables and of different decision goals on the character of the simulated faunal assemblage, with respect to the frequency of different animal species.

175

SIMULATING PREHISTORIC HUNTER–GATHERER SOCIETIES

I will now consider these simulation models with respect to the six issues noted above.

1. Aims of computer simulation

Simulation models must have clearly defined aims to be of substantial value. There are three types of aims represented in these models.

Hypothesis testing

Thomas's simulation model of Shoshonean subsistence–settlement patterns was constructed to test whether that model was appropriate for the prehistoric foragers of the Great Basin of central Nevada. To this end, he attempted to simulate the annual subsistence activities of the foragers including the discard or loss of artefacts. The distribution of these artefacts in the landscape, and in particular their averaged frequencies in different microenvironmental zones, could then be compared with the archaeological record to test the applicability of Steward's model under the assumption that it was "correctly" translated into a simulation model.

Mithen's simulation could also be seen in a hypothesis-testing framework, though it was originally described as an inductive exercise. He suggested that Mesolithic foragers of southern Scandinavia may have used different decision goals during their foraging activity, such as attempting to improve their overall foraging efficiency, or to reduce the risk of failing to kill large game on any particular day. His simulation was geared towards defining the archaeological "signature" of these goals in terms of the frequencies of species within faunal assemblages. He then determined which of these simulated signatures was the best fit to the real data and consequently inferred one of the decision-making goals for these foragers.

Methodological

The simulation developed by Aldenderfer was aimed at developing methods to evaluate the use of multivariate statistics for the identification of "tool kits" from lithic assemblages. The idea that inter-assemblage variability of artefact frequencies may relate to different tool kits has been prevalent in archaeological thought since Binford & Binford (1966) proposed this in a seminal paper discussing Mousterian variability. A variety of multivariate statistical tests have been used to attempt to identify these tool kits from the archaeological data. A major problem with using such techniques is that their ability to identify functional variability has never been verified. Ideally,

SIMULATION STUDIES OF PREHISTORIC HUNTER–GATHERERS

this would require recording the daily usage and discard of tools by a group of hunter–gatherers, collecting the lithic assemblages created by their activities and examining whether the use of multivariate methods could allow one to infer correctly the functional patterns of behaviour that had occurred. This research is impossible, however, since there are no living hunter–gatherer groups with a sufficient reliance on stone tools. Aldenderfer's simulation consequently created lithic assemblages from known sets of activities which could then be analyzed by multivariate methods as if they were real archaeological data. He could then examine whether the multivariate techniques were able to identify the tool kits and pattern of activities that had occurred to create these simulated assemblages.

Exploratory or theory building

Reynold's model appears to have been primarily concerned with theory building. As noted earlier, it was constructed to help explore the processes of plant domestication in Mexico between 9000 and 6500 BC, as had been recorded through the excavation of the Guila Naquitz rock shelter. At one level, this simulation aimed to replicate the processes of plant gathering by the prehistoric foragers. Consequently the test of the model was whether it could predict the specific character of the palaeo-botanical assemblage at various levels in the Guila Naquitz site. Yet the absence of sensitivity analyses of the model and the limited comparison between the real and simulated data suggest that this aim was of less importance to Reynolds. Although certain aspects of model sensitivity were explored in an associated paper (Reynolds 1981), it appears that his main aim in building this simulation was to contribute towards the development of a general understanding of the origins of agriculture, the character of culture change, and archaeological explanation. In this regard it drew heavily on the model for agricultural origins proposed by Flannery (1968) which had emphasized the problems of scheduling plant-gathering activities. As such, the simulation provided a vehicle for the further exploration of those ideas, notably the relationship between decision making on a micro scale and long-term culture change. That is, can a model based upon micro-scale decision-making be sufficient to describe the long- term changes in resource use observed in the archaeological record?

Similarly, there are features of Mithen's simulation model that fall into this category of exploration and theory building. His model had been constructed in a theoretical framework that had been critical of optimality studies of human behaviour (e.g. optimal foraging theory), and that had argued

177

that an evolutionary ecological perspective was important for the study of hunter–gatherers. Consequently, in putting forward a general theoretical framework concerning decision-making processes in states of uncertainty, the simulation was used to develop that theoretical framework as much as to test specific hypotheses about past behaviour.

We should note that these simulation models were centred on very specific questions concerning the archaeological record. In Reynolds's case he was concerned with the variability in plant remains within successive levels of a single site, while Mithen's interest was the variability in faunal remains between sites. Yet both were also concerned with much broader issues: the origins of agriculture and of social differentiation respectively. In essence, they used computer simulation to facilitate the conceptual and methodological leap between the details of the archaeological record and general theoretical issues.

In looking towards the future, we should expect that simulation models will continue to have diverse, though well defined aims. As we have seen, simulations often have multiple aims and can contribute to each of the three categories defined above. Hypothesis testing will probably be the least, and theory building the most prominent, aims of future simulations. As we learn more about hunter–gatherers and appreciate the complexities of their societies, it becomes increasingly apparent that predictions concerning their behaviour are inherently difficult to make, and consequently that hypothesis testing is an inappropriate research strategy. This becomes particularly apparent as we digest the significance of the nonlinear elements in models which can make the simulations very sensitive to minor changes in parameter values. As archaeologists, we are forced to work with rather gross estimates for the values of many of our most important parameters. However, recognizing such complexities means that the theory-building rôle of simulation is of even greater importance than at present. We need simulation to explore how sets of variables interact and to delimit the bounds to the behaviour of a model, in order to help explore the relationship between short and long-term processes of culture change.

2. Time scales

These four models adopted a range of time scales for their simulations. A trend can perhaps be seen (which follows, or maybe precedes, that in archaeological thought in general during the past decade) of reducing time scales to simulate shorter and shorter time units. Thomas's simulation was

SIMULATION STUDIES OF PREHISTORIC HUNTER–GATHERERS

based on an annual framework; he simulated the yearly cycle of subsistence activities for 5000 years. The central time scale in Aldenderfer's model was the day; he modelled each forager undergoing a sequence of activities during each of the simulated days of his model. Similarly Mithen also focused on the day, although within this frame he tracked the activities of simulated foragers minute by minute.

The time frame in Reynolds's model is rather complex. The model has several levels of activity and the time scale for each was different. Each pass through the model did the following: (a) modified the cognitive decision-making plans; (b) modified the plant acquisition strategies; and (c) applied a subset of the existing strategies during the months that the cave was occupied. Each plan was constrained to be performed over a 10-day period. A number of strategies could be applied during the several months that the cave was occupied at the end of the summer. The time frame over which the plans and decisions were re-evaluated remained ambiguous; it is unclear as to whether this was modelled as an annual process or on one occurring on a finer time scale. Reynolds demonstrated that a stable pattern of foraging activities arises after 500 time steps and argued that this shows a pattern of long-term learning by the foragers as they improve their foraging efficiency. He implied that this time duration is equivalent to that between initial occupation in the Oaxaca valley and the period immediately prior to plant domestication – but this is a period of several millennia.

Paradoxically, Reynolds's simulation is the most interesting with respect to time frames since it is the only one that attempts to deal with long-term change, a uniquely archaeological (as opposed to anthropological) problem. The simulations of Thomas, Aldenderfer and Mithen do not address long-term change, although they imply that there are no separate processes occurring over such time scales.

This issue of time scales is one of the major issues in the simulation of prehistoric hunter–gatherer societies and culture change. If we wish to model change over several centuries or millennia, such as in the gradual formation of agricultural economies or social differentiation, what is the most appropriate time scale to adopt? Do we see these long-term processes as nothing more than the accumulation of short-term events, which can be simulated only at the micro scale? Recent models, and much theoretical discussion in archaeology, suggests that this is indeed the case. There are of course long-term processes that can be included in such models, such as environmental cycles (e.g. of glaciation). The difficulty facing archaeologists is that our understanding of modern hunter–gatherers suggests that it is not

179

the general climatic trends that are critical, but the very particular sequence of weather events, such as rainfall or temperature. In our simulation models we may be able to mimic a series of fluctuating environmental variables, but we cannot replicate the specific sequence of events that occurred.

3. Social unit

Along with the increasing concern with smaller time scales, recent simulation studies have shown greater concern with the individual rather than the group. Thomas modelled the activities of a group of foragers, with little concern for explicitly modelling the size and character of the group. Similarly, Reynolds focused on the group but felt a need to justify this by invoking a consensus-based decision-making process; hence he was attempting to remain consistent with the theoretical framework he adopted, which concerned decision-making by individuals, while reducing the complexity of his model by simulating group rather than individual behaviour. Aldenderfer and Mithen both focused on individuals and tracked the behaviour of each individual of the group through the model.

This concern with micro time scales and individuals is directly opposed to the character of the archaeological record, in which the long term and aggregate behaviour of groups is the most accessible. It is, however, in conformity with various strands of recent theoretical developments in archaeological thought (e.g. Hodder 1985; Mithen 1989) and simulation provides the most appropriate (perhaps the only) means of operationalizing these with archaeological data.

4. Subsistence activity

All four simulation models have a prime concern with the subsistence activities of the prehistoric foragers, either directly or indirectly through a functional approach to stone artefacts. Thomas's model for the Shoshonean foragers was based on a cycle of subsistence activities, Reynolds simulated plant foraging, Mithen simulated hunting and Aldenderfer used simulation of plant gathering and hunting to determine activities concerning the manufacture, repair and discard of stone tools. Indeed, practically all computer simulations/mathematical models of prehistoric and living hunter–gatherers have had a major concern with subsistence, the models by Wobst (1974), concerning palaeolithic demography, being a notable exception.

There are several reasons for this concern with subsistence. Perhaps of

SIMULATION STUDIES OF PREHISTORIC HUNTER–GATHERERS

greatest importance is that this is the "easiest" type of behaviour for archaeologists to deal with. As I noted above, the most abundant type of archaeological data concerning prehistoric hunter–gatherers relates to subsistence activities. (This is not to argue that such data are not also informative about social organization or ideology.) If those building simulation models wish to make a connection between data generated by the simulation and the archaeological record, it is difficult to see how this can be achieved without an explicit simulation of subsistence activities. Consequently, even if the prime focus is with modelling the development of, say, social complexity and the theoretical framework in which the model is developed suggests there is no causal relationship between this and subsistence, it may nevertheless be necessary to model the implications of developing social complexity for subsistence if one wishes to test the model against archaeological data.

A second reason relates to the theoretical framework in which prehistoric hunter–gatherer studies are conducted. Most archaeologists adopt an evolutionary–ecological framework which, while not necessarily functionalist, emphasizes the critical importance of the interaction between humans and their natural environment. Consequently the character of subsistence activities, social organization and settlement patterns are seen to be heavily influenced by the character of the resources being exploited. The concern with subsistence activity in simulations appears to be a consequence of this theoretical framework as much as a pragmatic stance to connect simulations with the real world.

5. Environmental reconstruction

Since subsistence activity has been a central theme in these simulation models, there has been as much attention to modelling the environment of the prehistoric foragers as to human behaviour itself. The means by which these four simulations modelled past environments share two characteristics: a use of Markov transition matrices and a heavy reliance on analogies from the modern world.

In building his simulation, Thomas's initial concern was to model the resources within the four micro environments exploited by the Shoshonean foragers. He chose to model only three of the possible resources/activities as annually fluctuating: pinon nut harvesting, Indian rice grass harvesting and antelope driving. The others (e.g. deer hunting, root gathering) were assumed to be constant, i.e. to occur in every single year of the simulation. The probability of there being a Pinon nut crop to harvest was modelled

SIMULATING PREHISTORIC HUNTER–GATHERER SOCIETIES

using modern data on the frequency of Pinon nut crops. This was achieved by a Markov matrix which defined the probability of good, fair or failed crops in successive years. Thomas also used modern ecological data to simulate the frequency of Indian rice grass crops. This was shown to depend upon spring rainfall; a sufficient crop arose only if rainfall exceeded 3 inches and Thomas derived the probability that this will occur. For modelling the probability of antelope driving, Thomas used Steward's records which showed that this only occurred on the average only every 12 years, since this was the time required for antelope numbers to recover to levels that would make a drive once again economically viable. Consequently Thomas used a 0.08 ($^1/_{12}$) probability that antelope driving will occur.

This methodology for reconstructing past environments, drawing on as much data in as similar environments as possible and using probabilistic models for environmental events, has been followed in the other simulation studies. Aldenderfer's principal input data for his model concerned the distribution of rainfall in the western desert which he believed was the principal cause of movement between sites by Aboriginal foragers. Aldenderfer used empirical rainfall data from the western desert within a Markov chain approach to produce a pseudo-random sequence of rainfall events at each site. This prevented sequences of rainfall events from following each other too closely. Each site was treated independently for rainfall. Aldenderfer refined this model to distinguish between two types of rainfall events: effective, which was sufficient to stimulate plant growth, and non-effective, which helped to fill up water catchments but was insufficient to affect vegetation.

Similarly, Reynolds's simulation required data on the plant communities and the climate of the region around the Guila Naquitz cave where prehistoric foraging took place. These were argued to be analogous to the modern environment, and data on the spatial distribution and yield of most of the available plants were acquired during a decade of fieldwork on the modern plant communities. Exceptions to this were for plants such as Pinon nuts which no longer grow in the area, and for these the required data were estimated by using measures taken from relevant literature. Similarly, Reynolds argued that the modern rainfall pattern is sufficiently similar to that in prehistory to be able to use recorded frequencies of wet, average and dry years as a model for prehistoric rainfall patterns.

Mithen drew on a diverse set of ecological studies to model five characteristics of the prey items available to his simulated hunters. He needed to define the following for each of his game species at each time step of the simulation: probability of encounter, stalk time, probability of successful kill,

SIMULATION STUDIES OF PREHISTORIC HUNTER–GATHERERS

field butchery time and the utility of the carcass. These were modelled by a series of equations which drew on a range of ecological and ethnographic studies and focused on two parameters of the prey: body size and aggregation size. This environmental model is in contrast to Thomas's and Aldenderfer's, since it does not make a strict separation between environmental and technological variables. For instance, the probability of successfully killing a stalked animal was shown by ethnographic date to relate principally to maximum running speed, which in turn is related to body size. Yet the character of the technology employed is also critical, for rifles are more efficient than bows and arrows. Consequently Mithen included parameters in his equations modelling "environmental" variables which could be varied to simulate technological change.

Reynolds also integrated environmental and technological variables. He modelled technological change in terms of differences in plant productivity that result from decisions to use incipient agricultural techniques as opposed to plant collecting.

It is apparent from these four studies that the need to simulate past environments has created two major problems for archaeologists. The first is simply the complexity of modelling the distribution and behaviour of past resources, particularly in the context of environmental change. As our modern ecological knowledge becomes more sophisticated, this challenge grows. For instance, if we wish to simulate the hunting of red deer, we may feel it necessary to model the population dynamics of a red deer herd to explore the consequences of different hunting strategies or culling practices. Yet these population dynamics may be complex in themselves, dependent upon a range of environmental parameters. This becomes yet more difficult if we wish to model several animal populations which interact, i.e. to construct simulations of ecological communities in which human foraging takes places, as our evolutionary ecological framework suggests we should.

The second problem is that many species that were exploited in the past are now extinct and past environments may have no modern analogues. For instance, by definition, simulating the extinction of mega-fauna at the end of the late pleistocene, as done by Mosimann & Martin (1975), requires models for the behaviour of extinct species such as mammoths and woolly rhino. Similarly, many late Pleistocene environments appear to have been far more diverse in their array of plant and animal species than any environments today. For instance, the late Pleistocene environment of southwest Europe, in which many cultural developments took place and current simulations studies are based (Mithen 1990, Part 3; Doran 1991; see also

183

SIMULATING PREHISTORIC HUNTER–GATHERER SOCIETIES

Ch. 9 below), had a constellation of large game species including horse, reindeer, bison and red deer living within a single ecological community of a type unknown today. Guthrie (1984) has argued that the pattern of vegetation in the late Pleistocene was substantially different from the zonation typical in the modern world upon which models of hunter-gather subsistence–settlement patterns are often based. Simulation studies play a vital rôle in the reconstruction of these unique ecological communities; yet simulating them is an enormous task in itself, let alone modelling their exploitation by human foragers.

6. Decision-making

The simulation models by Aldenderfer, Reynolds and Mithen had an explicit focus on the decision-making process. This was particularly developed by Reynolds and Mithen, though in very different ways. We can consider this aspect of the simulation under two headings: decision goals and information flows.

Decision goals
The assumption in each of these three simulations was that foragers attempt to improve their foraging efficiency, in terms either of increasing their net rate of energetic intake or reducing the risk of foraging failure. Aldenderfer's model came closest to an optimality approach in which foragers are concerned not with the improvement, but with the relative maximization of some variable using local information. In modelling the movement of foragers across the landscape, he conditioned their choice of a new settlement location by ranking these in terms of available food resources and moving the foragers to the site with the highest rank within a 40 km radius. The availability of food was modelled as dependent upon rainfall events and the duration since the last occupation. If two sites tied for the highest ranking, foragers moved to the nearest.

Reynolds chose a similar method for modelling the choice of 10-day plant-collecting strategies by his simulated foragers. For each possible strategy he devised a "performance index", by which he could then compare strategies in terms of their efficiency at acquiring food in addition to their ability to obtain the minimal requirement of proteins and calories for the group. For instance, if the protein yield of a particular strategy was less than the average of all strategies, its performance index was incremented by 1. This index ran from a value of 6, marking the worst of the available strat-

SIMULATION STUDIES OF PREHISTORIC HUNTER–GATHERERS

egies, to 0, denoting the best. The probability of a particular strategy being adopted was then directly related to its performance index.

In Mithen's simulation three alternative decision goals were explored for their relative performance and consequences for the archaeological record. These were the goals adopted by the simulated hunters when they had the choice of either stalking and attempting to kill an animal, or continuing to search for other opportunities. The first goal, denoted UIS (utility increasing and satisficing), stated that the animal should be stalked if the expected return from doing so (taking into account the probability of not successfully killing it) was greater than that currently attained from foraging in general. This defined a "stalk probability" of either 0 or 1 for each prey type. Second, a goal denoted UISR (utility-increasing, satisficing and risk-reducing) modified these probabilities with respect to the time of day, i.e. the number of simulated minutes left for foraging. As these passed, all stalk probabilities were gradually increased so that, in the final minute available for foraging, all stalk probabilities were equal to 1. This acted, therefore, to reduce the risk that no kills would be made on any one particular day. Both the UIS and UISR goals were also modified by a satisficing element which reduced stalk probabilities in relation to the amount of game already killed. A third goal, denoted NULL, was also explored. This simply stated "stalk every resource", and provided a base line against which the performance of the other goals could be compared.

As is apparent, Mithen attributed his simulated foragers with goals that had multiple elements, the UI parts relating to the long term (i.e. increasing the rate of utility gain over several days) and the S and R parts relating to the short term, i.e. the events of the current day itself. This attempted to capture the real situation in which hunters are often attempting to satisfy multiple and conflicting goals simultaneously.

Reynolds, Aldenderfer and Mithen adopted foraging efficiency as the decision goal for their simulated foragers. Mithen was the most explicit about the rationale for this. He based his modelling on Darwinian principles and argued that being an efficient forager is a proximate means by which hunters gain reproductive success since it improves their capacity to compete for mates. It is a weakness of Aldenderfer's models that he leaves the rationale for adopting foraging efficiency as a decision goal rather deeply embedded in his text, with no justification for why it, as oppose to other types of goals, was adopted. Reynolds was also less explicit than is desirable about his use of foraging efficiency. He explains, however, that "the whole idea was to use a machine learning technique based upon Darwinian prin-

SIMULATING PREHISTORIC HUNTER–GATHERER SOCIETIES

ciples as a framework for decision-making adaptations. Above average strategies were reproduced and recombined based upon performance. This corresponds to the idea of reproductive success" (Reynolds 1992, personal communication).

Information flows

Aldenderfer's model assumed that foragers had perfect knowledge of their environment, in that they could always move to the highest ranked settlement location. He justified this by asserting that in arid environments good decision-making is essential to survival and foragers do indeed have near-perfect information. As he noted, information about rainfall and resources is constantly being passed within and between groups living in such environments. Consequently, he felt that, although such information flows were not explicitly modelled, his movement algorithm included its effects. This appears reasonable, but Aldenderfer may be underestimating the investment foragers make in the process of acquiring information. In arid environments, mobility between settlements is often motivated by the need to acquire information, rather than to exploit resources. Consequently foragers may not wish to move to the highest ranked settlement site, but to a site within an area about which more information is desired.

Information flows played a much larger and more critical part in Reynold's simulation. At the centre of his model was the notion of "multi-generational memory". Information about the performance of different plant-collecting strategies, and the means by which these had been improved, were used to increase the foragers' efficiency at plant gathering gradually through time. Hence from a starting point of ignorance, when the selection of collecting strategies was determined in large part by a random process, foragers used the ever increasing amounts of multi-generational memory to select those strategies that performed the most effectively. Consequently Reynolds simulated a long-term learning process.

This is one of the most interesting parts of Reynold's simulation. The notion of multi-generational memory concerns not just the memory capacities of the human brain but cultural and social activities whereby information is maintained within a society. These may include story telling, ritual and visual arts. Consequently Reynolds includes in his model something that is distinctly human, setting this model of foraging apart from those used to explore the foraging behaviour of other animal species.

One of the major weaknesses of Mithen's simulation is that it does not do this; the types of information flows and memory are not distinct from

OVERVIEW AND FUTURE DIRECTIONS

those that appear to be used by a broad range of non-human animal species. The foragers in his model maintain an estimate for their current foraging efficiency derived from their past experience. Essentially, this is a running average of their daily foraging efficiency in which more weight is put on the most recent foraging, so that they are able to adjust their foraging behaviour as game is depleted. This estimate of foraging efficiency made by simulated hunters is used to derive stalk probabilities for each of the game species that may be encountered during foraging activity. At the end of each day, each individual in the model calculates the stalk probabilities (initially 0 or 1) for each of the resources that may be encountered the next day. These are then adjusted so that a consensus is reached about the worth of stalking an encountered animal. In reaching this consensus, the influence of each individual is defined by his hunting success in terms of the amount of resources he has contributed to the group. (It is assumed that all meat, hide and antler resources are shared between group members.) A weighted average of stalk probabilities for each resource is calculated and these are adopted by each forager at the start of the following day. This model, therefore, simulates the acquisition of information from past experience and the sharing of information between individuals at the end of each foraging day. During the day no information flows are modelled between foragers, so that the satisficing and risk-reducing decisions are taken without knowledge of the success or otherwise of other foragers with whom food is shared.

8.4   Overview and future directions

In this body of simulation work it is apparent that there are certain themes and trends which we can expect to be developed in future simulation work. The concern with the micro scale (individuals and short time frames) is perhaps the most significant. And this is indeed appropriate, for the great power of simulation is to allow archaeologists to simulate centuries or even millennia so that the relationship between the short and long term can be explored. Hand in hand with the micro scale is the concern with decision-making processes and learning. We should expect the modelling of these to become more sophisticated than it is at present. Greater attention should be paid to specifically human aspects of decision-making with particular emphasis on information flows between individuals. A further feature that must remain prevalent is the modelling of subsistence activity. Even if this is thought to be largely irrelevant to the particular issue being explored, its inclusion in the model greatly enhances the possibility that the model may be tested, evaluated or simply discussed with data from the archaeological record and be made to impinge upon the interpretation of that data rather than remaining an isolated theoretical exercise. A consequence of maintaining a concern with subsistence activity is the need to continue to improve the manner in which the environment and resources are modelled.

In general, we can see future simulation models as requiring five elements, each of which may be more or less developed in any particular model:

- a model for the formation of decision goals.;
- a model for the processes of decision-making, or cognition in general, by individual foragers to achieve their goals. This should include variables such as beliefs and attitudes which are largely absent from current models;
- a model for human behaviour in terms of interactions with the social and natural environment – in essence, the consequence of the cognitive processes;
- a model for the natural environment in which such actions take place;
- a model for the formation of the archaeological record.

In searching for ways in which models including these features can be developed, two fields (which archaeologists have so far drawn on only sparingly) appear to be of greatest value for the first three of the above elements: artificial intelligence and models of cultural transmission. I will briefly comment on their possible value.

8.4.1 Artificial intelligence and computational psychology

Future simulation models are likely to be concerned with the explicit modelling of multiple interacting individuals and cognitive processes. The concepts and modelling techniques of artificial intelligence and the related field of computational psychology are likely to play a substantial rôle in developing this aspect of simulations. Indeed, Reynolds's simulation has already provided one example of how such concepts might be used. Doran has argued the importance of using AI concepts and is illustrating their value in the current EOS project (Ch. 9). He has particularly stressed the value of distributed artificial intelligence (DAI):

DAI is about the study, in computational terms, of sets of agents and their properties. DAI agents are programmable on a computer, and are typically able (albeit in very limited ways) to sense and react to

OVERVIEW AND FUTURE DIRECTIONS

their context, to communicate with one another, to accept and set themselves goals, to generate, reason about and execute plans of action in pursuit of their goals, and to maintain and update individual belief sets. (Doran 1991: 2)

As he argues, the repertoire of concepts and techniques provided by DAI seems the best tool kit available to meet the types of modelling requirements that have been discussed above. One can easily imagine how Aldenderfer's or Mithen's models could be substantially improved if the modelling of decision-making was developed in this manner. For instance, it would appear to facilitate the modelling of meta-decision-making, i.e. decisions about how to make decisions, a rather critical feature of human thought (Mithen 1990; Johnson-Laird 1988) which Reynolds has already begun within his simulation. While specific AI modelling languages and techniques are likely to have a vital contribution to play, so are more general concepts developed in AI research which help us to develop conceptual models for cognitive processes.

One of the principal challenges in current models is to simulate the storage of large quantities of information in the human mind and embedded within cultural practices, and the retrieval of *relevant* information from this store by individuals for solving a particular problem. This issue arises in Reynolds's model in the context of plant gatherers attempting to choose strategies that are most appropriate to the particular set of current environmental variables, and in Mithen's work when discussing the problems concerning hunter–gatherer patch choice (Mithen 1990, 1991). It is also one much discussed in AI (e.g. Schank & Abelson 1977; Boden 1990), and various concepts have been developed which will greatly benefit these archaeological studies. For instance, the notions of semantic nets which can be used to model spontaneous conceptual association and of scripts, i.e. sequences of behaviours that are initiated by a particular cue without requiring decision-making about each separate step in the sequence, may be useful. Archaeologists involved in modelling or concerned with more general issues about the rôle of cognition in cultural behaviour are likely to benefit substantially by a greater familiarity with such concepts.

One of the challenges is to model processes that are distinctively human, rather than those shared by many animal species. For instance, effective models of human problem-solving need to simulate creative thought, analogous thought and inference as well as simple calculation. Precisely the same environmental and social conditions never re-occur, and consequently when individuals face problems similar to, but not the same as, those faced in their

189

past, they must recognize analogies between past and present conditions. Recent work in computational psychology has argued that such cognitive processes can indeed be modelled effectively (e.g. Johnson-Laird 1983; Boden 1990). The need to include these can again be seen in the context of Mithen's and Reynolds's models. Both simulated foragers in environmentally changing landscapes, but neither could model the foragers making inferences from trends in weather conditions to predict future environments and prepare for them; rather their simulated foragers were purely reactive in nature.

8.4.2 Cultural transmission

A related area of theory and modelling which is likely to contribute to the development of more sophisticated simulations of prehistoric hunter–gatherer societies concerns cultural transmission and social learning. A problem with current models is that they cater to only one of the many processes of culture change: economic decision-making by individuals in which the benefits and costs of each possible action is taken into account. This is goal-directed learning, involving the use of decision rules and heuristics, as modelled in AI. However, as Boyd & Richerson (1985) argue, this is just one of several processes of culture change; in many circumstances it may be of limited significance. They developed a broad theoretical framework to explore cultural change within a Darwinian framework in which processes of social learning were prominent and referred to this as a "dual inheritance theory" since it invoked both biological and cultural evolution. They argued that processes such as frequency-dependent bias and indirect bias are often critical for the behaviour of individuals and the patterning of behaviour within and between groups. Frequency-dependent bias refers to the tendency of people to imitate the more common, rather than the rarer, types of behaviour they observe, while indirect bias refers to the tendency to imitate a whole set of traits of another individual as a consequence of consciously copying just one. These types of processes are important since, on the one hand, in certain contexts they provide a much more efficient learning process for individuals than trial and error, and on the other, they indicate how maladaptive patterns of behaviour can spread within human populations. They are clearly relevant for any model purporting to be modelling information exchange between individuals.

Shennan (1992) has argued that an understanding of such processes of cultural transmission is crucial for interpreting the archaeological record. In

CONCLUSION

a simulation of multiple interacting individuals the inclusion of frequency-dependent or indirect bias may enable us to develop far more effective models for past societies with particular regard to the spread of ideas about technology, and material culture in general. This, in turn, should allow us to make more effective contact with our archaeological data.

My reference to the work of Boyd and Richerson is made also to invoke a wider issue that requires discussion: the relationship between biological and cultural evolution. This is particularly pertinent when dealing with prehistoric hunter–gatherers, because the archaeological record monitors the evolution of hominid species as well as the cultural behaviour of those species. Consequently, for the earlier part of the record it is often unclear whether the behaviour we witness, such as early stone technology, should be thought of as largely genetically fixed for the hominids concerned, or variable within that species, as is tool behaviour among modern humans. More generally, the development of human society involves, as Boyd and Richerson argue, a dual inheritance by individuals of information embedded in genes and contained in learned patterns of behaviour. Simulation models are needed to help understand this complex process (see Reynolds, Ch. 10, below).

8.5 Conclusion

The fields of artificial intelligence and cultural transmission overlap in their concepts and should enable us to build more effective models for prehistoric hunter–gatherers with regard to cognitive processes and social interaction. These will have to be embedded within models for past environments and resources if we wish to construct a holistic simulation model and to generate data that can be compared with that in the archaeological record. This aspect of simulation requires archaeologists to become more familiar with the practice of modelling in ecology and with how it can be adapted for an archaeological context. Ideally, collaboration is required between archaeologists and specialists in various fields of modelling.

What has been, and will be, the value of computer simulation of prehistoric hunter–gatherer societies? The main contribution of such models is that they provide a means to think through the immensely complicated issues that we deal with – not only those concerning the nature of past societies, but also the formation of the archaeological record. Prehistoric hunter–gatherers are intimately linked to their natural environment via their social and economic behaviour. Simulation provides an effective way to manage a large number of variables and explore the conceptual space we create concerning the development of such societies. In particular, these models can allow us to explore the critical relationship between the short-term behaviour of individuals and the long-term processes and patterns of culture change we see in the archaeological record. To do this, they need to be firmly embedded in a theoretical context and based on empirical data. Reynolds's Guila Naquitz model provides an excellent example of such a model, allowing us to examine the processes of agricultural origins by being embedded in Flannery's theoretical discussions and excavation reports.

While hunter–gatherers may be thought of as a relatively simple type of society, simulating them provides some particularly difficult challenges arising from this "simplicity". There is rarely any defined rôle for individuals to play which would make simulating their behaviour easier; there are very intimate links between the character of these societies and the natural environment, requiring that many features of the natural environment be simulated in detail; and many biological and physical processes are involved in the formation of the archaeological record which must be deciphered if inferences about prehistoric hunter–gatherers are to be used in the construction and evaluation of simulation models. Such formation processes ought to be an integral part of the simulation model. As I noted earlier, these difficulties should not be taken as reasons for not simulating, but quite the reverse, because they indicate that simulation is essential for understanding the interactions between the many variables that condition the behaviour of hunter–gatherers and the character of the archaeological record.

In many respects, simulating prehistoric hunter–gatherer societies presents precisely the same problems as simulating any society. These include decisions by the model builder about which specific questions to address, which variables to include, how complex the model should be and whether one is seeking realism or generality. Yet there are also issues that are particular to the nature of these societies and the data we have concerning them: these concern long-term change in human society, the integration between cultural and biological evolution and the often sparse and biased character of the archaeological record.

Perhaps the most significant impression from the study of these four models is the tension that exists between the need to construct simulations that are theoretically respectable (as for instance in the wish to focus on individuals) and the desirability of maintaining a certain pragmatism about including features that generate data that are directly comparable with the

CONCLUSION

archaeological record. The balancing of this tension is one of the major challenges facing those who wish to simulate prehistoric hunter–gatherer societies.

Acknowledgements

I would like to thank Bob Reynolds and Jim Doran for their comments on an earlier version of this manuscript and Mark Lake for discussing the problems of simulating prehistoric hunter–gatherers.

Chapter 9
The EOS project:
modelling Upper Palaeolithic social change

Jim Doran, Mike Palmer, Nigel Gilbert, Paul Mellars

The objective of the EOS project (Doran 1982, 1992) is to investigate the growth of social complexity and, in particular, to formulate and experiment with an abstract computational version of an informal model proposed by Paul Mellars (1985) of the growth of social complexity in the Upper Palaeolithic period in southwestern France. At the heart of the project is the use of the concepts and techniques of distributed artificial intelligence (DAI) (Bond & Gasser 1988) to enable cognitive factors to be incorporated into the computational version of Mellars's model. The computational model has been programmed to run on a computer, and its behaviour studied.

The EOS project is still in progress and this chapter should be read accordingly. The chapter is a development of Doran & Palmer (in press) and of Palmer & Doran (in press). We shall describe a computer software testbed which has been created, the way in which the Mellars model has been formulated within it, the initial experiments that have been performed and the insights that they have given us, and our plans for the immediate future.

It will become apparent that the EOS project is not a straightforward computer modelling exercise (if there is such a thing). The utilization of only partly developed DAI techniques, although we believe them entirely appropriate, means that interpreting the Mellars model becomes a DAI research investigation in its own right. In the short term the project is therefore perhaps best seen as a piece of exploratory DAI research motivated and guided by an archaeological problem, with the contribution of the DAI research to the solution of the archaeological problem taking place in the longer term. This is a not unusual relationship between an archaeological problem and a piece of mathematical or computer science research.

9.1 Sociocultural trajectories to complexity

Much effort has been put into the study of the long-term dynamics of human society. Although there seem to be the foundations of general theory (e.g. Johnson & Earle 1987), much remains to be done. We are concerned here only with the spontaneous transition from a relatively simple egalitarian hunter–gatherer society to one with a more complex structure. Even this restricted problem has attracted much debate and more controversy than proven insight.

The problem must first be stated in more detail. We follow Cohen (1985: 99) in defining an "egalitarian" society as one characterized by fluid group organization, freedom of movement, relatively immediate and easy access to resources, immediate consumption, simple division of labour, and relatively direct personal leverage on other individuals. By contrast, a more "complex" society features centralized decision-making, ranking, technological specialists and other rôle differentiation, territoriality and ethnicity (Cohen 1985: 105; Mellars 1985: 285–6). These are, of course, anthropological characterizations and are uncomfortably imprecise from a computational standpoint. However, it is far from trivial to translate them into formal mathematical or computational terms, as will become apparent.

How can an egalitarian society, thus characterized, be transformed or transform itself into a more complex one? There have been certain recurring suggestions concerning, for example, the impact of population increase and/or concentration, of sudden resource scarcity and of specific climatic changes. In the time spans at issue, the possibility of significant development in basic cognitive function seems remote, but this does not exclude rapid fulfilment of pre-existing cognitive potential.

9.1.1 The case of southwestern France

There is archaeological evidence for at least one and perhaps several transitions from relatively simple to more complex society during the course of the Upper Palaeolithic period of southwestern France and northwestern Spain, that is, between about 15,000 and 30,000 years ago. This was over the period of the last glacial maximum when the evidence suggests a unique concentration of animal populations within southwestern Europe.

The evidence for this transition (only to be sketched here; for details readers may refer to Mellars 1985) is a matter of comparing the archaeological record at the end of the period with that at its beginning. At the end we find:

SOCIOCULTURAL TRAJECTORIES TO COMPLEXITY

- larger and more abundant archaeological sites;
- increased wealth, density and stratigraphic complexity of archaeological material in sites;
- abundant and sophisticated cave art (e.g. at Lascaux);
- elaboration of stone, bone and antler technology;
- abundance of "trade" objects (e.g. marine shells).

What explanation can be given for the emergence of complexity in this particular case? Before giving Mellars's answer, we should note first that the significance of the archaeological evidence cited is itself a matter of controversy. Not all would agree that it implies the emergence of genuine social complexity. Secondly, the environmental circumstances were less continuously severe than at first appears. There is evidence of short-term temperature rises, which Mellars suggests may have had a marked effect on the economic, residential and social structures of the local human groups (1985: 289), an implication being that the emergence of social complexity may have been both irregular and recurrent.

9.1.2 The Mellars model

Mellars has suggested that in the case of southwestern France a particular combination of ecological conditions led to population concentration and stable and relatively large co-residential units involving sedentism over a substantial part of the annual cycle, and that this was the crucial step in the emergence of more complex social structures. The ecological conditions were specifically:

- an exceptional wealth and diversity of food resources;
- a strong pattern of concentration of these resources, both at particular locations and at particular periods in the annual cycle;
- a relatively high degree of stability and predictability in the spatial distribution of these resources from year to year, (Mellars 1985:284–5).

The second part of the Mellars proposal, which is less elaborated, is that population concentration (however caused) leads to social complexity as defined earlier. He suggests as "'appropriate' and perhaps even 'necessary' . . . the emergence of certain individuals with increasing status or authority to organize and coordinate the activities of other members of the group . . . [for example] communal hunting activities" (Mellars 1985: 285).

It is highly relevant to what follows that Cohen (1985) has persuasively discussed the impact of cognitive stresses and physical congestion in population concentrations. Such problems, he suggests, were solved by aspects of

197

MODELLING UPPER PALAEOLITHIC SOCIAL CHANGE

complex organization such as social stereotyping (a form of cognitive economy) and the coordination of groups through differentiation. In effect, Cohen adds to the Mellars model the idea that the central issue faced by a group with high population density is the interaction between specific problems of logistics and cognitive overloading. A society that fails to solve these problems will fail comprehensively.

9.1.3 The importance of cognitive factors

It is important that both Mellars and Cohen introduce cognitive factors into their discussions of emergence. Cognition has been much more emphasized in such studies in recent years, notably by Renfrew (e.g. 1987, and in press). And Mithen has recently commented that "part of the reason that archaeologists continue to have difficulty in explaining change is that they have neglected one locus for that change – people making decisions about what to do" (Mithen 1990:2). This new emphasis is substantially a consequence of frustration with the limitations of non-cognitive explanations. However, there is also some feeling that cognitive science and artificial intelligence studies are starting to provide useful means to handle these cognitive factors (see Mithen, Ch. 8 above).

Some of the particular insights deriving from cognitive science and artificial intelligence work are:

- that a precise account can be given of cognitive processes in computational terms and made operational in computer programs;
- that the cognitive ability to "distance" reasoning from the immediate situation, notably the ability to predict and to plan (compare Alexander 1989: 459) should not be identified, as too often happens, with natural language use. The use of language requires, but should not be confused with, more fundamental cognitive abilities (Bloch 1991);
- that the concept of "cognitive limitation" is of fundamental significance; the meaning of cognitive limitation is that any information-processing device (including the human brain) has limitations on its capacity and speed, and must therefore embody various heuristic methods to overcome its limitations, for example heuristic generalization, types of information discard, suboptimal reasoning and the re-use of past problem solutions in similar problem situations. These heuristic methods are fundamental to human behaviour, including social behaviour (Doran et al. 1991; Cohen 1985).

Thus, to formulate more precise models of the type proposed by Mellars and Cohen, requiring the modelling of cognition, strongly suggests recourse to the concepts and techniques of cognitive science and artificial intelligence, with due attention to issues of cognitive limitation, but without being deflected into surface issues of language use. This line of thought is at the heart of the EOS project.

9.2 Computer-based modelling

As stated, we are using a computer as the means by which we formulate and objectively test the consequences of our model and its assumptions. In general, we see the objectives of modelling as being to clarify, test the coherence of and rigorously establish the consequences of a set of precise assumptions. By so doing, particular combinations of assumptions may rigorously be related to ertain types of outcome, and hence in a particular application initially tenable hypotheses may be eliminated by discovering that the outcomes they imply are contrary to empirical observation. Doran (1990) has reviewed previous experience with computer-based modelling in archaeology.

Our procedure involves four steps (compare e.g. Zeigler 1976):

(i) ABSTRACT: isolate the essentials of the target entity;
(ii) TRANSLATE: cast these essentials into an outline model within the chosen formal conceptual repertoire (in this case DAI);
(iii) STUDY: establish the properties of the model by writing and running a computer program which embodies it under varying circumstances;
(iv) COMPARE: compare the behaviour of the model with the target.

As will be seen in the following, in this project we have not yet reached stage (iv) in any substantial way.

Building a computational model from an informal theory is no trivial matter for several reasons. The informal theory is often too wide-ranging to be put into computational terms and so it is necessary to pare it down to a few limited features which contain the essence of what is being said. The selection of these essential features may be very controversial. Further, it is not until an attempt is made to put an informal theory into computational terms that many of its ambiguities will emerge.

9.2.1 Computer modelling using DAI

The research field of artificial intelligence is somewhat misleadingly named and is often misunderstood. It is largely concerned with non-numeric sym-

MODELLING UPPER PALAEOLITHIC SOCIAL CHANGE

bolic computation and, in particular, with achieving operational computational interpretations of aspects of cognition such as planning, memory, learning and induction. An important concept of artificial intelligence studies is that of an "agent": a process, however simple, which collects information about its environment, makes decisions about its actions, and acts. This use of the term "agent" differs somewhat from its use in other areas of science, where it is often used to denote anything endowed with causal powers (Bhaskar 1978: 49).

Distributed artificial intelligence is a relatively recent development of artificial intelligence studies. It concerns the properties of sets of intercommunicating agents ("multiple agent systems") coexisting in a common environment. The aim may be to study the properties of such systems in an abstract way, or to design systems of immediate practical use, or – the more relevant case here – to use such a programmed multi-agent system as a model of a human or other real-world system. The potential impact upon the social sciences is obvious.

An important facet of DAI research has been the development of various "software testbeds" (e.g. Bond & Gasser 1988, Ch. 1 and Sect. 6.3; Doran et al. 1991). In this context a testbed is a computer program which provides a platform upon which one can build and experiment with multi-agent systems. Typically it will provide some means of defining and creating a number of agents, their capabilities, an environment in which these agents are to exist, one or more protocols which they can use to interact with one another, and means of monitoring the agents' collective behaviour when the system is run. Testbeds differ in their degree of generality or specificity. General testbeds give the experimenter greater flexibility in the range of experiments that can be set up. Specialized testbeds are designed to support experiments in a particular domain or with particular agent architectures or communication protocols.

It seems clear that DAI (especially of the "experimental testbed" variety) should be able to contribute to the study of social change generally, and to the processes of change suggested by Mellars in particular, since it enables the integrated study of both environmental and cognitive factors and their impact.

9.2.2 The need for DAI theory development

Unfortunately, the situation is less straightforward than the preceding would suggest. DAI -based models typically embody agents capable of cognitive

THE EOS SOFTWARE TESTBED

processes such as planning and learning. But how to program such processes is only partly understood. Hence the requirements of a model may not be fully achievable within the present state of the art. It follows that model building within a DAI context easily comes to include an element of theory development – new DAI itself. And several aspects of the EOS project are indeed innovative as regards DAI.

9.3 The EOS software testbed

The EOS software testbed was motivated by our wish to experiment with a computational version of the Mellars model. However, to facilitate comparison with other testbeds, we shall initially describe it independently of that objective.

The EOS testbed allows the creation of an environment, and of resources and agents within that environment. Agents can move and acquire resources and need to do so in order to survive. They have rules thathich determine their behaviour, and in particular they can send and receive messages and can sense their local environment and act upon it. They can hold internal representations of themselves, of other agents and of their locality and can carry out a limited form of planning. The agents in the testbed are partly standardized in that they all have the same structure and rules and work with the same underlying concepts. However, their internal representations of their own local environment (including other agents) are dynamic and vary from one agent to another.

The testbed has been implemented in "Object-oriented" style in the Prolog language and runs on a Sun SPARCstation ELC. A scheduler simulates the concurrent activity of objects by activating each in turn. We equate the passing of one unit of time within the testbed to one cycle of the scheduler activating each object (e.g. agents, resources) in turn for a limited amount of computation.

The testbed is designed to facilitate experiments involving variations in the behavioural and representational repertoires of the agents, and the dynamics of resources in their environment.

We now describe the features provided within the testbed in more detail.

9.3.1 The environment

The environment is a two-dimensional square and the experimenter can

201

MODELLING UPPER PALAEOLITHIC SOCIAL CHANGE

specify its size. A typical height and width is 10,000 by 10,000 units. Agents and resources have locations within the environment specified by pairs of coordinates.

9.3.2 Resources

The essential characteristics of resources in the testbed are that they occur in clusters at fixed "resource locations", and that they can vary from one to another as regards the type of energy they embody, the number of agents that must act simultaneously to acquire one of them, and their availability though time.

A resource location comprises a cluster of resource instances, analogous, say, to an apple tree or a (static) reindeer herd: when an agent acquires an instance of the resource the number at the locality is reduced by 1. The testbed also includes provision for resources that require a group effort for their acquisition, that is, simultaneous action by several agents. The number of agents required we call the "complexity" of the resource. We shall often loosely refer to a resource as "complex" meaning that it requires a number of agents for its acquisition. More precisely, a complex resource is acquired when a number of agents equal to or greater than its complexity (and which are within range of the resource location) simultaneously attempt to acquire it, and then each of those agents acquires a resource instance.

The testbed is parameterized accordingly. Thus, the following must be specified by the testbed user:

- the number of resource locations of each type that should exist in the environment and their distribution (e.g. randomly distributed);
- the number of resource instances each resource location comprises;
- the type of energy each resource location can supply;
- the quantity of energy an instance of a particular resource type can supply;
- the minimum number of agents that must simultaneously "attack" a resource locality of a particular type before any of them can acquire a resource instance (i.e. its complexity);
- how close to a resource location an agent must be before it can be effective in acquiring that resource;
- the time period for which a resource cluster exists and then the time it takes to renew itself.

By varying these parameters very many resource patterns in time and space may be specified. One pattern it is natural to specify is a "resource cycle", whereby the resources are co-ordinated to fail and be renewed at regular intervals. Our experiments using the testbed, described below, have used only some of these facilities. We have not yet, for example, looked at the case of resources of several different energy types.

9.3.3 Agents

Agents "seek to stay alive" by acquiring and consuming one or more types of resource energy. In each testbed time unit an agent's energy levels are decremented. If it fails to acquire enough new energy by resource acquisition it will eventually "die", i.e. cease processing. Acquiring energy is the only inbuilt goal of agents; all others are derivative.

An agent embodies of a set of production rules (cognitive and action) each of which reacts to a particular set of conditions in working memory. The main constituents of the agent's working memory are the social and environment models.

The agents have a "production system" architecture in the AI sense (see Fig. 9.1). Each agent has a number of production rules of the form

IF condition THEN action

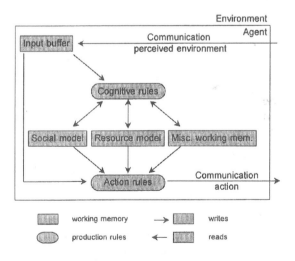

Figure 9.1 The EOS testbed agent architecture – a production system (in the AI sense).

MODELLING UPPER PALAEOLITHIC SOCIAL CHANGE

and a working memory which consists of (possibly many) facts which can change dynamically. If the condition part of a rule is satisfied by the facts in the working memory, then the rule can be "fired", meaning that its action part is performed.

Cognition and action are both achieved by production rules. By definition, cognitive rules have an effect only on an agent's working memory, whereas action rules have an effect on the environment. In each testbed time unit each agent will fire all fireable cognitive rules (including multiple instantiations of the same rule), but only one action rule. This difference is intended to capture, however crudely, the tendency of action to take more time than thought. If more than one action rule is fireable, then that with the highest (user set) priority is chosen.

Message passing between agents is via the environment; that is, a message sent from one agent to another is passed first to the environment, which is designed to determine whether the message is indeed to reach its intended recipient and, if so, when. An agent "acts" by sending a suitable message to the environment which reacts appropriately. When the environment changes (spontaneously or in response to actions by agents), corresponding messages are sent to agents within sensory range of the change.

The working memory of an agent is divided into four main areas:

- RESOURCE MODEL, where an agent keeps a record of resources it knows about including their types and locations;
- SOCIAL MODEL, where an agent stores its beliefs about itself and other agents;
- MESSAGE BUFFER, where incoming messages from other agents and the environment are stored; this is cleared at the end of each scheduler cycle;
- MISCELLANEOUS, where other information associated with the agent is stored, for example, its hunger level, its behaviour mode and its perception range.

The social model is particularly important. It is designed to record an agent's beliefs about the existence of groups of agents and the identities of their leaders. Associated with beliefs about leaders is other information, for example the size of its immediate following. Some followers may themselves be leaders. An agent may well appear in its own social model as a leader or follower in particular groups. Also held within the social model are beliefs about territories. There is no expectation that the information held in an agent's social model will be either complete or accurate.

Notice that, whereas the generic concepts of a "leader" and a "follower" are inherent in the structure of a social model, particular instances of these

THE EOS MODEL

concepts normally arise dynamically and differ from one agent's social model to another.

The agent parameters specified by the experimenter determine the number of agents of each type and, for each type:

- their initial locations in the environment (randomly set within a specified region);
- the speed with which they can move in the environment, that is, the distance they can move in one testbed time unit;
- sensory range: at what range an agent can detect other agents and resources;
- a list of skills: a resource whose energy is of a certain type can be acquired only by an agent with the corresponding skill;
- the number of energy "stores" with their initial levels;
- a critical "hunger" level for energy stores: if the energy in a store falls below this critical level the agent will try to replenish it by consuming appropriate resources;
- the particular set of rules (both cognitive and action) which determine the agents' behaviour.

The last of these is the most complex and important.

In all our experiments with the testbed so far (see below), each of the foregoing characteristics, other than initial location, has been set to be the same for all agents in the community.

Facts, the condition and action parts of rules, and messages are all held as Prolog structures. All knowledge/belief epresentation within agents is therefore within a subset of first-order logic. Matching of conditions is by Prolog unification.

9.3.4 The testbed interface

A graphical interface provides the experimenter with a dynamic view of the environment with its agents and resources. This is updated with the passage of testbed time. The interface also provides the ability to interact with the system during experimentation. There are simple measurement facilities.

9.4 The EOS model

Our computational version of the Mellars model exists at two levels: as a set of core abstract processes, which we propose as embodying the growth

MODELLING UPPER PALAEOLITHIC SOCIAL CHANGE

of social complexity and which are based upon the Mellars and Cohen formulations and on DAI concepts, and as detailed rule specifications for agents implemented in the EOS testbed, from which we intend the core processes to develop.

9.4.1 Core processes

We consider abstractions of the Palaeolithic environment and its resources, the people living in that environment and the interactive processes between them. We directly follow Mellars (1985) in taking crowding and central decision-making to be at the heart of the matter. Our computational model therefore focuses on what can happen when agents with elements of human-like cognition share a common environment, are strongly aware of one another and need collectively to perform one or more complex resource acquisition tasks if they are to survive.

We have not attempted to capture within our model processes of reproduction, or kin structures. We find that we need not address these issues to explore essential processes of the development of social complexity. Nor is conflict explicit in our model, although it arises in a secondary way.

We propose three core processes which, we suggest, arise naturally from population concentration:

(i) temporary planned co-operation between agents, involving a temporary group leader, to achieve effective resource acquisition and to avoid negative interactions, for example too many agents seeking to acquire the same resource;

(ii) conversion of temporary groups into semi-permanent groups, with a leader, with agents forming internal representations of the groups, so that, once formed, a group continues to work together unless something causes otherwise;

(iii) the repeated use of the processes just specified to support the "recursive" development of hierarchical structuring: groups of groups of groups, etc.

A central point is that an agent's representations of other agents and of groups of agents, in our terms its "social model", will have a determining effect on how it behaves in relation to other agents and ultimately on how effective it is in acting and surviving in its environment (see Fig. 9.2). For example, group permanency (see process (ii) above) is a matter of agents becoming aware of their membership of a group and then treating fellow group members differently and having useful knowledge about them. And

THE EOS MODEL

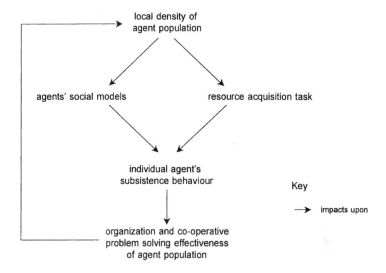

Figure 9.2 The heart of the EOS model. Population concentration impacts upon the characteristics of the environmental resource acquisition task, and both impact on agents' social models. These in turn affect the agents' behaviour and hence community effectiveness, which has an effect on on population density, closing the loop.

agents within a group have expectations about how the others may behave, enabling quick responses to resource opportunities.

9.4.2 The EOS model in the testbed: the agents' rules

It is the agents' production rules that provide them with their specific behavioural repertoire from which emerges the complex behaviour that interests us. Currently there are about sixty rules, including both cognitive and action rules.

The recruitment process
Much agent behaviour is organized around the recruitment of a group of agents for the performance of a complex resource acquisition task. The recruitment process (see Fig. 9.3) is based upon the contract net task delegation protocol (R.G. Smith 1980): an agent with a resource requirement ini-

207

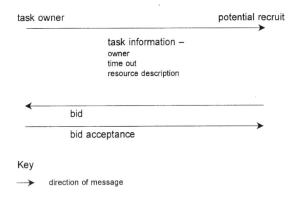

Figure 9.3 The resource acquisition task recruitment protocol.

tiates a plan for a resource acquisition, invites bids from others who may wish to take part, and then chooses those who are to do so.

Agents achieve co-operation as follows. An agent that has planned the co-operative acquisition of a resource sends out information about the task to other agents. These other agents evaluate the information and may decide to bid for a part in the task. If the task owner has received enough bids by some specified time, then it will accept those that it favours.

If an agent already has an established following (meaning that both it and its followers recognize the existence of a group with the agent as leader), then, in a specific way, the recruitment process is biased towards use of that existing following – followers are more likely to receive proposals than are non-followers, and are more likely to accept them if they do. When a (new) group is successfully recruited by an agent, then, subject to certain conditions, e.g. no spatial dispersal, that group has a continuing existence.

For programming convenience and conceptual clarity, the rules have been written so that an agent will normally be in one of a number of modes. We briefly describe each mode in turn.

- *Autonomous mode* This is the default mode. In this mode an agent acts in an independent non-co-operating way. For example, it can move around at random looking for resources.
- *Recruiting mode* An agent may go into recruiting mode if it believes it can organize a sufficiently large team of agents to perform some resource acquisition task it has planned.
- *Bidding mode* An agent may go into bidding mode if it receives a mes-

THE EOS MODEL

sage from another agent inviting it to take part in some planned resource acquisition task.

- *Executing mode* An agent goes into executing mode when it has recruited a full team or when its bid has been accepted. In executing mode agents go ahead and execute a planned task.

The "planning" referred to in these mode descriptions is very simple. Essentially, it involves no more than the choice by an agent of a particular resource to be targeted for acquisition by an appropriate number of agents, together with a time period within which the acquisition is to take place.

Information flow

There are a number of rules which deal specifically with information flow. We mention three groups of rules of this type:

- rules that handle agents' perceptions of the environment (agents and resources) and consequent updating of their social and resource models;
- rules that pass up information (about resources, agents and groups) from followers to leaders;
- rules that pass on information about changes in groups to nearby agents and thus lead to the updating of agents' social models. Since the information that is passed on in this way is not guaranteed to be accurate or timely, agents' social models may well be inaccurate.

Territories and their use

A third set of rules capture a notion of agent and group territory. We represent territories as "subjective" in the sense that they exist as beliefs in agents' social models, but not in any way as structures in the environment.

Every agent, in its social model, keeps as part of its beliefs about agents and groups a representation of the territory associated with them. For initial simplicity territories are assumed to be rectangular. The territories for single agents are determined by cumulative observation of resource collection – that is, one agent believes another's territory to be where it has observed that agent to collect resources. Group territories are determined as the composition of the territories of group members.

Territories are primarily of significance when an agent chooses a resource to target for acquisition by itself or its following. Resources believed to be in an agent's (or an agent's group's) own territory are preferred, with resources believed to be in another agent's or group's territory are avoided if possible.

An effect of this use of territories is to reduce the tendency of agents or groups to undermine one another's resource acquisition plans by accident. When there is no resource acquisition plan to execute, territories also provide a default direction of movement for an agent, back towards the centre of its territory.

Choosing and assessing rule sets

The rules that we have described, and the processes that they collectively specify, determine the behaviour of individual agents and hence of the agent community. They can, however, be formulated in many different ways. We have selected and parameterized rule sets that we find plausible and effective, in line with the core processes we have put at the heart of the EOS model, and we have conducted experiments to establish the impact of variations in some of the parameters involved. We now describe these experimental trials.

9.5 Experimentation

9.5.1 Initial experimentation: group-coordination

The following agent behaviour has been demonstrated within the EOS testbed. It directly follows from the rules specified for the agents.

Agents start with no knowledge of any groups or other agents. If they are able to collect resources individually, they will do so. If the resources that look the most promising require the co-operation of several agents and an agent has received a request to co-operate, then it will do so. If it has not already received a request to co-operate, then it will attempt to recruit others to a plan of its own.

Agents that successfully recruit a group to their plan become group leaders, with all members of the group adjusting their social models accordingly. Agents that have become group leaders expect their followers to do as they suggest. Those that have become followers will normally acquiesce in the plans of their leaders, but will not always do so. For example, a follower agent that has become spatially separated from its leader may be recruited by a new leader, in which case it will, temporarily at least, reject proposals from its old leader.

A leader can receive a request to co-operate involving its whole group rather than just itself and can respond on its group's behalf. It is this step,

EXPERIMENTATION

of course, that leads to the formation of multi-level groups (i.e. hierarchies). Once an agent becomes a leader, it will no longer respond to a request as an individual. It follows that the exact number of agents required for the acquisition of a particular resource sometimes cannot be recruited but more can (e.g. three groups of 6 are available for a resource of complexity 16). In such a case the recruitment and acquisition will go ahead but with "over-manning", and therefore inefficiency.

Figure 9.4 illustrates collective behaviour generated in the testbed. It shows a situation where the leader of a group of three agents (agent20), in order to acquire a resource requiring coordinated action by six agents, recruits another agent (agent7) which is itself the leader of a group of three, thus forming a two-level hierarchy. The social models of both agent20 and agent7 contain references to the fact that agent20 is the leader of a group of four agents, one of which is agent7, and that agent7 is itself the leader of a group of three.

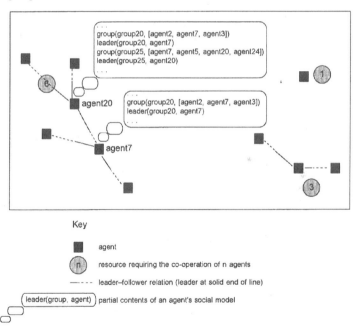

Figure 9.4 A view of the EOS testbed environment showing agents and resources and fragments of associated social models.

MODELLING UPPER PALAEOLITHIC SOCIAL CHANGE

In our initial trials we demonstrated:

- agents acting autonomously;
- crowding: many agents moving into a restricted area to acquire resources limited to that area;
- "clobbering": agents accidentally and negatively interfering with one another in their attempts to acquire resources;
- agents forming groups to acquire complex resources;
- groups attaining some degree of permanence.

The important concept of clobbering needs some comment. It is entirely possible for two agents, or two groups of agents, to set out independently to acquire the same resource at roughly the same time. Since normally only one of them can in fact acquire it, there must be a loser. If the losing agent or group had relinquished another possibility in order to make its (failing) attempt, there has clearly been a failure of coordination from the standpoint of the agent community as a whole. As mentioned earlier, the use of territories reduces clobbering, but by no means eliminates it. We shall return to the significance of clobbering later.

9.5.2 Further experimentation: hierarchies and their properties

In more systematic, though still exploratory, experimentation we have tried to address several questions involving hierarchies, their properties and effectiveness.

The following preliminary points should be noted concerning our experimental trials:

- A typical experimental trial (i.e. set up a community and resources, and run through a number of resource cycles) takes from a few hours to several days. This explains why the number of agents involved in our trials is relatively small and why all the trials to be described have been replicated only two (sometimes three) times.
- The number of agents involved in trials ranged from 32 to 50, located in a 10,000 × 10,000 environment.
- The initial spatial distribution of resource is a random scatter (different scatters on different trials). All resources provide the same energy type, the only type needed by agents.
- Resources ranged from simple resources requiring a single agent for their acquisition, to those of complexity 48 (i.e. requiring 48 agents to act simultaneously at the resource location).
- Resources arise, die and are then renewed over a "resource cycle", typi-

EXPERIMENTATION

cally lasting 500 or 800 testbed time units.

- Agent communities *always* die off over a small number of resource cycles. This is because there is always some degree of mismatch between the organization of the agent community and the current pattern of resources, and there is no process of reproduction to make good agent "deaths".

Do hierarchies form?

Starting with a set of autonomous agents (i.e. no joint plans or awareness of one another), under what circumstances, if any, will one or more hierarchies emerge and to what extent? By a hierarchy we mean a combination of agents which is at least a group of agents with a leader, but that may well be groups of groups of agents, to several levels, with an overall leader.

To address these questions with some precision, it was necessary to define a measure of the existence of hierarchies. This proved less straightforward than might at first appear. After some experimentation we fixed upon the following. Each agent is assigned a depth; all agents which are not followers of any other agent are of depth 0, their followers are of depth 1, their followers' followers depth 2, etc. The hierarchy measure is then the sum of all $N*D$ where N is the number of agents at depth D.

We performed a series of experimental trials each with 50 agents and a combination of simple and complex resources randomly scattered: 16 resource locations of complexity 3, eight of complexity 6, four of complexity 12, two of complexity 24 and one of complexity 48. We found that multi-level hierarchies will regularly arise, but to an extent depending strongly upon certain contextual factors. The two most important of these factors are the distribution pattern of resources and the perceptual range of the agents, that is, the distance over which they can perceive both resources and other agents.

As regards the first of these two factors, it is important to notice that hierarchies will *not* form if there are only complex resources and no simple ones. This is because agents, if not already organized into small groups, have insufficient awareness and time to form the large groups needed to acquire complex resources. Thus there must, in effect, be an element of facilitation in the way resources are distributed.

Regarding the second factor, the greater the perceptual range, the stronger the initial growth of hierarchies. Notice that this is equivalent to: "the greater population concentration, the stronger the growth of hierarchies", because population concentration essentially means greater awareness of others, which is exactly what a greater perceptual range implies.

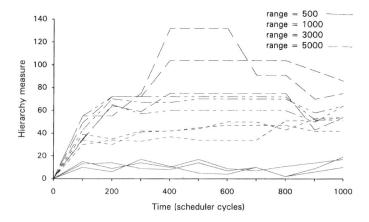

Figure 9.5 The degree of hierarchy formation is affected by the perception range of 50 agents in a 10 000 × 10 000 environment. A small perception range results in a low level of hierarchy formation, whereas a large perception range leads to more hierarchy formation.

Figure 9.5 shows the degree of initial hierarchy formation plotted against increasing perceptual range (with each trial replicated three times). The length of the resource cycle is 800. (At the start of a new resource cycle, some disintegration of existing hierarchies often takes place as subordinate agents leave to acquire simple resources which have become available again.)

The length of the resource cycle is 800 time units in all cases. There are fewer hierarchies after 800 time steps because the reappearance of simple resources causes some hierarchies to break down into smaller units so that individual agents can collect them.

When hierarchies form, do they persist?

When hierarchies form, do they persist from one resource cycle to the next? The answer to this question is "yes", but the degree to which persistence occurs is strongly dependent upon (a) the length of time followers retain the belief that they are part of a group even when not in contact with it, (b) how easily agents decide to operate independently of their leader (e.g. agreeing to be recruited by another agent) and (c) when separated from their group and without any plan to follow, whether agents head back towards the centre of the group territory. We use the word "commitment" to describe the

EXPERIMENTATION

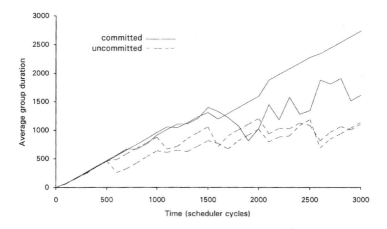

Figure 9.6 The persistence of groups depends upon the "level of commitment" of the group members. "Commitment" is a composite of three parameters: (1) a parameter that determines how long an agent will continue to believe itself to be a member of a group after losing contact with the group; (2) one that determines the tendency of a follower to accept plans suggested by another agent or formulate plans of its own; and (3) one that determines the probability that an agent will return to the centre of its group's territory when there is nothing else it can do. As may be seen, a large degree of commitment leads to greater group persistence.

degree of adherence which an agent has towards its group and leader. Commitment is thus a combination of the three factors just described.

Figure 9.6 shows the results from experimental trials involving 32 agents in which we examined how the persistence of hierarchies depends upon individual agent commitment. "Committed agents" are highly committed on all three dimensions. Uncommitted agents are uncommitted on all dimensions. We employed a measure of group survival defined as the average "age" (in testbed time units) of each existing group. As one would expect, the results suggest that group and hierarchy persistence is much less when the agents are uncommitted.

Are hierarchies effective?

This question may be interpreted in at least two different ways.
  (i) Do hierarchies facilitate the acquisition of resources? In a simple sense

MODELLING UPPER PALAEOLITHIC SOCIAL CHANGE

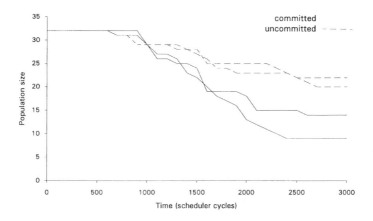

Figure 9.7 Agent survival is affected by the commitment of agents to their groups. Low commitment leads to longer survival.

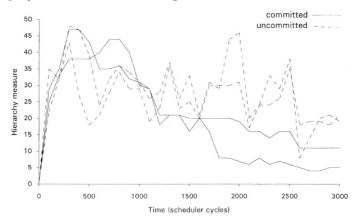

Figure 9.8 Low commitment leads to higher average levels of hierarchy formation. Note, however, that there is a greater degree of fluctuation than with high commitment.

the answer is "yes". Without hierarchies, the more complex resources would never be exploited by the community. Hierarchies are the means by which the community organizes itself to acquire more complex re-

EXPERIMENTATION

sources, and their existence is prompted by the gradation of resources from simple to complex.

(ii) Does persistence of individual hierarchies benefit the agent community? Somewhat unexpectedly, the answer to this question is "no". Maintaining hierarchies over long periods is too inflexible. Agents and groups of agents need to be able to break away from their existing commitment and reorganize, in order to adapt to changing environmental circumstances.

Our results bearing on this later interpretation of the question appear in Figures 9.7 and 9.8. We have found that lower agent commitment, and therefore *lower* persistence of hierarchies, leads to *greater* agent survival and, paradoxically, to *greater* average levels of hierarchy formation.

How important is it for agents' social models to be accurate?

In general, there is nothing that guarantees that social models are accurate. For example, they may record the existence of groups that in reality do not exist, or they may assign wrong leaders to them.

Intuitively, faulty models may arise in various ways: when an agent's beliefs are not updated as a group's membership and other properties

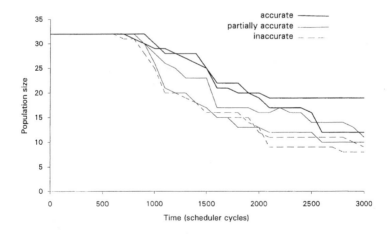

Figure 9.9 The accuracy of agents' social models affects the survival of the population.

change, by misleading initial observation, by faulty generalization (e.g. about territories) and so on. It seems likely that inaccurate social models will give rise to attempts at recruitment and to plans that fail on execution. Plausibly, they may be worse than useless.

To gain some understanding of this key issue, we have experimented with the "unreliable" transmission of updating information from one agent to another, with the degree of unreliability adjustable. Figure 9.9 shows the results of our experiments. They show that unreliable inter-agent information transfer about changes of group allegiance, and hence the development of faulty social models, undermines the survival of the community. However, the size of the effect is less than one might initially expect.

Accuracy of social models is measured indirectly by a parameter that controls the reliability with which updating information is passed from agent to agent. As may be seen, inaccurate social models decrease the survival rate.

9.5.3 Discussion of experimental results

It is tempting to draw general conclusions from our experiments, for example that they support our initial hypotheses that population concentration promotes the development of centralized decision-making, that the effectiveness of social models is crucial to the growth of social complexity, and that over-strong adherence to hierarchies is counter-productive. But the computational intensity of our experimental trials has meant that we have only very limited results using a particular set of assumptions on which to base such conclusions. At best they are suggestive.

However, even our limited experiments clearly demonstrate the complexity of the relationship between agent characteristics, multi-level hierarchies and their dynamics and effectiveness, and the resource environment. This relationship is far from simple. Thus, there is much to be learned about the dynamics of problem-solving hierarchies in the abstract, potentially yielding elements of new theory.

9.6 Future work

At this point in the project we have a choice: to experiment in more detail with the model as it exists, or to develop the model further. Our commitment to building a computational version of the Mellars's model prompts the latter course, since there are a number of important topics in Mellars'

FUTURE WORK

account which our existing computational model does not address at all. We now indicate briefly how we need to develop our model as regards both the social processes it simulates and its essential technical content.

9.6.1. Needed developments

We need to overcome several limitations in our existing testbed and model.

First, the hierarchy formation process can form a hierarchy involving N agents only if there exist resources of complexity N to be acquired in the environment. This is unrealistic. We have identified the avoidance of clobbering as the underlying reason for a community of agents to form large hierarchies in the absence of resources of corresponding complexity. Quite simply, overall efficiency of resource acquisition requires coordination between large numbers of agents even if no individual task requires the coordination of many agents.

Related to clobbering is conflict. Conflict between agents is not a primary feature of our model, but it is inherent in the fact that agents and groups undermine one another's plans when acquiring resources. Were agents provided with the ability to harm other agents directly (e.g. with an action that immobilizes), planning to acquire resources would become a matter of finding the best mix of harming others (in order to prevent their interference) and acquiring resources oneself.

Secondly, our present handling of territories is clearly too simple. The issue of territory is, obviously, a most important one (see e.g. Dyson-Hudson & Smith 1978; Sack 1986), and we need to introduce a more realistic framework enabling a deeper study of the relationship between territoriality and resource acquisition efficiency.

Thirdly, not yet explicitly demonstrated, but inherent in the model as implemented, are the essentials of ranking and specialization. A hierarchical group necessarily implies a ranking by levels of the agents within it. Further, once an agent joins a group it will tend repeatedly to be allocated tasks requiring just a subset of its particular skills – this a consequence of leaders' partial knowledge of their followers and the requirement for cognitive economy. We need to demonstrate and extend these mechanisms.

Fourthly, our existing model does not address relationships between agents other than those of mutual autonomy and leader–follower. This is too simple, and we need to implement a wider range of relationship concepts within agents' social models to enable agents to take part in a correspondingly wider range of actual relationships.

To overcome these limitations we require new and more powerful processes of planning and of social model manipulation within agents. Thus, to control clobbering an agent must consider and plan for the actions of others not under its control. Furthermore, agents need to compare plans from different sources and choose between them (or merge them, should that be possible). And social models must contain a wider range of generic concepts with complex and flexible criteria for instantiating them. All these developments are technically difficult and close to the AI planning and DAI research frontier. Nevertheless, we are implementing a new version of the testbed in which agents can embody such processes.

Finally, there is the issue of how to relate the behaviour of the model to the Upper Palaeolithic archaeological record. Certainly it will be possible to specify deposition rules within the testbed which build up a "simulated archaeological record" (Mithen, Ch. 8 above) from the multi-agent activity – indeed, we have already done so in very simple ways. That opens a door to the identification of which model processes correspond in their record to actuality. Nevertheless, convincingly relating the simulated to the real archaeological record is another matter and a major challenge which we have yet to address.

9.7 Conclusions

We have stated that this is a report of work in progress. And as yet we can conclude nothing definite about the Mellars model. But our results do tend to support the view that population concentration encourages the growth of social complexity, and that having accurate social models is a necessary condition for that growth. We also have also obtained some suggestive specific results, for example that in certain circumstances stable hierarchies do not enhance survival. And we can begin to address in computational terms such anthropological issues as territoriality, ranking and specialization.

Simple though these findings are, they have implications that should not be underestimated. They mean that there is a new resource available to social science which combines computer simulation and its power to handle massive detail rigorously with the ability of cognitive science and artificial intelligence to address in precise terms some of the most subjective and essentially human aspects of society. That takes us to the very heart of social science and its problems.

CONCLUSIONS

Acknowledgements

The EOS project is funded by the UK Joint Council Initiative in Cognitive Science/ HCI, Grant SP8930879.

Chapter 10
Learning to co-operate using cultural algorithms

Robert G. Reynolds

In this chapter an approach to evolutionary programming based upon principles of cultural evolution is developed. In cultural algorithms evolution takes place at two levels: at a micro-evolutionary level, in terms of changes in traits associated with individuals in a population, and at a macro-evolutionary level, in terms of beliefs. In such multiple-inheritance systems there are evolving populations of trait sequences as well as associated belief spaces. The belief spaces are derived from the performance of individual trait sequences and are used to constrain the traits acquired in future populations. There can be changes in the representation of the belief space and in the trait sequences.

In the second half of the chapter, this approach is used to illuminate the evolution of co-operation among llama herders on the punas of Ayacucho, Peru. Using this example, the cultural algorithms approach is compared with a micro-evolutionary approach implemented using genetic algorithms, an evolutionary learning model proposed by Holland (1975). The results suggest that cultural-algorithms can be fruitfully applied to situations where the problem to be solved possesses both a micro- and a macro-evolutionary component.

10.1　Cultural and genetic evolution

Culture can be defined as "a system of symbolically encoded conceptual phenomena that are socially and historically transmitted within and between populations" (Durham 1991: 8–9). Since the 1970s there has been considerable debate about the relationship between cultural and genetic processes. A prominent issue is whether or not the process of human evo-

LEARNING TO CO-OPERATE USING CULTURAL ALGORITHMS

lution is the result of a combination of two independent, but interacting, inheritance systems, one genetic and one cultural. Some specific questions are: (1) Is culture a *bona fide* second inheritance system? (2) If so, what are the appropriate units within which to represent the transmission and adaptation of cultural information? (3) What is an appropriate framework within which to describe their interaction and how does the nature of this interaction affect the overall process of evolution?

Evolutionary models that contain more than one mode of inheritance are called multiple-inheritance models. This is because information can be transmitted in several modes. A number of multiple-inheritance models proposed in the literature support an affirmative answer to the first question above. While all these models assume an underlying genetic inheritance system based upon Darwinian principles, they differ in terms of how they represent the cultural component. One group of models represents the cultural system as a non-genetic inheritance system where the units of inheritance are culturally heritable traits observable in an individual phenotype (Boyd & Richerson 1985; Cavalli-Sfarza & Feldman 1981).

The popularity of this class of models is the result of several factors. First, the models allow information on traits to be easily acquired, studied and related directly to cultural activity. Second, the models are micro-evolutionary in scale and can be viewed as analogous to the process of genetic evolution. That is, cultural change can be described as the replacement of traits through a process analogous to the substitution of alleles in genetic evolution. Alternative traits are viewed as alleles whose frequencies differ as a result of their relative rates of transmission through the population.

Reynolds (1986) used a trait-based approach to model the evolution of strategies for incipient agriculture within a traditional hunter–gatherer economy. This was a micro-evolutionary model, implemented using genetic algorithms (Holland 1975), which focused on the learning of new economic strategies by a group of hunter–gatherers residing in a particular cave, Guilá Naquitz, in the Oaxaca valley of southern Mexico. The plant yields produced using the collecting strategies learned by the simulated group corresponded closely with the actual distribution of plant remains found in the cave.

The trait-based approach, while successful in modelling micro-evolutionary changes in individual behaviour, is less successful when dealing with macro-evolutionary processes that pertain to groups of individuals. Cultural change at the macro-evolutionary level involves changes in the regulatory or control activities that govern the interaction of individuals. These changes can have major effects on a society's economic and political structure. The

224

CULTURAL AND GENETIC EVOLUTION

modelling of change at this level requires that a group's ideational or belief structure be constrained to the collective combination of traits that the individuals in a society can exhibit.

For example, in the Oaxaca valley, a change in subsistence strategy from hunting and collecting to incipient agriculture led to marked changes in the political and social structure (Flannery & Marcus 1983). In the trait-based approach, one can indirectly represent the results of a shift in the belief structure of a group by changing the frequencies of individual resource-collecting strategies. This was accomplished in the genetic algorithm implementation through modifying the way in which various operators were applied to change the trait sequences in the population of collecting strategies.

While such a tactic is useful in situations where changes in a group's belief structure affect a limited number of traits and where only a few beliefs are relevant to the process being described, it does not scale up well to situations where a complex belief structure must be modelled and where a given belief can influence a variety of traits. As a result, researchers interested in macro-evolutionary processes have proposed a second category of co-evolutionary models in which the units of cultural inheritance can be ideational (Durham 1991).

In this chapter a new class of evolutionary learning algorithms, cultural algorithms, is proposed to model the interaction between the micro- and macro-evolutionary scales. In principle, cultural algorithms can be used to describe explicitly the effect that a group's belief structure at the macro-evolutionary level has on the transmission of traits between individuals at the micro-evolutionary level. The belief structure is represented as a network of structured, hierarchically organized behavioural constraints in which the society's current set of acceptable behaviours can be expressed. This belief network can be viewed as an extension of the idea of version spaces (Mitchell 1978).

In the following section, cultural algorithms are introduced. The structure of the micro- and macro-evolutionary components of the dual inheritance system and their interaction is described. Section 10.3 introduces a problem concerning the cultural evolution of co-operative behaviours among llama herders on the punas of Ayacucho, Peru. It then describes how this problem can be expressed in terms of an implementation of cultural algorithms. Section 10.4 presents results from this implementation and compares its performance against an implementation of the trait-based approach using genetic algorithms.

LEARNING TO CO-OPERATE USING CULTURAL ALGORITHMS

10.2 Cultural algorithms

Cultural algorithms support two modes of inheritance, one at the micro-evolutionary level in terms of traits, and the other at the macro-evolutionary level in terms of beliefs. The two modes interact via a communication channel that enables the behaviour of individuals to alter the belief structure and allows the belief structure to constrain the way in which individuals behave.

A cultural algorithm operates on three components: a belief structure, a population structure and a communication channel. The basic algorithm is as follows:

```
CULTURAL ALGORITHM
begin
t=0;
Initialize population POP(0);
Initialize belief space BLF(0);
Initialize communication channel CHL(0);
Evaluate (POP(0));
t=1;
 repeat
  Communicate (POP(t), BLF(t));
  Adjust (BLF(t));
  Communicate (BLF(t), POP(t));
  Modulate fitness (BLF(t), POP(t));
  t = t+1;
  Select POP(t) from POP(t-1);
  Evolve (POP(t));
  Evaluate (POP(t));
 until (termination condition)
end.
```

In the remainder of this section the algorithm is described in detail. Prior to entering the learning loop (the steps from repeat to until), the population, belief space and communication channel are initialized. Sections 10.2.1–10.2.3 explain how these components are represented. The basic processes involved in the learning loop are discussed in Section 10.2.4.

10.2.1 Representation of the population space

Each individual in the population is characterized in terms of a set of properties or traits. A trait is a value taken over a hierarchically structured collection of terms called a *term hierarchy* where the most general term is found in the root and the most specific terms are found at the leaves. Each term hierarchy

226

Figure 10.1 The term hierarchy for a binary valued trait.

is well structured in that there is a simple path from a given term to the root. This is called the term hierarchy for a given term i. For example, the term hierarchy for a binary valued trait is shown in Figure 10.1. The symbol # corresponds to the set that contains all the possible values for that term.

Given that certain traits require other traits as prerequisites, one can define a prerequisite graph as a directed acyclic graph (DAG) where an arc from a trait i to a trait j exists if trait i is required for the development or description of trait j. An example of such a structure is given in Figure 10.2. This prerequisite structure consists of four traits, labelled T1–T4, as well as a dummy node, O, representing the individual. In this structure T3 needs T1 and T2 as prerequisites, and T4 has no prerequisites.

A topological sort is the assignment of a linear ordering to the vertices

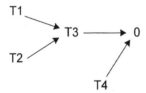

Figure 10.2 The prerequisite graph for a collection of four traits.

of a directed acyclic graph so that, if there is an arc from trait i to trait j in the graph, then i must appear before j in the linear ordering. Therefore the ordering of traits in the sequence depends on the traversal procedure used. Here, a basic post-order traversal is selected. The ordering of traits for an individual will therefore be T1, T2, T3, T4. Other orderings are possible depending on the traversal procedure used. For example, another possible sequence could be T2, T1, T3, T4.

A *trait network* is produced by augmenting the prerequisite graph with the set of trait values found on the leaves of the term hierarchy for each trait. Assuming that the prerequisite structure in Figure 10.2 is defined over a set of binary valued traits, the resulting network is given in Figure 10.3. Given the trait network, the population of possible trait sequences is specified by the selection of a topological sort that determines the ordering of traits in the trait sequence. For each trait visited during the sort, one of its leaf node

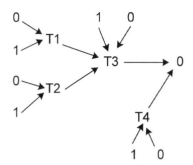

Figure 10.3 The trait network for the four binary valued traits.

values is selected. The population of all possible sequences, the *population space*, constitutes the space of individuals from which each current population can be drawn. For the trait network in Figure 10.3, the individual trait sequence 1011 is produced by selecting a 1 for T1, a 0 for T2, a 1 for T3, and a 1 for T4.

10.2.2 Representation of the belief space

The *belief network* consists of the prerequisite structure for the trait sequence described above, augmented by the entire term hierarchy for each of the traits. If it is assumed that all of the traits are defined over a binary alphabet, then the belief network for the example trait network in Figure 10.3 is shown in Figure 10.4. Just as the trait network is used to describe the set of all possible individuals, the belief network is used to describe the set of all possible beliefs, the *belief space*. The generation of the belief space is done using the same topological ordering as that for the population space and corresponds to the set of all unique combinations of term assignments that result from traversals of the belief network. The combinations of term assignments are called beliefs because generalized descriptors are allowed for a trait sequence in addition to the leaf node values used to describe the population. Thus, a sequence can represent a collection of individual descriptions and stands for an equivalence class of individuals, all of whom share the same properties.

For example, the sequence ##11 can be produced from the belief network given in Figure 10.4. This represents the set of all individuals with a term value of 1 for traits 3 and 4, regardless of the values for traits 1 and 2. Using the subset operation, one can order these sequences as a lattice in which the root node is that sequence that contains all other sequences. In

CULTURAL ALGORITHMS

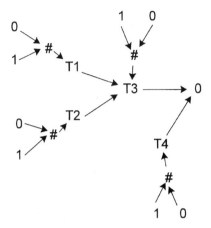

Figure 10.4 The belief network for the four binary valued traits.

this example it is ####. Each pair of sequences in the lattice has a greatest lower bound (GLB) that is produced by taking their intersection and a least upper bound (LUB) that is produced by taking their union. The belief space is the lattice defined over the set of all possible sequences, the power set, for a given topological sort.

In Figure 10.5 a belief network defined over two traits is given along with a lattice that describes their GLB and LUB. This is the belief space initially generated from the network. Note that for convenience the null set, which

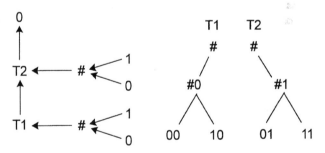

Figure 10.5 A belief network defined over two binary valued traits and its corresponding belief space.

229

is the GLB for all pairs of leaf nodes, is not represented explicitly in the graph. During the learning process those hypotheses that do not exhibit acceptable performance are pruned from the space. Therefore, subsequent belief spaces will contain only those beliefs that are deemed acceptable based upon the past performance of individuals that represent those beliefs.

10.2.3 The communication protocols

The belief space is used to constrain the combination of traits that individuals can assume. Likewise, the performance of individuals can affect the performance of the beliefs that they represent. This is the standard form of interaction between the two systems during the learning process and it is termed the VIP or vote–inherit–promote protocol. During the voting phase, performance information about specific trait sequences in the population is associated with a subset of beliefs in the belief space. In the inheritance phase, beliefs in this subset inherit the performance of the specific traits in the current population, so altering their performance and resulting in the deactivation of some beliefs that no longer give an acceptable performance. This process can also induce the activation of new beliefs. In the promote phase, the new structure of the belief space is used to influence the production of new trait sequences. The performance of individual sequences is modified based upon the performance of the beliefs with which they are associated, and individuals with unacceptable beliefs are removed.

Other forms of interaction between the two systems are possible and each type of interaction can be supported by particular protocols. These interactions can involve the modification of the term hierarchies, the prerequisite graph, the acceptance function or the fitness function (see Reynolds & Sverdlick 1993). However, only the vote–inherit–promote protocol is used in this chapter.

10.2.4 The learning loop

The learning activity has three goals. The first is to preserve those beliefs associated with "acceptable" behaviour at the trait level and to prune away currently unacceptable beliefs. The second goal is to use these acceptable beliefs as constraints to direct the generation of new trait sequences at the population level. The third goal is to maintain the expressive power of the belief and trait networks in the wake of a shifting performance environment by changing aspects of these networks.

CULTURAL ALGORITHMS

In the learning loop of the cultural algorithm the performance of individual trait sequences are used to modify the set of currently acceptable beliefs as well as the belief structure. These modifications are propagated back to the population of trait sequences and trait structure. Assuming that the VIP communication protocol is used, the learning loop begins with the communication of the results of the Evaluate function for the current population at time t. The Evaluate function evaluates each trait sequence relative to a fitness function that determines the sequence's performance in a given problem environment. The VIP protocol then passes the information to the belief system as indicated by Communicate (POP(t),BLF(t)).

At this point the Adjust procedure is performed. This procedure has several steps. First, each of the individual sequences is associated with a subspace of the belief space that it represents. This process is called *outlining*. It presupposes the existence of an acceptability function that associates each belief in the space with a value over the range {ACCEPTABLE, UNACCEPTABLE}. The goal of outlining is to determine how the performance of an individual sequence is affected by the values for a given trait. The result is to identify a region of the belief space, expressed as a sub-lattice, that shares the same acceptability result as the individual trait sequence. The Outline function maps a trait sequence (TS), with a fitness value of F, into an ordered pair of beliefs, BP and BG:

$$\text{outline(ts,f)} \rightarrow \text{(BP,BG)}$$

This pair of beliefs determines a subspace of the belief space where the Accept function value for the individual is preserved. BP is the most specific belief in the space whose ACCEPTANCE value corresponds with that of the individual trait sequence. It may be the trait sequence itself. BG is the most general belief for which the Accept function returns a result the same as that for the original trait sequence. All beliefs that lie on a path in the belief space between BP and BG are assumed to be homogeneous relative to the Accept function.

To illustrate how the Outline function works, take the belief space defined over a set of binary values described in Figure 10.5. Assume that the trait sequence to be outlined is 00 with some fitness value, f. Also assume that the application of the Accept function to the ordered pair $(00, f)$ returns the value ACCEPTABLE. The Outline function will identify an equivalence class of acceptable beliefs. It can be decomposed into two subfunctions:

$$\text{Outline\_BP: (TS,f)} \rightarrow \text{(BP)}$$
$$\text{outline\_BG: (TS,f)} \rightarrow \text{(BG)}.$$

LEARNING TO CO-OPERATE USING CULTURAL ALGORITHMS

`Outline_BG` is defined as follows for each of the i traits in the binary sequence, BG(i):

```
BG(i) will return # if the value of the Accept function is
not changed by altering the bit value for trait i;
otherwise it will return the current bit value for trait i.
```

`Outline_BP` is defined to return the individual trait sequence, TS.

For the individual sequence 00, BP(00, f) will be 00. In order to perform BG(00,f), each of the two bits are flipped, one at a time, and the value returned by the `Accept` function for the new sequence is examined. If the value is the same as that for the old sequence, then a # (don't care) symbol is substituted for the original bit. For the sequence 00, the sequences 10 and 01 are generated. If the values returned by the `Accept` function for these are the same as those for 00, then BG will be ##. Note that, relative to the belief space given in Figure 10.5, ## is an educated guess since 11 has not yet been explored. If the value returned by the `Accept` function for 11 is not the same as that for 00, this over-generalization will have to be adjusted. The adjustment takes place in the next stage of the `Adjust` procedure.

The pair of beliefs, BG and BP, describe a *stable class* relative to the `Outline` function. That is, the value of the `Accept` function is postulated to remain stable for all beliefs within the sub-lattice described by BG and BP. The `Outline` function can be seen as analogous to dreaming where alternative versions of reality are examined. The stable class description does not have to be precise. What is important is that the results of the `Outline` function can be integrated into what is currently known about the world. This `Merge` process constitutes the second phase of the `Adjust` function. In this phase, the generated stable class is merged into the current set of stable class descriptions. This is accomplished by comparing the BP and BG descriptors for each of the sequences in the current population with the set of existing stable classes in the belief space. During the first pass through the learning loop, the stable classes for each of the individual sequences are the existing sets. From then on, the new stable classes are integrated with those classes that are currently active.

The integration process proceeds as follows. Each new stable class described by the pair BG and BP is compared with the currently active stable classes and one of the following actions is taken based upon this comparison:

(a) If, for one of the N currently active stable classes, i, BG(i)=BG and BP(i)=BP, then discard the new class.

(b) If for one of the currently active stable classes, i, BG(i) overlaps with BG or BP(i) overlaps with BP, or both, then `Merge` the two classes by taking

THE CO-OPERATION PROBLEM

their union if they fall into the same Accept category.

(c) If they do not fall into the same Accept category, then identify their intersection and adjust the two sets to remove this overlap. How the sets are adjusted will depend upon the application. An overlap will occur if the Outline function can produce over-generalizations.

The performance of the stable class with which a sequence is associated is passed back to the population of individuals using the communication channel and the VIP protocol. The performance information is then used to Modulate the performance of individuals in the population. There are many ways in which this can be done. For example, if an individual trait sequence is associated with an UNACCEPTABLE stable class, its fitness might be reduced to zero to guarantee that it will not be reproduced.

After the fitness of the population has been modulated, the new population of trait sequences is produced by first Selecting individuals that are to reproduce. Then this set of parents is operated on by the Evolve function to produce new offspring. There are several evolutionary paradigms, such as genetic algorithms (Holland 1975) and evolutionary programming (Fogel 1993), that can be used to produce this new population. Then the Evaluate function can be applied to this new population. If the state of the belief space and the population of traits do not satisfy the termination conditions, the learning loop will be repeated.

Having summarized the basic operation of cultural algorithms, the next section will show how they can be used to solve a particular problem in the evolution of co-operation.

10.3   The co-operation problem

In this section cultural algorithms are used as a framework within which to express a problem concerning the evolution of co-operative behaviour in human societies. The problem is the emergence of a ritual called sunãy observed by Flannery et al. (1989) among llama herders in the Peruvian Andes. The herders live at elevations above 4000 m in alpine meadow zones that have nine to 12 months of frost each year. In this harsh environment the local flora consist primarily of grass, lichens and mosses. Plant cultivation is generally restricted to root crops such as the potato. Local fauna include deer, geese, ducks and other waterfowl .

The herding of llamas is the principal economic activity. Many factors, including disease, predators and rustlers, threaten the size of existing herds. Sunãy takes place in August during the annual marking ceremony. One of

LEARNING TO CO-OPERATE USING CULTURAL ALGORITHMS

the herders in the region will host a ceremony where llamas are decorated as an expression of thanks to the Wamani, the supernatural owner of the animals. During the ceremony a person, possibly unrelated to the host, receives the gift of a llama in return for contributing food and beverages to those present. This is an opportunity for a visiting herder to acquire a fertile female to restock his herd.

A question arises about how the process of sunãy emerged within this environment when there seems to be no direct advantage for a herder to give an animal to a non-relative. Flannery et al. developed a hierarchically structured model of a regional herding community. The hierarchy is shown in Figure 10.6 and is described in detail in Flannery et al. (1989). Simulation of the herding system yielded a curve (Fig. 10.7) that describes the relationship between regional herd stability and the likelihood that a herder will donate a llama to others that need them. The greatest herd stability occurs when all the herders co-operate with donations when needed, regardless of their relationship to the recipient. Even slight deviations from 100 per cent co-operation cause marked reductions in herd stability.

Once a regional herding system has attained 100 per cent co-operation, there is a great incentive to maintain that level. The problem is how the system can attain this level, since there are several obstacles to its doing so. First, the immediate impact on a donor is a reduction in his herd size, po-

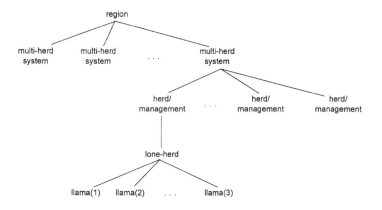

Figure 10.6 The hierarchy of models used to simulate the regional llama herding system.

THE CO-OPERATION PROBLEM

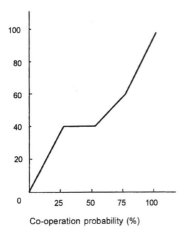

Figure 10.7 The percentage of surviving herds in a four-herd regional system as a function of the probability of co-operation.

tential productivity and local stability. Second, while some co-operation (up to 25 per cent) can produce a noticeable increase in herd stability to compensate for those reductions, little further increase in herd stability is produced until everyone co-operates all the time.

While the maximization of herd stability may not be an easy problem to solve, the occurence of sunãy suggests that the culture has in fact solved it. In the remainder of this chapter, the way in which the process of sunãy might have emerged is modelled in terms of both a multiple inheritance system using cultural algorithms and a trait-based approach using genetic algorithms. The performance of these two approaches is compared in Section 10.4.

10.3.1 Representation of the belief space

The goal is to see whether the beliefs fundamental to the support of sunãy can emerge from individual experience using cultural algorithms. The model system under consideration consists of four herders. Each herder possesses a plan for co-operation. This plan determines how the herder will interact with the others in the region. A regional plan consists of the plans for all four herders. The population of interest is the set of co-operative traits for regional groups of four herders. A description of the trait network for a regional plan is given in Figure 10.8. Since the description is the same for each of the four herders, only one of the sub-networks is described in detail.

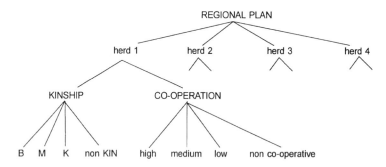

Figure 10.8 The trait network for a four-herd regional plan.

Herders can be biologically related (B), related through marriage (M), related in some other fashion (K), or unrelated (N). The set of relationships between all the herders is called the kinship matrix. The example matrix shown here is for a four-herd regional system. The entry in column 1 and row 2 shows how herder 1 is related to herder 2. The matrix is symmetrical because herder i is related to herder j in the same way that herder j is related to herder i.

	Herd 1	Herd 2	Herd 3	Herd 4
Herd 1	–	M	B	N
Herd 2	M	–	K	N
Herd 3	B	K	–	N
Herd 4	N	N	N	–

Associated with each type of kinship relation (B, M, K and N) is a level of co-operation (low, medium, high or no co-operation) that determines how the herders will accommodate requests from other herders, depending on their kinship.

The regional plan is produced by collecting together each of the four individual plans. The structure of the trait sequence that describes the regional plan will be determined by the selection of a given topological sort for the trait network. The specific sequence of traits used here will be discussed in Section 10.4. The population of trait sequences represents a collection of regional plans. These plans are used as input to the simulation. The performance of a plan is measured by the total number of llamas present in all the surviving herds after running the simulation for a given period of time. Note that the number of surviving herds is not used directly in measuring performance although it is important indirectly since the environment places a limit on the size of any one herd.

The regional belief space is described by the belief network shown in Figure 10.9. The presence of non-leaf node values, such as the don't care symbol (#), from the term hierarchies allows the system to generate beliefs concerning successful and unsuccessful strategies for regional co-operation. The Accept function for a given belief simply uses the average yield of all those instances associated with that belief during the simulation run. A belief is ACCEPTABLE if the performance of all of its instances is above average and UNACCEPTABLE otherwise.

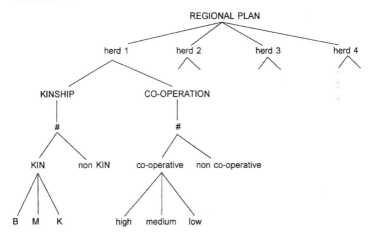

Figure 10.9 The belief network for the four-herd regional system.

Figure 10.10 shows part of the belief space generated by first elaborating the trait for co-operation (levels 2 and 3) and then elaborating the trait for kin relations at lower levels. Note that other portions of the space can be produced by the elaboration of traits in a different order.

10.3.2 The learning loop

In the multiple inheritance model of cultural change employed here, the belief and trait subsystems communicate exclusively via the VIP protocol. At the population level, the performance of each regional plan is evaluated by

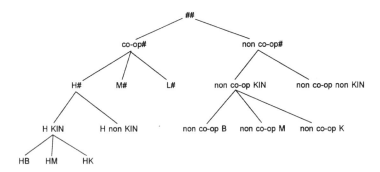

Figure 10.10 A portion of the belief space for the four-herd regional model.

running the regional simulation for a fixed period of time (the observation window) using the regional plan as input. Details about the regional simulation can be found in Savatsky & Reynolds (1989). Since the simulation is stochastic, the same regional plan will yield a distribution of values over time rather than a single fixed value. The number of llamas remaining in the system at the termination of the simulation run reflects the performance of the plan. This performance is communicated to the belief space by the VIP protocol.

Given the relatively small size of the belief space, the outlining process was not employed. Instead, the performance information for each plan was used to update (inherit) the average performance of all the more general beliefs in the space for which it was an example. This was done for each of the current regional plans. Next, the promote phase of the VIP protocol involved adding an increment to the performance of each regional plan for each of the above-average beliefs that it was currently associated with. This augmented performance was used as the basis for reproducing and modifying regional plans. Thus, regional plans associated with high numbers of acceptable beliefs had their performances promoted while those representing unacceptable beliefs did not receive any promotion.

The reproduction and modification of the regional plans were carried out using a genetic algorithm framework. Each of the regional plans was expressed as a binary string. Copies of each plan were made, the number depending on its performance relative to the adjusted average. These copies were used as the basis for generating new plans for the next generation, using mutation and crossover operations. Mutation involves changing a bit

EXPERIMENTAL RESULTS

value at a randomly specified point in the plan. This is equivalent to changing the level of co-operation for one of the interaction types. Crossover is the random exchange of bit sequences between regional plans. This corresponds to the exchange of trait sequences. After these modifications are made, the new regional plans are evaluated using the fitness function and the process begins again.

Since it was of interest to assess the contribution of the belief structure to the evolutionary process, an alternative model that did not use the belief space was also developed. This model evolved the population of regional plans using exactly the same genetic algorithm framework as that described above, except that the performance of individual plans was not modified according to the belief structure. Instead, regional plans were reproduced relative to their unadjusted performances. This approach reflected the basic micro-evolutionary process and ignored the macro-evolutionary control activities performed by the belief space. In the next section, the performance of the two approaches will be compared in a variety of situations.

10.4 Experimental results

In this section, the value of applying the cultural algorithm approach to explain the emergence of sunãy will be investigated for a given set of problem environments. The results will be compared with those for the micro-evolutionary trait-based approach for the same set of problem environments.

The main obstacle facing both models is the harshness of the environment, which places limits on the size of the population of regional plans and the length of time taken to adapt a plan to the environment. Ten is clearly an upper bound on the size of the regional plan population and was the size of the population for both models. As for run length, 100 iterations or model years is a definite upper bound on the time that a group can take to propose a successful adaptation. The key question is which of the two models is able to produce results that support an optimal adaptive strategy within these limitations.

A problem environment consists of two major pieces of information: a kinship matrix and an initial population of trait sequences. A regional plan describes how each of the four herders responds to requests from another herder and will produce different results depending on how the herders are related, as defined by the kinship matrix. The kinship matrix employed for a given run is generated from a discrete probability distribution over the set of kin relations. This distribution is supplied by the user. For example, if the probabilities are equal (B=0.25, M=0.25, K=0.25, and N=0.25), although each type of relationship will be equally likely, the arrangement of kinship relations in the matrix will vary from run to run. In addition, two other forms of matrix were used. One was where all the herders are related by birth (B=1.0) and the other was where no herders are related (N=1.0).

The other major determinant of the input configuration is the initial set of regional plans. The plan for a given herder specifies his level of co-operation with those related to him by birth (B), by marriage (M), by other kin relationships (K) and with non-kin (N), in that order. For each of these relations a certain level of co-operation is specified in the plan. The basic levels of co-operation are encoded as a pair of bits: 00 represents no co-operation, 01 represents a low level of co-operation, 10 represents a moderate amount of co-operation and 11 represents complete co-operation. Thus, for example, 11||10||01||00 represents an individual's regional plan where || is used to separate the codes. This individual would co-operate completely with requests from individuals related by birth, co-operate moderately with requests from those related by marriage, and so on.

Taken together, the set of four individual plans constitutes a regional strategy. A sample regional strategy might be:

Herd 1				Herd 2				Herd 3				Herd 4			
B	M	K	N		B	M	K	N		B	M	K	N		B	M	K	N
00		00		00		00						11		11		11		11						10		10		01		01						11		10		00		00					

In this example, the topological sort visits the herds in numeric order, and the kin relations in order of birth, marriage, other kin relations, and no relation.

Three sets of initial trait sequences were presented to both models. In the first, the entire trait population consisted initially of 10 plans, all of which specified complete co-operation by all herders with all others regardless of kin relation. In this situation each sequence consists of all 1's. In the second set, the population consisted of 10 plans, all of which specified non-co-operation with all herders regardless of their kinship relation. For these, each sequence consisted of all 0's. In the third set, a random mix of 0's and 1's was generated for each of the 10 plans.

Table 10.1 presents the results of the cultural algorithm for all pairings of the three classes of kinship matrices and the three sets of initial population (IP) configurations. Table 10.2 presents the results for the micro-evolutionary model, where the belief space is not used, for the same set of nine

EXPERIMENTAL RESULTS

Table 10.1 Summary of the dominant beliefs produced by Cultural Algorithms for each of the nine problem classes.

Relation	$IP = 0$	$IP = 1$	$IP =$ random
$B = M = K = N = .25$	Coop#	High#	High#
$B = 1; M = K = N = 0$	Coop#	High#	Some co-operation[a]
$B = M = K = 0; N = 1$	Coop#	High#	Some co-operation[b]

[a]High 5, medium 2, no co-operation 4.

[b]High 2, medium 5, low 1, no co-operation 3.

Table 10.2 Summary of the performance of the Trait-Based approach, omitting the belief space, for the nine different problem classes.

Relation	$IP = 0$	$IP = 1$	$IP =$ random
$B = M = K = N = .25$	Inconclusive	High	Inconclusive
$B = 1; M = K = N = 0$	Inconclusive	High	Inconclusive
$B = M = K = 0; N = 1$	Inconclusive	High	Inconclusive

input situations. Eleven experiments were conducted for each model in each of the nine categories of problem scenario. Each run of the two models was executed for 100 generations. For each iteration, a 100-year simulation of the regional herd simulation model was employed to produce the final payoff for each regional plan.

For each of the input situations in Table 10.1, the most general above-average strategy remaining in the belief space after 100 iterations is given. Note that the most general above-average belief will be the most influential in determining regional strategies produced by the system. It is called the dominant belief because it will augment the performance of more individual regional plans than any other belief at a given time step. Let us look first at the situation where the set of input strategies specifies complete co-operation (all 1's). The dominant belief generated by cultural algorithms for all classes of kinship matrix is "always co-operate (H) regardless of the kinship relation (#)", or H# in Figure 10.10. As mentioned earlier, this strategy produces maximum herd stability for the four-herd regional system. Note that, while specific instances of the strategy were present in the initial population, the corresponding generalization in the belief space was not. These initial instances allowed sufficient observations to be made about the performance of this generalization for an assessment of its performance relative to that of other beliefs to be achieved in all the runs.

241

LEARNING TO CO-OPERATE USING CULTURAL ALGORITHMS

The next three cases start with an initial set of regional plans showing no co-operation (all 0's). According to the stability curve given in Figure 10.7, these initial plans will produce regional systems with the lowest overall herd stability. For this initial population, all 11 simulations for each of the kinship categories produced the belief, "co-operate at some level (C) regardless of kinship relation (#)", or Coop# in Figure 10.10. While this belief does not require the highest level of co-operation from each herder, it is just one level removed from that. It also supports the concept of sunãy since co-operation with all is encouraged. Since the system began in a state of complete non-co-operation and ran for only 100 generations, it is possible that with more time it would have produced enough examples to cause the performance of C# to become less than H#. Nevertheless, the dominant belief after 100 generations is sufficient to support sunãy.

The last three cases start with a randomly generated initial set of regional plans. In the previous two sets of environments, the results were the same regardless of the state of the kinship matrix. However, for these three cases the structure of the kinship matrix exerts a strong effect on what can be achieved in the 100-generation run. For example, in the situation with the most variability (random plans and a random kinship matrix), the most general above-average belief is always the optimal one, H#, or "always co-operate regardless of kinship".

Since the complexity of this situation is closer to that of real-world situations than the other more constrained examples, its performance is likely to be indicative of how the system will work on average. In the other two situations the herders are either all related or all unrelated. When the herders were all related, seven of the 11 runs produced conclusions that supported sunãy. Of those seven, five concluded with the optimal result, H#, and two with M# (moderate co-operation with all). When the herders were all unrelated, the system was still able to produce a conclusion that supported sunãy in eight of 11 runs. However, the level of support was suboptimal, M# or L# (low co-operation with all), in six of the eight cases.

The performance of the trait-based model, the one without the belief space, was assessed in terms of the most successful regional plan that it produced (see Table 10.2). "High" in the table represents the existence of an optimal regional plan (all 1's). The "inconclusive" result shown in Table 10.2 indicates that no level of co-operation dominated any other by more than 3 per cent at the end of 100 iterations. None of the experiments using random or non-co-operative initial plans produced an optimal plan (all 1's) after 100 iterations. However, when started with an initial set of optimal

CONCLUSIONS

plans, it did retain an optimal strategy. In other words, the system was not able to generate the optimal plan within 100 iterations unless it started with it. Although it is quite likely that the optimal plan would have been produced if the run had been continued, the rate of learning was clearly slower than that for the cultural algorithm.

In this section a multiple-inheritance model using cultural algorithms was applied to a difficult problem of co-operation found in a real-life situation among llama herders in the punas of Peru. In 99 experiments, 11 for each of nine problem environments, this model produced a dominant belief that supported sunãy in 92 of them. In the situation most closely resembling the real world, a random kinship matrix and a random initial population, the optimal belief was produced for all 11 runs. The trait-based approach, without the belief system, was not able to produce a maximally co-operative strategy in any of the runs if it was not there to begin with. While both approaches would have done better had they been given more time, the 100 generations used in the simulation is longer than the real society would have had to find a solution in the harsh environment in which it was located. If a solution had not been found relatively quickly, the society itself would have disappeared. It is clear that, without a belief system to guide the cultural evolution process, the production of beliefs that support sunãy would not have been likely.

10.5   Conclusions

Both trait-based and ideational approaches to the modelling of cultural change have been proposed during the past twenty years. In this chapter, a computational paradigm for cultural evolution, cultural algorithms, that combines both a trait-based and an ideational approach is described. An operational version of this model was applied to a complex problem concerning the evolution of co-operation among llama herders living in the Peruvian Andes. It was shown that a trait-based model by itself was not able to find the optimal strategy for co-operation in the time frame allowed for adaptation in this harsh environment in any of the 99 runs unless the strategy was there to begin with. However, the addition of the belief system to this model using cultural algorithms produced a dominant belief that supported the optimal strategy in 92 out of 99 runs. The presence of the belief structure played an important rôle in allowing the model group to produce an optimal co-operative strategy in this situation.

LEARNING TO CO-OPERATE USING CULTURAL ALGORITHMS

From the above, it is clear that, when describing the adaptation of groups to life in harsh environments, where successful adaptations must be generated quickly in order to ensure survival, the belief structure of the individuals will be an important factor in determining the groups' success. If one presumes that each novel environment has some element of risk associated with its colonization, one might expect that the presence of mankind in so many diverse environments today is due to the existence of a strong belief system that controls how groups can co-operatively adapt to new and potentially stressful situations. The use of modelling techniques such as cultural algorithms, which allow us to model explicitly the way in which our beliefs affect our actions, will certainly afford us a better understanding of the evolutionary process as a whole.

Chapter 11
The simulation of trade in oligopolistic markets

José Castro Caldas & Helder Coelho

People of the same trade seldom meet together, even for merriment and diversion, but the conversation ends in a conspiracy against the public, or in some contrivance to raise prices.

Adam Smith, *The Wealth of Nations*, 1776

11.1 Microeconomics, oligopoly and rational choice

Neoclassic microeconomics is the prevalent theory for the functioning of economic systems. In microeconomics, the laws of the system are deduced from assumptions about the behaviour of individual economic agents. The economic agents – producers and consumers – are the micro elements of the system. According to the theory, the behaviour of agents depends on the market structure. For instance, if there are a large number of producers on the supply side of the market, it is assumed that they are unable to change the state of the market through their individual decisions. The equilibrium price depends on the aggregated supply and demand, and individual changes in supply are too small to unbalance the market. Therefore, the agents' decisions are independent, each agent maximizing profit given a market price. However, if there are only a few producers in the market, the market state will depend on each agent's decisions and therefore the agents' decisions are interdependent.

Oligopoly is a market in which there are only a few producers selling a given product and a great number of consumers. In such a situation it would be unrealistic to assume that the producers act independently. When deciding what to do, each producer has to consider not only the consumers' re-

THE SIMULATION OF TRADE IN OLIGOPOLISTIC MARKETS

sponse to the action, but also his competitors' decisions and their responses to his action. This kind of strategic interaction among producers makes oligopoly complex and hard to model.

As a result of this complexity, there are many conflicting theories and models of oligopoly. Economists generally believe that the equilibrium price in oligopolistic markets tends to be higher than the equilibrium price in perfect competition, but lower than the price in a monopolistic situation. This belief has its roots in Cournot's model, the first and most famous model of oligopoly (Cournot 1838). However, other theories maintain that the oligopoly price may not differ from the competition price (Bertrand 1883) or even from the monopoly price (Chamberlin 1933).

The classical models of oligopoly are static models. They assume that the agents are perfectly informed and the environment stable so that the agents are able to make lasting decisions.

The first game-theoretic models of oligopoly were also static, but soon the need for dynamic models was acknowledged. However, game theorists have been facing serious problems when trying to develop dynamic theories – theories of infinitely repeated non-co-operative games or "supergames". The problem is that they are unable to predict the outcome of these games. "There is the difficulty of selecting among the vast multiplicity of equilibria. The huge number of supergame equilibria must be considered a major liability of this whole theoretic development" (Shapiro 1989: 379).

Both the classical theories of oligopoly and the game-theoretic developments are based on logical rationality axioms. According to these axioms, rational decision-makers are optimizers. This means that they must be always able to enumerate extensively all the alternatives of choice; measure the consequences of each alternative; order the complete range of alternatives according to preferences; and have the computational means to select the best alternative.

Simon (1983) and other authors questioned these axioms, stating that, if economic theory is to explain how and why decisions are taken in the real world, it must take into account that most decisions are taken in a context of, first, a lack of information on the available alternatives and the consequences of each alternative, second, an imperfect perception of available information and, third, a lack of time or resources to explore the whole range of alternatives and consequences. This means that in most situations decision-makers are simply unable to optimize. They decide using rules of thumb or intuition. Simon speaks of an economic agent whose rationality is bounded, in opposition to the omniscient rational economic agent of neoclassical economics.

METHODOLOGY

Neoclassical authors (Friedman 1953) reacted to this criticism by stating that, although economic agents in the real world may not make their decisions by optimizing an objective function, they act as if they were optimizing since they are driven to optimal decisions as a result of a learning adaptive process. They concluded that models based on rationality axioms served economic theory well because, although they might not describe decision-making procedures accurately, they could predict the outcome of the decision process.

However, the main points of Simon's argument remain relevant for two reasons. First, the optimal outcome of economic decision processes has never been proven, either theoretically or empirically. There is experimental evidence to show that the outcome of repeated decisions can be sub-optimal (Herrnstein 1991). Secondly, it is not enough to predict the outcome of the decision processes. The adaptive processes leading to these outcomes are of interest to economists, since understanding them will help to understand many other kinds of dynamic situations. Research on bounded rationality therefore remains on the agenda. Our aim has been to contribute to this research, focusing on the topic of oligopoly (Caldas 1992).

We believe that the experimental method is a good way to acquire knowledge about the behaviour of economic agents. We also believe that the tools and ideas of distributed artificial intelligence can be very useful for modelling and simulating economic systems.

In the following pages a framework for the modelling and simulation of strategic interaction among economic agents in markets is described. The results of a first implementation of this framework, applied to the modelling of producers in a duopoly market, are also presented (Caldas 1992; Caldas & Coelho 1992).

11.2 Methodology

One may conjecture that decision-makers use heuristics rather then maximization procedures. These heuristics may evolve as knowledge accumulates and beliefs change as a result of learning. But in order to understand the real decision-making processes we must know exactly which heuristics are used and how they evolve with learning. This means that the starting point must be analyses of real decision-making processes and not abstract theorizing. We must learn by watching how real people decide, before we theorize. This can be done through either case studies (Cyert & March 1970) or laboratory experiments (Plott 1982; V. L. Smith 1982).

247

THE SIMULATION OF TRADE IN OLIGOPOLISTIC MARKETS

Laboratory experiments have huge advantages. The experimental environment can be controlled and simplified. Experiences can be repeated, and the subjects of the experiment are easier to find and more co-operative than real managers.

The experiment is not aimed at testing any theory. It is used to observe the decision-making procedures used by subjects. In spite of the fact that we are unable to watch inside people's heads, the reasoning behind each decision becomes clear just by following the experiment. It is also possible to question the subjects on their reasoning processes and choices.

Once understood, the decision-making procedures can be modelled. This modelling is difficult, if not impossible, with the standard mathematical tools. However, ongoing research on distributed artificial intelligence, namely on societies of autonomous agents "viewed as complex entities capable of communicating, reasoning, acting, defining preferences and, also, capable of changing gradually during their life" (Gaspar & Coelho 1991: 1), provide new ideas about ways of modelling interaction in economic systems (Sernadas et al. 1987; Monteiro 1989; Coelho et al. 1992). Other previous research on market modelling and simulation (Cyert & March 1970) and on "artificial adaptive agents" (Holland & Miller 1991; Arthur 1991; Marimon et al. 1990) and on knowledge-based systems for market simulation also provide a valuable inspiration (Star 1986; Miller 1986a, 1986b).

A model of the decision-making process can be formalized using a programming language and can then be tested by running the program. The program is a system that can simulate the previous experiments with human subjects. The simulation system is identical to the experimental setting, except that the experimenter is replaced by a program and the human subjects (the real agents) are replaced by their models (the artificial agents). The results of the simulation can be used to improve, reject or validate the model.

Therefore, the method consists of the following five steps:
1. Define an experimental setting with human subjects.
2. Run the experiment a limited number of times.
3. Analyze the experimental results. What was the outcome? What was the reasoning behind the decisions taken by the subjects?
4. Build models of the agents using a programming language.
5. Replace the human agents by their models (artificial agents) and simulate the experiment. Does this simulation fit with "reality"?

11.3 Experimenting, modelling and simulating duopoly

In order to test this kind of methodology, a comparatively simple situation was selected: duopoly, a market with two producers and many consumers. The analysis focused on the behaviour of the producers and their interaction in a sequence of time periods. The producers' only decision variable was price.

11.3.1 Set-up of the experiment

The experimental market included three components: demand (the consumers), supply (the producers), and the experimenter (Fig. 11.1).

Demand was simulated by a computer program (a 7.4 Kbyte program written using Arity-Prolog 5.1 in the MS-DOS environment). Two human subjects acted as producers. The experimenter stood between supply and demand. He announced the prices to the consumers (inserted data into the computer) and informed the producers of the market results.

The experiment consisted of a sequence of market periods with indefinite limit. The market referred to an unspecified, normal differentiated product. Decisions were taken separately by the producers before each

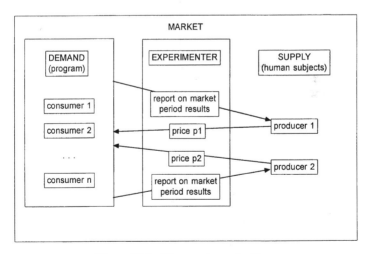

Figure 11.1 The experimental setting.

THE SIMULATION OF TRADE IN OLIGOPOLISTIC MARKETS

market period, taking into account the information on the past market periods. The producers were unable to communicate with each other since they were in different locations.

A general description of the experimental context was made to each subject before the experiment started. They were given the following information:

- Before each market period they would have to decide at what price to sell their product. This price should not be placed above a certain upper limit and it could not be changed during the market period.
- There would be instant adjustment of supply to demand, as if they were selling inventory, and therefore they would not have to decide how much to produce.
- They would not be able to change the product specification, technology or consumers' preferences; aAll they could do was to change the price between market periods.
- Since the product they were dealing with was a normal product, they should expect that sales reductions might follow price increases, depending on what the competitor did with his price.
- Their average unit cost was information not available to their competitor and was constant in time and independent of quantities.
- After each market period they would receive a report containing their sales, total market sales, profit and the competitor's price in the previous period.
- In the first market period they would not know the demand for goods from each producer, but since demand was deterministic they could count on a repetition of previous outcomes.

Demand was modelled in a simplistic way as a collection of agents (consumers). The decision process and the specification of the agents was in accordance with the following assumptions:

(a) Each agent had a utility scale such that she would buy in the market period increasing (but limited) quantities of the product depending on its offer price. For each consumer a preference was defined, that she would rather consume producer 1's or producer 2's product. A preference coefficient was also defined expressing the strength of preference. Each consumer would buy the product she preferred unless the ratio

preferred product price / alternative product price

was greater than the preference coefficient. Utility scales, preferences and the number of consumers were fixed during the experiment.

EXPERIMENTING, MODELLING AND SIMULATING DUOPOLY

(b) demand was symmetric; that is, the number of consumers with a preference for producer 1's item was equal to those who preferred producer 2's, and although utility scales and preference coefficients might differ within each group, their distribution was identical inside both groups.

(c) The total demand in the market depended on both unit prices (producer 1's product unit price and producer 2's product unit price). The preferences assigned to consumers and the values of the utility scales and preference coefficients were such that when both prices were equal the market was split into equal halves: both producers would sell the same amounts and achieve the same profit. Only one of all the possible pairs of equal prices maximized joint profits. If one of the prices was lower than the other the corresponding producer would have a larger market share.

(d) In each market period consumers went shopping sequentially and always in the same order. The consumer associated a utility value to each unit purchased, and when this value was lower than the offer price of the item she preferred (or the one she was led to prefer on account of the price relation) she left the market place. When there was no remaining demand, the market closed for the period.

So far, this society is apparently as simple as the economies in any standard economic model. However, as the experiment showed, the dynamics of repeated decisions gave it a more complex nature. A sequence of price decisions, a sequence of actions and reactions, is a sequence of acts with its own semantics. Prices are messages that can be and are understood by both producers, and therefore the absence of talk and negotiation is only apparent.

11.3.2 The experimental results

Three replications of the experiment, involving six subjects, were held. The subjects had different levels of expertise: three of them were professional economists and the other three were qualified in other social sciences. There was no material incentive involved.

The analysis of the experiment was aimed at finding the most suitable model for the decision-making process, by discovering the heuristics used by the subjects and how they evolved during each run of the experiment. The sequence of price decisions in the three runs is shown in Figures 11.2, 11.3 and 11.4.

The experiment revealed three interesting facts:

(a) In all three runs we can observe two stages: an initial stage where prices

251

THE SIMULATION OF TRADE IN OLIGOPOLISTIC MARKETS

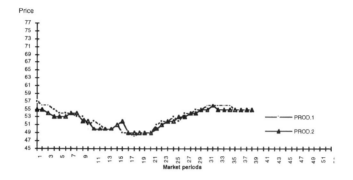

Figure 11.2 Sequence of price decisions in the first run of the experiment.

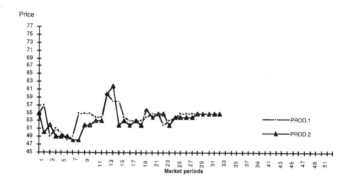

Figure 11.3 Sequence of price decisions in the second run of the experiment.

were lowered by both producers, and a final stage where prices tended to be raised. In the first run (see Fig. 11.2), the first stage lasted until the 18th market period. From this period onwards, prices were raised gradually until the 33rd market period where they stabilize. In the second run (Fig. 11.3), the first stage was shorter: it lasted until the 5th market period. In the second stage, prices were initially very unstable but eventually stabilized on the 29th market period at a higher level. In the third run (Fig. 11.4), the first stage was present until the 5th market period, but it is unclear whether there was second stage or not.

EXPERIMENTING, MODELLING AND SIMULATING DUOPOLY

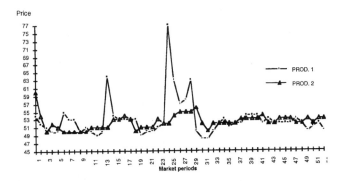

Figure 11.4 Sequence of price decisions in the third run of the experiment.

(b) The pattern of the sequence of price decisions is quite different in the three runs of the experiment. In the first run, the two stages were clearly differentiated. The changes in price were taken carefully: a maximum of a two-point shift per period. In the second and third runs, the second stage was very unstable, with sudden jumps in price.

(c) In the first and second runs the prices converged to an equilibrium (both producers selling at a price of 55), while in the third run no equilibrium was reached until the 53rd market period.

How is the existence of two stages in the experiment to be explained? In the initial stage, both subjects have an incomplete understanding of the situation. They know that demand increases as the price is reduced, but they underestimate their competitor's reaction. They believe that they can achieve a larger market share through price cuts. However, price cuts tend to be followed by competitors and therefore the result of this strategy is disastrous to both producers: profits decrease as prices are reduced (see Fig. 11.5). Both producers soon understand (perhaps, one of them more quickly than the other) that they must replace this type of competition by some kind of co-operative agreement.

Since they are unable to communicate verbally, they must use a non-verbal way of negotiating. The following procedure is used. One of the subjects increases his price and sustains this new price during at least two market periods. This message must be interpreted by the competitor as: "let's stop the price war and try jointly to find the pair of equal prices that grants the highest possible profit".

THE SIMULATION OF TRADE IN OLIGOPOLISTIC MARKETS

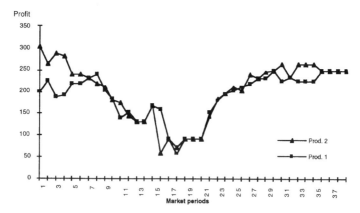

Figure 11.5 Evolution of profits of both producers in the first run of the experiment.

This message may or may not be understood, and even if it is understood it can be rejected. If it is understood and accepted, a process of joint search for the best compromise solution (a pair of equal prices that maximizes joint profit) is initiated. If it is not understood or if it is rejected, a process of negotiation starts. If the competitor refuses to follow the price increase decision, insisting on a lower price, in the next market period the price will be lowered to the level of the competitor's. Retaliation is the argument used to persuade the competitor that he has no choice but to co-operate in the joint search for optimum profit.

The two stages of the experiment show that the producers learn about both the behaviour of demand and the competitor's behaviour. This learning process leads to the evolution of producer strategies. The first strategy, cut-throat competition, corresponding to the first stage of the experiment, is based on the belief that the maximization of profits can be achieved by obtaining a dominant position (market share greater than 50 per cent) through price cuts. The second strategy, co-operation, corresponding to the second stage of the experiment, is based on the belief that a compromise is necessary (the market must be shared) if a mutually satisfactory level of profits is to be achieved.

The different patterns in the three runs of the experiment may result from different initial conditions (different initial price decisions) and from individual characteristics of the subjects. Subjects can differ in their learn-

EXPERIMENTING, MODELLING AND SIMULATING DUOPOLY

ing and leadership abilities and they can use a different language in their message-sending. These differences in the type of language used can be clearly observed in the sequence of price decisions in runs 1, 2 and 3 of the experiment. One producer may use careful shifts in price to signal an intention to raise prices, another may use "loud" signals, that is, sudden shifts upward in his price. There is a "calm" type of language and a "nervous" type.

The equilibrium price obtained in the first and second runs (55, 55) is the point of joint maximization of profit. When both subjects are co-operating, that is, if they accept even shares of the market, they can explore the price space in order to find the point that maximizes profits. Once they find it, they have no incentive to move away from it.

A detailed analysis of the third run of the experiment reveals that the failure to co-operate and to reach the equilibrium is due to the nervous signalling procedure adopted by producer 1 and to mistakes committed by both subjects.

11.3.3   A model of the decision-making process

One interesting point about this experiment is that it tends to confirm Chamberlin's conjecture that the equilibrium price in oligopoly could be the monopoly price, achieved through what Chamberlin called "tacit collusion":

> If each seeks his maximum profit rationally and intelligently, he will realize that when there are only two or a few sellers his own move has a considerable effect upon his competitors, and that this makes it idle to suppose that they will accept without retaliation the losses he forces upon them. Since the result of a cut by any one is inevitably to decrease his own profits, no one will cut, and although the sellers are entirely independent, the equilibrium result is the same as though there were a monopolistic agreement between them.   (Chamberlin 1933: 48)

However, we must try to move beyond the analysis of the outcome and understand the process that led to it. The experiment shows that most decisions taken by the subjects are rational; that is, they can be justified, given the information available at each stage of the experiment. But, mistakes and random moves could also be observed. It is possible to model the processes that led to rational decisions. Mistakes and random moves cannot easily be modelled.

255

THE SIMULATION OF TRADE IN OLIGOPOLISTIC MARKETS

In this case, the main features of the decision-making process seem to be the following:

- During the experiment the subjects go through a learning process about the behaviour of demand and on the behaviour of the competitor.
- This learning process leads to an evolution of strategies. The subjects start with "cut-throat competition" (they believe they can maximize profit by achieving larger market shares through price cuts) and end by co-operating (they discover they must share the market and keep balanced prices if they are to secure long-run maximum profits).
- The subjects' actions are determined by the situation at the end of each market period.

There are four basic types of action which producers can take. For the next market period, each producer may decide to keep the same price, raise the price, lower the price, or retaliate by drastically lowering the price. The choice of the appropriate action depends on the situation at the end of the market period. The situation is the set of the relevant internal and external factors:

- the beliefs of the agent concerning the best strategy, the strategy of the competitor, and the direction the prices should move in order to secure higher long-run profits;
- the state of the market: the market shares and the price in the market period;
- the "personality" of the agent: his type of language and leadership ability.

The situation is altered by changes in the state of the market and by changes in the belief state of the agent. Beliefs concerning the best strategy tend to mature as the results of the strategy are evaluated. Beliefs concerning the competitor's strategy may change by observing her actions. Beliefs concerning the direction of improvement of profits evolves as knowledge about demand, given specific pairs of prices, builds up. These changes in belief must be made through the assimilation of the results of the strategies, the actions of the competitor and information about demand.

The decision-making process can be described as a sequence of three phases: assimilation, definition of the situation, and choice of the action. Assimilation includes the evaluation of the results of the strategy, an analyses of the actions of the competitor and analyses of demand. This assimilation phase defines three of the elements of the situation: preferred strategy, competitor's strategy, and direction of improvement of profits. In addition to these elements, the situation is completely defined by the market share, the level of the price in the market period and the type of "language".

The decision-making process is described diagrammatically in Figure 11.6.

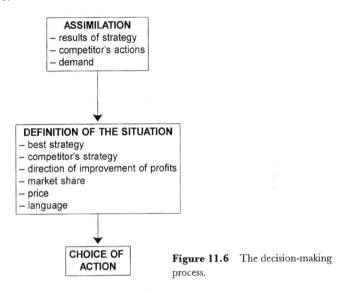

Figure 11.6 The decision-making process.

11.3.4 Creating artificial agents

Once the decision-making process of the subjects has been described and understood, it can be formally modelled using a programming language. This corresponds to the creation of artificial agents able to replace the real agents in the experimental system, so that it can be simulated.

The artificial agents must be able to assimilate the information about demand, the results of their strategies and the behaviour of their competitors; identify the situation in the end of each market period; and select an action. The program to implement each of these artificial agents consists of a personality module, an assimilation module, an action module and a notebook (Fig. 11.7). It was inspired by a modular architecture proposed previously by Gaspar & Coelho (1991).

In the personality module, each producer is defined by two personality parameters: an initial level of credit assigned to strategies which expresses

THE SIMULATION OF TRADE IN OLIGOPOLISTIC MARKETS

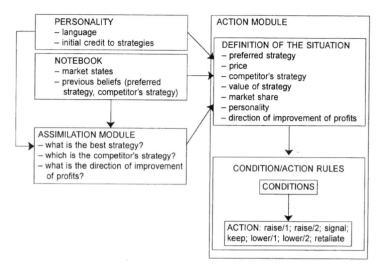

Figure 11.7 The architecture of one agent (producer).

the strength of the producer's belief concerning the best strategy, and one of two possible language types: "nervous" (causing fast price shifts) or "calm" (slow price shifts).

The action module performs two different tasks: it defines the situation (the state of the market, the personality of the agent and his state of beliefs) and selects the corresponding action, and it identifies the actions of the competitor. The actions are selected by condition–action rules. These rules are represented in a frame structure, with the following slots: preferred strategy, competitor's strategy, price set by the agent in the last market period, current value of strategy, market share, language, direction of improvement, and action. The rule selection process is carried out through the pattern-matching (unification) mechanism of the Prolog language.

In Prolog these rules were implemented with the structure shown in Fig. 11.8, where the underscores are anonymous variables standing for "don't care".

Each strategy corresponds to a set of rules. The rules are common to, and assumed to be known by, both agents. The present model includes the three key strategies: cut-throat competition, co-operation/leader, and co-operation/follower. There are 26 rules to implement these strategies (see Fig. 11.9).

EXPERIMENTING, MODELLING AND SIMULATING DUOPOLY

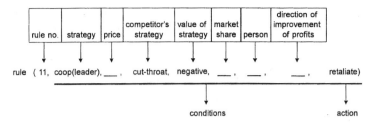

Figure 11.8 Structure for implementation of rules in Prolog.

rule no.	preferred strategy	price	competitor's strategy	value of strategy	market share	language	direction	actions
1	cut throat comp.	48	–	–	> 0.8	nervous	–	raise/2
2	cut throat comp.	48	–	–	–	–	–	raise/1
3	cut throat comp.	–	–	–	> 0.8	nervous	–	raise/2
4	cut throat comp.	–	–	–	> 0.8	calm	–	raise/1
5	cut throat comp.	–	–	–	> 0.5	–	–	keep
6	cut throat comp.	–	–	–	= 0.5	–	–	lower/1
7	cut throat comp.	–	–	–	< 0.5	–	–	lower/1
8	cut throat comp.	–	–	–	< 0.2	–	–	lower/2
9	coop/leader	–	cut throat comp.	initial	–	nervous	–	signal
10	coop/leader	48	–	–	–	–	–	raise/1
11	coop/leader	–	cut throat comp.	negative	–	–	–	retaliate
12	coop/leader	–	–	–	> 0.8	nervous	–	raise/2
13	coop/leader	–	–	–	> 0.8	calm	–	raise/1
14	coop/leader	–	–	–	> 0.5	–	–	keep
15	coop/leader	–	–	–	= 0.5	–	don't know	raise/1
16	coop/leader	–	–	–	= 0.5	–	higher	raise/1
17	coop/leader	–	–	–	= 0.5	–	lower	lower/1
18	coop/leader	–	–	–	= 0.5	–	optimum	keep
19	coop/leader	–	–	–	< 0.5	–	–	keep
20	coop/leader	–	–	–	< 0.2	–	–	lower
21	coop./follower	–	–	–	> 0.8	nervous	–	raise/2
22	coop./follower	–	–	–	> 0.8	calm	–	raise/1
23	coop./follower	–	–	–	> 0.5	–	–	raise/1
24	coop./follower	–	–	–	= 0.5	–	–	keep
25	coop./follower	–	–	–	< 0.5	–	–	lower/1
26	coop./follower	–	–	–	< 0.2	–	–	lower/2

Figure 11.9 The condition--action rules for the three strategies.

THE SIMULATION OF TRADE IN OLIGOPOLISTIC MARKETS

The actions corresponding to the cut-throat competition strategy are essentially driven by the state of the market during the market period before the moment of the decision. If the market share is under 50 per cent the price will be lowered; if it is above 50 per cent the price will not be changed, unless the market share is greater than 80 per cent, when the price will be increased.

The actions corresponding to the co-operative/leader strategy are driven not only by the market share but also by beliefs about the competitor's strategy and the direction of improvement of profits. The agent must take the competitor's strategy into account, because he must know when to send price increase messages and when retaliation is necessary. The agent must know the direction for improving profits, because he must guide the search of the price space when the competitor is co-operating as a follower.

The actions corresponding to the co-operative/follower strategy are, once again, essentially driven by the market share. The follower raises her price when she has a larger market share, and lowers it in the opposite situation.

There are seven types of action:

- *raise price/ 1* − raise the price one point;
- *raise price/ 2* − raise the price, so that it is three points lower than the highest;
- *keep price* − leave price unchanged;
- *lower price/ 1* − lower price one point;
- *lower price/ 2* − lower price, so that it is three points higher than the lowest;
- *signal* − raise suddenly the price;
- *retaliate* − lower price, so that it is one point higher than the lowest.

The assimilation module performs the task of reviewing the beliefs concerning the best strategy, the competitor's strategy and the direction of improvement of profits. Beliefs concerning best strategies are reviewed in the following manner. A credit is initially assigned to each strategy and at the end of each market period this value is updated, as each producer evaluates results comparing the current profits with an aspiration level. The value of the strategy can be regarded as a measure of its effectiveness. Cut-throat competition must be dropped and replaced by co-operation when this value becomes negative. If the agent is the first to switch strategy he will assume the rôle of leader; otherwise he will act as follower. Co-operation can have a negative value and must be renewed when its value is lower than $- (2 \times$ initial credit).

EXPERIMENTING, MODELLING AND SIMULATING DUOPOLY

Beliefs concerning a competitor's strategies are reviewed in the following manner. Since the condition–action rules are common knowledge, each producer can use information on past market states and past beliefs to infer whether the action taken by the competitor in the previous market period matches the strategy he believes the competitor is using. If it does not, the producer checks which strategy it matches and reviews his belief.

If one of the producers is co-operating as a leader, he must decide in which direction to shift prices. When prices are equal in the current market state, the leading producer must check whether there is another pair of equal prices yielding bigger profits, using information from previous market states; if so, he moves towards this position.

In the notebook (a set of facts stored in a portion of the internal Prolog database), previous states of the market and previous beliefs are stored to be used by other modules. Each agent has a private notebook (Gaspar 1990).

11.3.5 The simulation system

The simulation system as a whole is composed of a demand module (the same one as was used in the experiments), a supply module including the artificial agents, and a graphic interface which makes possible to observe the sequence of price decisions, belief changes and rule selections during the simulation process (Fig.11.10).

The simulation process starts with the specification of the number of mar-

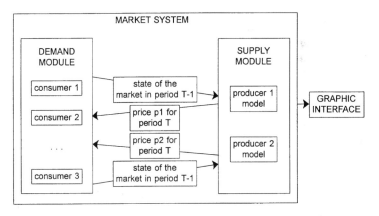

Figure 11.10 The market simulation system.

THE SIMULATION OF TRADE IN OLIGOPOLISTIC MARKETS

ket periods, the initial prices and the personality features of the producers.

11.3.6 The results of simulation

Simulation allows us to test the model to see whether it is correctly specified. If it is, it must be able to reproduce the overall patterns of the behaviour observed in the runs of the experiment with humans.

The results of simulation of runs 1, 2 and 3 of the experiment are shown in Figures 11.11, 11.12 and 11.13. The sequence of price decisions in the three runs of the simulation is shown in part (a) of these graphs. Although we did not obtain exact reproductions, the overall pattern of the human subjects' sequence of price decisions is reproduced.

The figures also show the sequence of strategies and the evolution of their respective credits in the three runs of the experiment. In simulation 1 (Fig. 11.11), which simulated the first run of the experiment, producer 1 had her strategies credited with the value 150 and producer 2 with 100 (different initial values of credit can be tested in order to "tune" the simulation), and both were defined as "calm". Producer 2 begins with a lower price (achieving larger initial profits), but suffers heavy losses as producer 1 lowers her price. Producer 1, as she adjusts her price, increases profits in market periods 3 and 4, cut-throat competition seeming to be a good strategy for her. In the 7th market period, cut-throat competition becomes negatively evaluated for producer 2 and he turns to co-operation, trying to lead an upward shift in prices. Since he is not followed by producer 1, he retaliates. Retaliation inflicts losses in both producers and persuades producer 1 to co-operate. After a period of misunderstanding that leads to an erosion of both co-operative strategies (producer 2 is not yet aware that producer 1 has changed strategy and hesitates to raise prices), both producers commit themselves to co-operation and find the joint profit optimum in the 35th market period.

If we compare the results of the simulation with the observed behaviour, we find that the major shortcoming of the model has to do with the rôles of the agents. While in the simulation the leading rôle is always played by producer 2, in the experiment producer 2 starts as a leader but swaps rôles with producer 1 in the final stages of the experiment.

In simulation 2 (see Fig. 11.12), both producers were defined as "nervous". Producer 1 has her strategies credited with 300 and producer 2 with 200.

In simulation 3 (see Fig. 11.13), producer 1 is "nervous" and producer 2 is "calm". Credit to both producers was 300. In contrast to what hap-

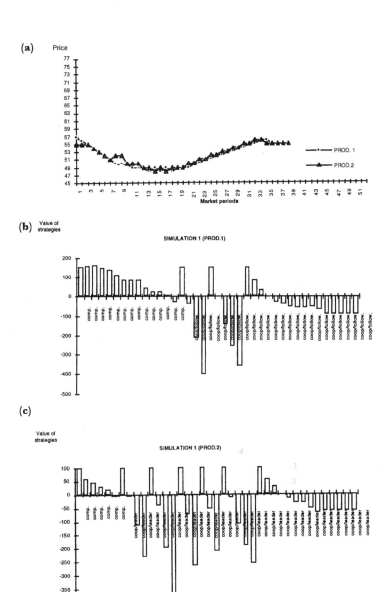

Figure 11.11 The sequence of price decisions and the evolution of strategies and credits in simulation 1.

263

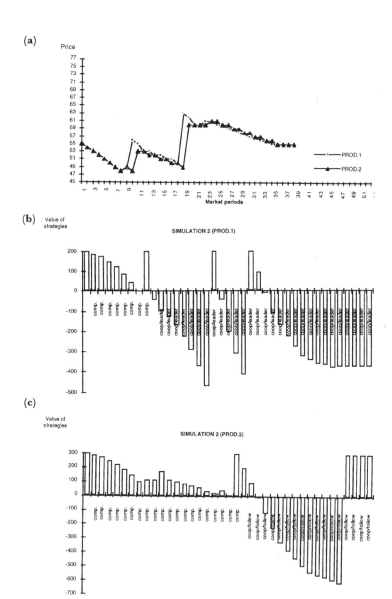

Figure 11.12 The sequence of price decisions and the evolution of strategies and credits in simulation 2.

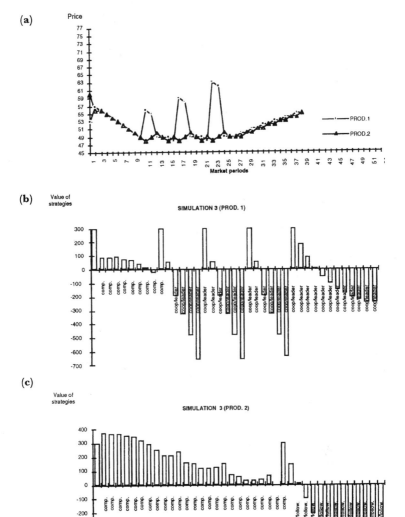

Figure 11.13 The sequence of price decisions and the evolution of strategies and credits in simulation 3.

THE SIMULATION OF TRADE IN OLIGOPOLISTIC MARKETS

pened in the experiment, producer 2 was induced into co-operation and joint maximization was achieved in the 39th market period. It is, however, interesting to note that co-operation was harder to achieve than in the other simulations. This has to do with the contrast between the "nervous" and the "calm" attitudes. Producer 1's "jumping up and down" tends to strengthen the competitive strategy of the "calm" producer, who enjoys large profits for a long while thanks to the nervous signalling procedure.

11.4   Conclusions

The results of this first implementation were satisfactory. The artificial agents exhibit some of the learning and adaptive abilities observed in humans; the overall pattern of the sequence of their price decisions fits the observed data.

The architecture of the agents and observations of their interaction and evolution during the simulation helped us understand a little better the process through which optimizing co-operative strategies can emerge out of repeated interaction, and how naive competition can evolve to the common-sense marketing rule: "If you don't have competitive advantage, don't start a price war".

However, the model still has some clear shortcomings. We assumed that the available strategies and the corresponding condition–action rules were known *a priori* and shared by both agents. In fact, within a learning situation, there is a process of discovery of strategies and rules that has not been modelled. The learning ability of the artificial agents will have to be designed and developed in future implementations.

The results, so far, encourage us to think that experimentation and DAI-based simulation can be powerful tools in modelling markets, and a new way of developing theories in economics. However, there is still much to be done before relevant theoretical results can be obtained. New experiments must be run with real agents, with different assumptions and in different contexts, and our modelling techniques will have to be improved and developed.

Chapter 12
Mind is not enough:
the precognitive bases of
social interaction

Rosaria Conte & Cristiano Castelfranchi

In this chapter, two fundamental aspects of AI's models of social action are challenged: the presupposition of agents' co-operativeness, and a hyper-cognitive view of agents as omniscient and fully rational.

In contrast to these views, which are exemplified in much work in distributed artificial intelligence (DAI) and computer supported co-operative work (CSCW), we argue for a gradual bottom-up approach to the modelling of social action. This approach consists of situating intelligent autonomous agents endowed with cognitive capabilities and endogenous goals in a common world (that is, in conditions where the effects of one's actions are relevant to others' goals) and letting them (inter)act. In a gradualistic, "emergent" approach of this kind, the weight of "objective relations" among agents, and between each agent and the external world, becomes more evident. The objective relations of interest and dependence are analyzed both in a social and a non-social context. Within the social context, both positive and negative interferences among agents' goals are examined.

Finally, the predictive force of objective relations is explored. Intuitively, factual concurrence among agents is likely to produce aggression, while the objective convergence of goals is a predictor of co-operation. Some processes leading from objective relations to cognitive social actions (e.g. from objective social dependence to the social goal of influencing) are analyzed at some length, and some beliefs and rules implied by these processes (in particular, a rule of adoption and a rule of influencing, the two most important rules of interaction) are identified.

THE PRECOGNITIVE BASES OF SOCIAL INTERACTION

12.1 The cognitive cart and the social horse

Over the past decade, AI has gained a significant rôle within cognitive science and has contributed to a general theory of intelligence and of cognitive processes. Unfortunately, this is not also true of social studies in AI. Human computer interaction (HCI), multi-agent modelling and CSCW are not good candidates for working out a general theory of social relations and interactions. In the following, we will examine some reasons for this.

12.1.1 Pre-established social architectures *vs.* "emergent" sociality

AI social studies often presuppose a common task, a pre-established co-operativeness, a collective intelligence and a capability for problem-solving. While it is true that one of the problems of DAI is precisely how collective or decentralized control is achieved in a distributed problem-solving system (Lesser & Corkill 1987; Durfee et al. 1987a; 1987b), what is usually presupposed is the need for coordination. In other words, in a distributed problem-solving system, agents must objectify themselves to see where they fit in a coordinated process (Bond & Gasser 1988). The underlying idea is that coordination must already be present and that agents must fit into it.

AI is concerned with optimizing communication as well as with task- and resource-allocation among intelligent co-operative agents. Task-allocation may be addressed either statically, by the designer, or dynamically (Bond & Gasser 1988), by a set of agents using specific methods such as contracting (Parunak 1987). But even in this latter type of dynamic approach, "tasks" and "rôles" are pre-established, and what is a matter of negotiation is matching agents to available rôles (Malone 1987, Gasser 1988).

There is little interest in a radically bottom-up approach. This approach consists of situating intelligent autonomous agents, endowed with cognitive capabilities and endogenous goals, into a common world, and letting them (inter)act. This is perhaps the only viable way for an observer to "discover" the agents' need for sociality, be it co-operative or competitive, without presupposing it.

In a gradualistic approach of this kind, the weight of objective relations among agents, and between each agent and the external world, becomes clearer. Although in some areas of DAI agents are involved in objective structural relationships (e.g. blackboards, global planners and contract nets), these are special architectures provided by the designer. The social structures

THE COGNITIVE CART AND THE SOCIAL HORSE

that arise are then compulsorily co-operative: co-operation does not come out of agents' goals and interactional practice.

12.1.2 The hypercognitive fallacy

When agents are not forced into a pre-established co-operative architecture, they are conceived of in terms of what we may call a "hypercognitive fallacy". The following features seem to characterize such a view, although they do not necessarily co-occur in each model:

- *Lack of a dynamic perspective* Agents are so fully aware of the conditions under which they interact that the evolutionary steps of social actions are substantially ignored. Levesque et al. (1990) derive joint intentions from individual intentions, and the question is raised of why it is rational for agents to form joint commitments (Cohen & Levesque 1991); whereas Rosenschein & Genesereth (1988) assume that what is rational for the group is also rational for the agent. Even in such attempts, however, precognitive relations among agents are ignored: joint action is reduced to the mental states of the participants, namely to a "shared mental state", which is not derived, but simply postulated.
- *Social subjectivism* Social relationships are investigated only inasmuch as they are mentally represented, that is, only starting from what are considered as "social" goals and beliefs. (Agent believes and wants what others believe and want.) This feature is linked to the preceding one, but instead of stressing the static character of hypercognitive agent modelling, it pinpoints its subjectivism: social relationships are those that are believed to be such by the agents involved.
- *Emphasis on communication* As a consequence of the previous features, social action is conceived of only in terms of communication aimed at modifying mutual beliefs and goals (Cohen et al. 1990; Galliers 1988; Werner 1989; Winograd & Flores 1986).

In contrast to both forced co-operation and the hypercognitive view of agents, we view social action as an emergent phenomenon. If intelligent autonomous agents are placed in a common world, social relations are likely to emerge automatically and implicitly among them. Over time, these relations will have an impact on the agents' actions and mental attitudes. A multi-level cognitive and extracognitive pattern of social action and relation then emerges.

The working out of a formal model of objective relations is relevant not only to social theory but also, owing to the predictive power of such a model,

THE PRECOGNITIVE BASES OF SOCIAL INTERACTION

to practical aims. For example, reducing the explosion of agents' communications in a distributed problem-solving network requires making predictions on the grounds of their objective relations: given certain situations of dependence and concurrence among (some) agents, it is possible to foresee what kinds of interactions will take place, what messages will be sent to whom, and for which goals.

In this chapter, a preliminary model of different types of objective relationships among cognitive agents is presented. In addition, and as a consequence, an attempt is made to predict some fundamental types of cognitive social interactions.

12.1.3   Society is out there, and not only in the mind

Our main aim is to argue for the study of extracognitive social relations. More specifically, we believe that the following two aspects ought to be investigated:
-   the *objective bases* of social interaction: any relation occurring either between two (or more) agents or between one single agent and the external physical world is defined as objective. To assess whether a relation is objective we must take the stance of a non-participant observer (i.e. the scientist's point of view): objective relations are those relations that are described only in the observer's mind;
-   the *emergent functionalities* of actions intended and planned by cognitive agents.

Elsewhere (Castelfranchi & Conte 1992), we have dealt to some extent with the second point. In this chapter we will concentrate on the first point. In particular, we will be dealing with *precognitive* objective relations, that is, those objective relations that are neither desired nor believed by the agents involved (Fig. 12.1).

A fundamental assumption concerning intelligent agents states that their actions are necessarily based on knowledge. It might be argued, to the contrary, that what matters are the agents' world models and not the world as such. So why bother with precognitive bases of social action? All we need to account for are the agents' beliefs. Even if false, beliefs are still necessarily implied in actions.

This reasoning is right but insufficient because the nexus between beliefs and actions is bi-directional. Action is regulated by, and is a testbed for, beliefs. In fact,
-   false beliefs are likely to lead to unsuccessful actions, and

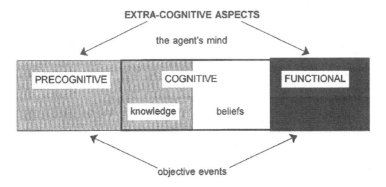

Figure 12.1 Cognitive and extracognitive aspects of social action.

- unsuccessful actions are, in turn, likely to lead to belief-revision; consequently
- an unknown situation that is relevant to (interferes with) the agent's achievements is likely to become known, and then
- to produce relevant actions.

Matters of fact predict to some extent not only agents' achievements and failures, but also their would-be mental attitudes, their acquisition of new beliefs and then their goals. As we will endeavour to show later, a factual concurrence among agents is likely to produce aggression, while factual social dependence is a predictor of manipulation, or at least the dependent agent's goal of influencing her social "resources".

The real predictive power of the precognitive bases of sociality is conditioned by the existence of a formal model of the processes sketched above. What we need to develop is a formal account ranging from unknown relevant situations and failures in planning to belief revision. Existing systems of belief revision are able to maintain coherence among beliefs, but are separated from planning. Only very recently has the problem of "pragmatic" belief revision (belief revision oriented to interaction) been raised (Galliers 1988). On the other hand, those planning systems that are concerned with learning from failures, that is with adjusting failed plans (Hammond 1986; Alterman 1986), are separated from the management of beliefs. As usual, an integrated model is what is lacking.

12.2 Precognitive notions

As previously noted (see Fig. 12.1), an objective relation is defined as precognitive when it is neither desired nor believed by the agents involved. Precognitive relations may be non-social (i.e. presocial) or social depending on whether they imply a single agent or more than one. In the former case, precognitive relations hold between the agent and the external (non-social) world. In the latter case, they hold between at least two agents' behaviours or mental attitudes.

As we will endeavour to show, social relations are based upon, and derived from, some fundamental non-social objective relations. Of all sorts of possible objective relations, therefore, we will take into account those we believe are relevant to the goals and destinies of social agents and thus to the modelling of social action.

12.2.1 Precognitive relations relevant to the social domain

There are at least two types of relations between one agent and the external world that are of some relevance from a social point of view: dependence relations and interest relations. Both produce social relations and will prove useful for describing sophisticated types of social interaction. In a sense, they lie at the bottom of sociality: from the least to the most complex, social relationships represent a series of steps starting from, and based on, presocial dependence and interest relations. The latter thus have a fundamental explanatory rôle in a theory of social action. It might justifiably be argued that the following concepts are partly overlapping and, to that extent, redundant. Nevertheless, we believe it is necessary to include all the concepts defined here in the model at the present level of its development, since they all have a long tradition in the social and behavioural sciences.

The relation of dependence

Dependence is undoubtedly the fundamental relation upon which the whole construction of sociality is based (Castelfranchi et al. 1992). As we have shown elsewhere (Conte et al. 1991), full co-operation necessarily implies mutual dependence. But dependence seems to be responsible for other types of interactions as well: it lies at the bottom of social exchange, influencing, and some forms of social exploitation (taking advantage of others' actions).

However, dependence is not necessarily a social notion: a relation of dependence may be said to occur whenever:

PRECOGNITIVE NOTIONS

- any object or event in the external world, if used, may increase the probability that a given state of the world be realized,and
- that world state is desired by at least one agent.

In such a case, we say that agent is dependent on the object or event. The latter will be called a "resource". Resources enter the structures of the actions (see also Parunak 1990). An action is a relation holding among agent(s), goal(s) and resource(s). Agents are said to be acting when using one or more resources to reach a given goal. We then say that anything that is involved in the action, except the agent, is a resource of that action.

In this chapter, we will mainly use the formal apparatus of Cohen & Levesque (1990a; 1990b). x and y denote agent variables with $x \neq y$ always implied, a denotes an action variable, r a resource, and p and q well formed formulae representing states of the world (with $p \neq q$). The predicate (RE-SOURCE r a) means that r is needed in order to perform a. (CANDO x a) means that agent x has the action a in his repertoire; that is, he is able to do it by himself. We use the following definition similar to the one in Cohen & Levesque (1990a; 1990b):

$$\text{(DONE-BY } x\, a) = \text{def (DONE } a) \wedge (\text{AGT } x\, a) \qquad \text{D1}$$

where (AGT x a) expresses the fact that x is the agent doing a. As in Cohen & Levesque, an axiom of action-ability holds:

Axiom of action-ability:

$$\text{(DONE-BY } x\, a) \rightarrow (\text{CANDO } x\, a)$$

In addition, we introduce a second definition:

$$
\begin{aligned}
\text{(DONE-FOR } x\, a\, p) = \text{def (DONE-BY } x\, a) \wedge \\
(\text{GOAL } x\, p) \wedge \\
(\text{BEL } x\, ((\text{DONE } a) \rightarrow (\text{EVENTUALLY } p))) \qquad \text{D2}
\end{aligned}
$$

which means that agent x performs action a in order to achieve his goal p.

As in Cohen & Levesque, action is always intentional:

Axiom of intentionality of action:

$$\text{(DONE-BY } x\, a) \rightarrow \exists p\, ((\text{GOAL } x\, p) \wedge (\text{DONE-FOR } x\, a\, p))$$

However, not all the consequences of one's actions are wanted, that is:

$$((\text{DONE-BY } x\, a) \rightarrow p) \nrightarrow (\text{DONE-FOR } x\, a\, p)$$

THE PRECOGNITIVE BASES OF SOCIAL INTERACTION

As we have specified in the definition of (DONE-FOR x a p), two further conditions should be true for the above conclusion to be allowed: that agent x has the goal p, and that x believes that the action done implies that later p will be true. This will have some important consequences for the discussion.

Agents are usually dependent on the existence of resources. We will call this type of dependence a resource dependence, to distinguish it from social dependence:

$$(\text{R-DEP } x\ r\ a\ p) = \text{def } (\text{GOAL } x\ p) \wedge$$
$$(\text{RESOURCE } r\ a) \wedge$$
$$((\text{DONE } a) \rightarrow (\text{EVENTUALLY } p)) \qquad \text{D3}$$

r is then a resource for x to perform an act, which implies that later p will be true. A set of resources is required for any act to take place. For instance, in the "blocks world" widely used in AI for experimentation with planning systems, the cubes and the table are resources (see Fig. 12.2). Adam is a one-armed robot. His goals are described on the left side of the figure, while the state of the world is described on the right side. In this world, (ON c_i c_j) stands for a state of the world in which a cube c_i is sitting on top of another cube c_j. Only two types of action are possible: (PUTON c_i, c_j), meaning put block c_i on block c_j, and (CLEAR c), which means clear the cube on top of cube c and put it on the table. One can put a cube on top of another only if both are clear. Therefore, in order to achieve his goal in the current state of the world, Adam must perform two actions: CLEAR and PUTON. To act, Adam needs the following resources:

- the resources required for PUTON (clear cubes);
- the resources required for CLEAR (clear cubes and table).

In the social world, as we will see, other agents may be used as resources. This happens not only in exploitation but also in prosocial action. For example, in the action of helping, the recipient is a resource of the action "give help".

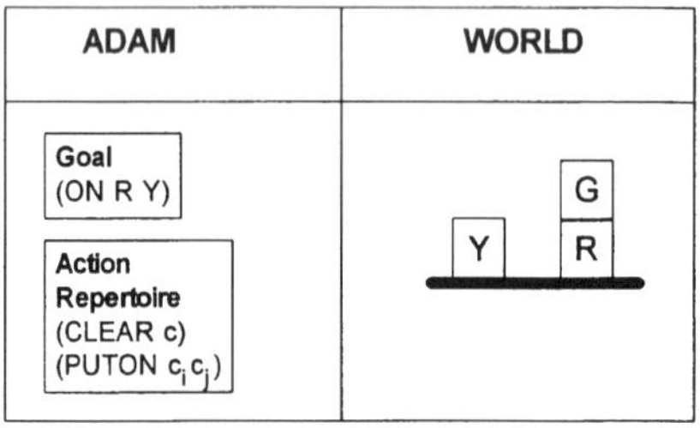

Figure 12.2 R-dependence and interest.

274

PRECOGNITIVE NOTIONS

The relation of interest

The notion of interest has a long tradition in social sciences. In the last few decades, owing to a typical hypercognitive misunderstanding, it has been considered anti-mentalist, anti-cognitive and heavily compromised with authoritarianism (both in politics and in philosophy; rational choice theorists wonder who is given the responsibility for spelling out what is your own interests). Consequently, its use is strongly discouraged in any sort of intellectual enterprise.

On the other hand, this rejection shows that interest is a typical objective notion, in the sense previously defined. Interest is not necessarily a social concept. A presocial relation of interest occurs between one agent with his mental states and some external state of affairs when a given state of the world q implies another world state p, and the latter is a (sub-)goal of the agent (when p implies a sub-goal, it often coincides with a precondition for a sub-plan):

$$(\text{INTEREST } x\, q\, p) = \text{def } (\text{GOAL } x\, p) \wedge (q \rightarrow (\text{EVENTUALLY } p)) \qquad \text{D4}$$

q (or, better, the event which instantiated it) is in x's interest.

On the other hand, a world state that goes against an agent's interests is a counter-interest of that agent's:

$$(\text{COUNTER-INT } x\, q\, p) = \text{def } (\text{GOAL } x\, p) \wedge$$
$$(q \rightarrow (\text{EVENTUALLY } \neg\, p)) \qquad \text{D5}$$

The notion of interest points to what is useful for the agent. A world state by itself sufficient to bring about a state desired by the agent is useful in the sense that it reduces the agent's costs: she finds (part of) her job done.

As an example, let us go back to Figure 12.2. Now, look at Adam's interests, that is, at matters of fact advantageous for Adam's goals: the fact that cube Y is CLEARTOP represents an interest of Adam's with regard to his goal of having R on top of Y. The fact that G is on top of R is a counter-interest of Adam's with regard to the same goal. However, cube G's being CLEARTOP is an interest of his with regard to the goal (CLEARTOP R).

Dependence and interest

The two notions of dependence and interest are similar and one may merge into the other according to the perspective taken by the observer. However, resource dependence is identified with respect to intended actions: an agent

THE PRECOGNITIVE BASES OF SOCIAL INTERACTION

is dependent on those resources that are needed to act. Interests are identified with regard to (sub-)goals and they refer only to useful conditions. Events and the resulting states sometimes achieve the agent's (sub-)goals, thus serving in her interests. Conditions that need be true for the agent to act create a dependence of that agent on them. She cannot do without them.

Of course, the existence of required resources may be seen as an interest of the agent. This is a truism: precisely because they are needed for the agent to act, existing resources reduce the agent's cost of acquiring them. A realized action condition is an interest, while an action condition to be realized is a resource.

12.2.3 Precognitive social relations

Let us now turn our attention to the social side of these ideas and to other social relationships that are based upon them.

Social dependence and social structure
Our basic definition of social dependence (Conte et al. 1991) is as follows:

$$(\text{S-DEP } x\,y\,a\,p) = \text{def } (\text{GOAL } x\,p) \wedge$$
$$\neg (\text{CANDO } x\,a) \wedge$$
$$(\text{CANDO } y\,a) \wedge$$
$$((\text{DONE } a) \rightarrow (\text{EVENTUALLY } p)) \qquad \text{D6}$$

That is: x depends on y with regard to an act useful for realizing a state p when p is a goal of x and x is unable to realize p, while y is able to do so. Look at Figure 12.3. Here, Adam is no longer able to clear cubes. However, the blocks world now includes a female robot, Eve, who is able to do so. In such a situation, we say that Adam is dependent upon Eve with regard to his goal of having R on G.

Social dependence is an objective dependence where resources are filled in by social agents. It sets up a social network among agents independent of, and often preceding, their awareness. Several dimensions are intertwined, such as the existence of alternatives, the degree of dependence, etc. (see Castelfranchi et al. 1992).

In particular, dependence may be either unilateral, when only Adam depends on Eve, or bilateral, when they depend on each other. Bilateral dependence is said to be *mutual* when agents depend on each other to achieve one and the same goal (cf. Conte et al. 1991). Bilateral dependence

PRECOGNITIVE NOTIONS

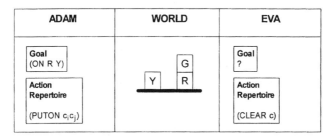

Figure 12.3 *S*-dependence.

is said to be *reciprocal* when agents depend on each other for realizing different goals. In Figure 12.3, if Eve's goal were identical to Adam's (ON *R Y*), the robots would be mutually dependent; If Eve's goal were (ON *Y R*), the robots would be reciprocally dependent (although their goals would have been contradictory).

Social interference

We say that there is an objective social interference between two agents, x and y, when the achievement of x's goals has some effect on y pursuing, and then achieving, her goals. Goals may interfere in a positive or negative way.

Positive interference: favour relationships.
In the positive case, we say that x favours y if he casually sets up a state of the world that is in y's interests. (Our notion of favour differs from Martial (1990), since the latter is a cognitive and intentional relationship of help.)

$$(\text{FAVOUR } x \, a \, y \, p) =_{def} ((\text{DONE-BY } x \, a) \to (\text{EVENTUALLY } p)) \qquad D7$$

That is, y factually benefits from x's doings. This relation differs from social dependence in that it is much weaker: y could reach her goal q on her own, without x's intervention. However, things are such that y may have (part of) her job done thanks to x's accidental help. For example, if you raise your hand to greet someone passing by and in doing so you stop the bus I am waiting for, you are giving me unrequested and unintentional help, but I cannot be said to be dependent on you.

In Figure 12.4, Eve's achievement of her goal to clear all cubes happens to favour Adam's goal. Although he does not need Eve's intervention, since he may accomplish his task by himself, Adam takes advantage of it.

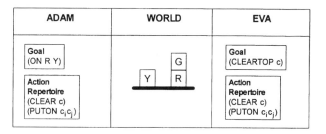

Figure 12.4 Favour and conflict.

Negative interference: conflict and concurrence.
Social interference is negative when *y* reaching her goal prevents *x* from reaching one of his goals. This gives rise to some interesting precognitive social situations, such as interest conflict and concurrence, which, once known by the agents involved, often produce antisocial interactions of different sorts.

There may be an objective conflict between two goals when agents have goals that are incompatible, that is, contradictory. However, the more general case is represented by the conflict of interests:

(INT-CONF $x\,y\,q\,p\,z$) = def (INTEREST $x\,q\,p$) ∧ (INTEREST $y \neg q\,z$)   D8

There are no examples of a conflict of interest in the blocks world because it is implausible that agents would not realize their conflicting interests, thus transforming them into contrasting goals. However, in Figure 12.4 we have an example of incompatible goals: Eve wants to have all cubes with their tops clear, while Adam wants to have at least one of them, *Y*, covered by a block. As a consequence, Eve destroys Adam's move by clearing *Y*, Adam in turn destroys her move, and so on in an infinite sequence.

In the real world, on the other hand, an objective conflict is more often a conflict of pure interests: people are frequently unaware of their conflicting interests. For example, the unemployed are interested in reducing wages because in the short run they can then find a job at a lower wage than employed people would accept. But at the same time, it is difficult to believe that the employed want their wages to be reduced: there is a conflict between the interests of the two categories rather than between their goals.

Often, conflicts depend on resource scarcity. An example is shown in Figure 12.5. Adam and Eve each want to put a different cube on another

PRECOGNITIVE NOTIONS

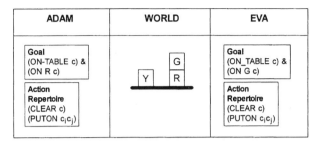

Figure 12.5 Concurrence.

cube sitting on the table. Given the scarcity of this sort of cube (there is only one), the two goals cannot be realized at once, even though they are not incompatible. From D3, we can derive:

$$(\text{CONC x y r a}) = \text{def} (\text{R-DEP } x \, r \, a) \wedge (\text{R-DEP } y \, r \, a) \wedge \\ ((\text{DONE-BY } x \, a) \vee (\text{DONE-BY } y \, a)) \qquad \text{D8}$$

It is easy to show that concurrence is a type of interest-conflict, since what is an interest to one agent is a counter-interest to the other: each robot wants to put its cube on Υ, and consequently either (DONE-BY $x\,r\,a$) or (DONE-BY $y\,r\,a$) is true. Thus, one doing it implies a counter-interest of the other's.

Concurrence could also be defined as a *shared dependence*: in Figure 12.5, Adam and Eve both depend on a resource which cannot be used at the same time for different goals. However, the sharing of interests or goals does not necessarily imply an anti-social relation. Indeed, the sharing of interests and goals tends to produce prosocial interaction or co-operation (Conte et al. 1991), at least in case of mutual dependence. This is true when goals and interests are effectively shared, that is, when they are overlapping. But it is not true when agents have parallel goals or interests, that is, when their goals are all identical but each mentions a different agent as the one who achieves the goal in question. With parallel goals or interests, there is no real sharing. Rather, there is often concurrence: when any two agents want to eat one and the same cake, their goals overlap almost perfectly except that the eaters are not supposed to be the same.

12.3 Social action

On the grounds of objective relations, agents construct social actions. But what is a social action?

We define a *social action* as an action such that at some level either an action performed by another agent y or some mental attitude of y (goal, belief or emotion) is mentioned in the chain of its goals.

12.3.1 Types of social action

We will now consider two types of social action, prosocial and antisocial, representing the two main origins, or bases, of sociality:
- Adoptive (or prosocial) action is derived from the sharing of interests. The general form of prosocial action is based on the goal adoption that we have defined elsewhere (Conte et al. 1991) as:

$$(\text{ADOPT } x\, y\, p) = \text{def } (\text{GOAL } x\, (\text{EVENTUALLY } (\text{OBTAIN } y\, p)))$$

where

$$(\text{OBTAIN } x\, p) = \text{def } (\text{GOAL } x\, p) \wedge (\text{EVENTUALLY } (p \vee (\text{BEL } x\, p)))$$

In prosocial action, x is acting in order for y to obtain her goal that p.
- Aggressive (or antisocial) action is based on x's aggressive goal to prevent y from reaching one of her goals:

$$(\text{AGGRESS } x\, y\, p) = \text{def } (\text{GOAL } x\, (\text{EVENTUALLY } \neg (\text{OBTAIN } y\, p)))$$

These are two fundamental types of social actions and they often occur combined in several ways: many actions are aggressive at a lower level of their goal chain, while their ultimate goal is prosocial, or vice versa.

12.4 Cognitive social actions (adding beliefs and desired effects)

Let us now address the questions of how and why precognitive relations of the type seen in Section 12.2 lead to various types of cognitive social actions. The process from precognitive relations to relevant social action includes two steps: the sub-process of the agents becoming aware of the social relations they are involved in, and the sub-process from relevant beliefs to social action. A satisfactory model of the first step ought to involve a formal

COGNITIVE SOCIAL ACTIONS

theory of causal reasoning, perception and learning which is far beyond the scope of the present work. In the following, however, we will express some preliminary ideas about pragmatic causal reasoning that are relevant for modelling the agent. More specifically, we will try to show the characteristics the agent ought to possess to acquire information relevant to her goals and interests. As for the second step, we shall endeavour to show some of the consequences of the agents' acquiring relevant information.

In all the situations described below, we shall assume the *postulate of introspection* (agents implicitly meta-believe all they believe and want). Secondly, we shall assume that agents have incomplete knowledge, but no false beliefs. (This is a more limiting assumption than that implied in Fig. 12.1, since we shall not be distinguishing between knowledge and beliefs.) Thirdly, we shall assume that the process under study is triggered by some event which interferes positively or negatively with some goal of one of the agents. To simplify matters, we shall also assume that this event will be perceived by at least one of the agents and that the event is believed by that agent to be consistently associated with a world state that is relevant to that agent's goals.

12.4.1   A rule of causal attribution

In the situations that we shall describe, agents are assumed to believe that there is a change in the state of the world. This will be expressed in the following way:

$$(\text{BEL } x \text{ HAPPENS } e; p)$$

where p is a state of the world that follows the event e which has just occurred. In our world, agents are also assumed to have the following rule:

Rule of causal attribution:

$$(\text{BEL } x \ \forall \ e_j (\text{HAPPENS } e_j; p)) \rightarrow$$
$$((\text{BEL } x \ \exists \ e_k((e_k \neq e_j) \land (p \rightarrow e_k))) \ \lor$$
$$(\text{BEL } x \ (e_j \rightarrow (\text{EVENTUALLY } p)))) \qquad \text{R1}$$

where e_j and e_k are instances of types of events E_j and E_k. This means that a state of the world that consistently follows a given event is believed to be implied by the latter unless a condition, different from the event that occurred, is believed to be needed for p to occur.

281

THE PRECOGNITIVE BASES OF SOCIAL INTERACTION

12.4.2 From interests to goals

One of the ways in which new goals are acquired via cognition implies that people learn that they have a so far unknown interest:

A goal-generation rule:

$$(\text{BEL } x \, (\text{INTEREST } x \, q \, p)) \rightarrow (\text{GOAL } x \, q) \qquad \text{R2}$$

This is a particular case of causal reasoning in planning. Like the action–precondition rule (Cohen & Perrault 1979), it is recursive: if x believes that a_1 is a preparatory action for the intended (or target) action a_2, a_1 becomes in turn a target action, and so forth. For example, if x believes that if it rains he will find mushrooms to gather, x will keep wanting it to rain.

The question is, how does x come to believe that q is an interest of his?

$$(\text{BEL } x \, \forall \, e_j \, (\text{HAPPENS } e_j; \, p) \wedge (\text{INTEREST } x \, e_j \, p)) \rightarrow$$
$$(\text{BEL } x \, (\text{INTEREST } x \, e_j \, p)) \qquad \text{T1}$$

From the first premises and the rule of causal attribution (R1), we derive that x believes that the event occurred is a sufficient condition for p to follow. Note that by definition x cannot have false beliefs and, given the second premises, a belief about a necessary condition for p would be a false belief. It is sufficient that x believes what is described in the first premises for him to arrive at the conclusion that the fact that the event occurred implies that p follows. From the second premises, given the definition of interest (D4), we can derive that p is a state desired by the agent and, given the postulate of introspection, the agent's belief that p is one of his goals. Therefore:

$$(\text{BEL } x \, (((\text{HAPPENS } e) \rightarrow (\text{EVENTUALLY } p)) \wedge (\text{GOAL } x \, p)))$$

which means that he believes that e is an interest of his.

12.4.3 From benefit to exploitation

Let us consider what happens when y is favouring x with respect to some goal of x's. Although this type of social relation might appear to be rather esoteric, it does allow for the interesting phenomenon of social parasitism: to the extent that x believes y will act in x's interests, he will probably wait for y to act in his interests. Thus, in the situation described in Figure 12.4, Adam will wait for Eve to do part of his job.

Here, too, the question arises of how x gets to believe that he benefits from y's action:

COGNITIVE SOCIAL ACTIONS

$$\forall \ a_j \ ((\text{BEL} \ x \ ((\text{DONE-BY} \ y \ a_j) \wedge (a_j; p)) \wedge (\text{FAVOUR} \ y \ x \ a_j p)) \rightarrow$$
$$(\text{BEL} \ x \ (\text{FAVOUR} \ y \ x \ a_j p)) \qquad \text{T2}$$

This is nothing but a special case of T1. From the first premises we derive that Adam believes that the action done by Eve implies later p . From the second premises, we derive that p is a goal of Adam's (see D7). Hence we derive Adam's belief that Eve's action is an interest of his, which means, by definition, that the agent believes that Eve is favouring him.

Note that Adam is not allowed to conclude that Eve's action is intended to produce p, since he has no reason to believe that Eve has any corresponding goal, or that she has any belief corresponding to the first premises. (See D2 and the axiom of intentionality of action.) Hence Adam is not allowed to believe that Eve wants to help him. All he has to believe is that he benefits from Eve's action.

12.4.4 From unilateral dependence to influencing and adoption

If people believe that they depend on others (irrespective of any belief concerning actual benefit), they will try to influence others according to their needs. (This has been shown in Castelfranchi et al. 1992).

Formally:

$$(\text{BEL} \ x \ (\text{S-DEP} \ x \ y \ a \ p)) \rightarrow (\text{GOAL} \ x \ (\text{DONE-BY} \ y \ a))$$

While in favour relationships (see Fig. 12.4) it is sufficient for Adam to wait and see, since he believes that, sooner or later, Eve will act in his interests, in social dependence this is not enough (Fig. 12.3). Consider the situation described in Section 12.2.3. Adam now has one more goal: that Eve has a new goal herself, i.e. to clear R.

The dual belief (x's belief that y is dependent on him) leads us to the well known problem of adoption: is this belief sufficient for x to act in y's interests? If this is not the case, what else is needed? As we have already argued (Castelfranchi 1990), we think another belief is needed in goal adoption, that y's achievement of her goal q is a means for x to achieve his goal p:

Adoption rule:

$$(\text{BEL} \ x \ ((\text{OBTAIN} \ y \ q) \rightarrow (\text{OBTAIN} \ x \ p))) \rightarrow (\text{ADOPT} \ x \ y \ q) \qquad \text{R3}$$

In Figure 12.3, if the agents were reciprocally dependent (e.g. if Eve wanted

283

THE PRECOGNITIVE BASES OF SOCIAL INTERACTION

to have Υ on G), Eve might decide to adopt Adam's goal that she clears R. Of course, such a decision usually implies a belief that the other is committed to adopt one's goal in reciprocation. A model of the process from reciprocal dependence to social exchange thus includes a model of commitment in social exchange which is beyond the scope of this work.

Another interesting process based on dependence is one from mutual dependence to co-operation. This was analyzed in some detail elsewhere (Conte et al. 1991). We derive Adam's belief that he is dependent on Eve from both precognitive social dependence and Adam's belief that a given p consistently follows Eve doing a given action:

$$((\text{BEL } x \ \forall \ a_j \ (\text{DONE-BY } y \ a_j; \ p)) \vee (\text{S-DEP } x \ y \ a \ p)) \rightarrow$$
$$(\text{BEL } x \ (\text{S-DEP } x \ y \ a \ p)) \qquad \text{T3}$$

From the first premises it follows that Adam has a belief that Eve's action implies later p (cf. T1 and T2). From this belief and the axiom of action ability, it follows that Adam believes that Eve is able to do an action implying later p. From the postulate of introspection and the second premises, two further beliefs of Adam's can be derived:

- that p is one of his goals,
- that he is not able to do an action implying later p, which means, given the definition of social dependence provided, that Adam believes that he is dependent on Eve with regard to his goal that p.

12.4.5 From conflict to aggression and from concurrence to competition

Finally, if Adam believes that there is a situation of conflict between his and Eve's interest(s) (cf. Fig. 12.4), Adam will also come to have an aggressive goal towards Eve. In formal terms:

$$(\text{BEL } x \ (\text{INT-CONF } x \ y \ q \ p \ z)) \rightarrow$$
$$(\text{GOAL } x \ \neg \ (\text{EVENTUALLY } (\text{OBTAIN } y \ z)) \qquad \text{T4}$$

From (BEL x (INT-CONF $x \ y \ q \ p \ z$)), it follows that Adam believes that if q is true either p or z follow (see D7). Since, by definition, p and z are desired by Adam and Eve respectively, and Adam believes so (first premises), Adam's belief,

$$(\text{BEL } x \ ((\text{OBTAIN } x \ p) \vee (\text{OBTAIN } y \ z)))$$

can also be derived. Consequently, Adam believes that Eve not obtaining

CONCLUSIONS

her goal implies that Adam will obtain his goal. With the goal-generation rule above, it is sufficient for Adam to have the goal that Eve does not obtain her goal that z. By definition, this goal of Adam's is an aggressive goal. In Figure 12.4, Adam ends up with the goal that Eve does not achieve her goal (CLEARTOP Y).

Adam's belief that there is a conflict between his own and Eve's interests is derived from the objective conflict and Adam's belief that $\neg q$ follows systematically from Eve's action:

$$((\text{BEL } x \ \forall \ a_j \ (\text{DONE-BY } y \ a_j; \ \neg p)) \land (\text{INT-CONF } x \ y \ a_j \ p \ z)) \rightarrow$$
$$(\text{BEL } x \ (\text{INT-CONF } x \ y \ a_j \ p \ z)) \quad \text{T5}$$

From the two premises, thanks to T1, it follows that Adam believes that Eve's action implies a counter-interest of Adam's. In addition, from the axiom of intentionality, Adam will also believe that there is a goal of Eve's whose achievement implies a counter-interest of Adam's. And vice versa: Adam's interest implies that Eve does not obtain her goal.

From believed concurrence (Adam wants to put his cube on the only clear cube existing and believes Eve wants to do the same; see Fig. 12.5), an aggressive goal is derived:

$$(\text{BEL } x \ (\text{CONC } x \ y \ r \ a)) \rightarrow (\text{GOAL } x \ \neg \ (\text{DONE-BY } y \ a)) \quad \text{T6}$$

which is a special case of T4.

Adam's belief that there is concurrence between his action and Eve's is derived from objective concurrence plus Adam's belief that Eve doing a given action is consistently followed by a state of the world which goes against his own interests (namely, the existence of a resource for an intended action by Adam). For a sketchy derivation, see the proof of T5.

12.5 Conclusions

In this chapter, current AI models of social action have been shown to suffer from either top-down (that is, pre-established) co-operativeness or the hypercognitive fallacy (a view of (social) agents as mutually transparent and endowed with built-in social awareness). In opposition to both these tendencies, we have advocated a gradualistic bottom-up approach to the modelling of social action. We have described elsewhere the rôle of emergent functionality among cognitive agents (Castelfranchi & Conte 1992). In this chapter, we have seen cognitive social action as an emergent phenomenon

THE PRECOGNITIVE BASES OF SOCIAL INTERACTION

which results from objective relations holding between each single agent and the external (social or non-social) world. This view can shed light on the sources of sociality, on why intelligent agents need to interact and on what steps gradually lead from static matters of fact to social action.

Objective social relations have been argued to have some predictive power; that is, they allow agents' social beliefs and cognitive actions to be foreseen. Furthermore, objective social relations pave the way to a reconsideration of social structures as not simply consisting of mutual knowledge, negotiations and commitments, but also resulting from common external conditions.

In other words, we believe that a model of multi-agent interaction confined within the limits of individual minds is insufficient. Mind is not enough. But shortcomings cannot be made good by simply constructing interactive subcognitive agents. The real methodological challenge consists of working out an integrated simulation approach. In such an approach, simulations of models of minds should be accompanied by dynamic simulations of the composite selective effects of agents' actions. More concretely, the following simulations should be integrated:

- the emergence of minds from subcognitive units;
- models of social minds;
- agents in interaction (the emergence of sociality);
- emergent functionality among intelligent agents in interaction.

The present work is intended to contribute to the third of these in that it both describes some external conditions of social action and attempts to derive interactions among the agents involved. The most natural next step would be to experiment on the basis of our conclusions using a multi-agent testbed. However, even in its present descriptive form, our work suggests how simulation methodology can inform the study of social action: sociality, and *a fortiori* society, can be seen to emerge from situating intelligent agents, rather than subcognitive systems, in a common world. A constructive simulation approach would shed new light on social action, stressing its problem-solving character, and would help in exploring the problems that agents will encounter in their common world and the solutions they will work out through coordinating with, and also taking advantage of, one another.

References

Abbott, A. 1990. A primer on sequence methods. *Organization Science* **1**(4), 375–92.

Abbott, A. 1992. From causes to events: notes on narrative positivism. *Sociological Methods and Research* **20**(4), 428–544.

Aldenderfer, M. 1978. Creating assemblages by computer simulation: the development and uses of ABSIM. In *Simulations in archaeology*, J. Sabloff (ed.), 67–117. Albuquerque: University of New Mexico Press.

Aldenderfer, M. 1987. *Quantitative research in archaeology: progress and prospects*. London: Sage.

Alexander, R. D. 1987. Evolution of the human psyche. In *The human revolution*, P. Mellars & C. Stringer (eds), 455–513. Edinburgh: Edinburgh University Press.

Allen, P. A. 1984. Vers une science nouvelle des sciences complexes. In *Science et pratique de la complexité*. Paris: La Documentation Française, 307-40.

Allen, P. M. 1976. Evolution, population dynamics, and stability. *Proceedings of the National Academy of Sciences of the USA* **73**, 665–8.

Alterman, R. 1988. Adaptive planning. *Cognitive Science* **12**, 393–421.

Aminzade, R. 1992. Historical sociology and time. *Sociological Methods and Research* **20**(4), 456–80.

Anderson, P. & G. Fisher 1986. A Monte Carlo model of a garbage can decision process. In *Ambiguity and command*, J. G. March and R. Weissinger-Baylon (eds), 53–71. Marshfield, Mass.: Pitman.

Anderson, P. & S. Thorson 1982. Systems simulation: artificial intelligence based simulations of foreign policy decision-making. *Behavioral Science* **27**(2), 176–93.

Arthur, W. B. 1991. Learning and adaptive economic behavior: designing economic agents that act like human agents: a behavioral approach to bounded rationality. *American Economic Review* **81**(2), 353–9.

Bailey, G. N. (ed.) 1983. *Hunter–gatherer economy in prehistory*. Cambridge: Cambridge University Press.

Baligh, H., R. Burton, B. Obel 1986. Designing organization structures: an expert system method. In *Economics and Artificial Intelligence*, J-L. Roos (ed.), 177–81. Oxford: Pergamon.

REFERENCES

Banerjee, S. 1986. Reproduction of social structures: an artificial intelligence model., *Journal of Conflict Resolution* **30**(2), 221–52.

Beer, R. D. 1990. *Intelligence as adaptive behavior*. New York: Academic.

Berkes, F. 1989. Community-based management and sustainable development: a framework for research. In *La Recherche face à la pêche artisannale*, J. R. Durand & J. Weber (eds), 525–49. Proceedings of ORSTOM–IFREMER symposium (unpublished).

Berkley, B. 1990. Analysis and approximation of a JIT production line: a comment. *Decision Sciences* **21**(3), 660–69.

Bertrand, J. 1883. Theórie mathématique de la richesse sociale. *Journal des Savants*, Septembre, 499–508.

Bhaskar, R. 1978. *A realist theory of science*. Chichester: Harvester Wheatsheaf.

Binford, L. 1980. Willow smoke and dogs tails: hunter–gatherer settlement systems and site formation. *American Antiquity* **43**, 330–61.

Binford, L. & S. Binford 1966. A preliminary analysis of functional variability in the Mousterian of Levallois Facies. In *Recent Studies in Palaeoanthropology*, J. D. Clarke & F. C. Howell (eds). Washington, DC: American Anthropological Association.

Blanning, R. 1990. *Human organizations as intelligent systems*. Working paper no. 19–16, Vanderbilt University, Nashville, Tenn.

Blanning, R. 1991. *Human organizations as physical symbol systems*. Working paper no. 91–02, Owen Graduate School of Managements, Vanderbilt University, Nashville, Tenn.

Bloch, M. 1991. Language, anthropology and cognitive science. *Man* (N.S.) **26**, 183–98.

Blundell, R., C. Meghir, E. Symons 1988. Labour supply specification and the evaluation of tax reforms. *Journal of Public Economics* **36**(1), 23–52.

Boden, M. A. 1990. *The creative mind: myths & mechanisms*. London: Weidenfeld & Nicholson.

Bond, A. H. & L. Gasser (eds) 1988. *Readings in distributed artificial intelligence*. San Mateo, Cal.: Morgan Kaufmann.

Bousquet, F. & C. Cambier 1990. Transfert d'echelle et univers multi-agents: le cas du système de la pêche du Delta Central du Niger. In *Seminfor ORSTOM*, Vol. IV. C. Mullon (ed.), 382–98.

Boyd, R. & P. J. Richerson 1985. *Culture and the evolutionary process*. Chicago: University of Chicago Press.

Bunn, D. & G. Wright 1991. Interaction of judgemental and statistical forecasting methods: issues and analysis. *Management Science* **37**(5), 501–18.

Caldas, J. 1992. *Oligopólio: experiências com agentes reais e artificiais*. MSc thesis, ISEG, Lisbon Technical University (in Portuguese).

Caldas, J. & H. Coelho 1992. Strategic interaction in oligopolistic markets: experimenting with real and artificial agents. Paper presented at the Fourth European Workshop on Modeling Autonomous Agents in a Multi-Agent World, Viterbo, Italy.

REFERENCES

Caniglia, A. 1988. The economic evaluation of food stamps: an intertemporal analysis with nonlinear budget constraints. *Public Finance Quarterly* **16**(1), 3–29.

Carley, K. 1986a. Efficiency in a garbage can: implications for crisis management. In *Ambiguity and command*, J. G. March & R. Weissinger-Baylon (eds), 195–231. Marshfield, Mass.: Pitman.

Carley, K. 1986b. Measuring efficiency in a garbage can hierarchy. In *Ambiguity and command*, J. G. March & R. Weissinger-Baylon (eds), 165–94. Marshfield, Mass.: Pitman.

Carlson, D. & S. Ram 1990. Modelling organizations as a social network of distributed knowledge-based systems. *Proceedings of the 23rd annual conference on Systems Science*, volume III, 271–80. New York: IEEE Computer Society Press.

Castelfranchi, C. 1990. Social power: a point missed in multi agent DAI and HCI. In *Decentralized AI*. Y. Demazeau & J. P. Mueller (eds), 49–63. Amsterdam: Elsevier.

Castelfranchi, C. 1992. No more cooperation, please! In search of the social structure of verbal interaction. In *Communication from an artifical intelligence perspective*, A. Ortony, J. Slack, O. Stock (eds), 205–29. Berlin: Springer Verlag.

Castelfranchi, C. & R. Conte 1992. Emergent functionality among intelligent agents. *AI & Society* **6**, 78–93.

Castelfranchi, C., M. Miceli, A. Cesta 1992. Dependence relations among autonomous agents. In *Decentralized AI*, vol. III, Y. Demazeau & E. Werner (eds), 215–27. Amsterdam: Elsevier.

Cavalli-Sfarza, L. L. & M. W. Feldman 1981. *Cultural transmission and evolution.* Princeton, NJ: Princeton University Press.

Cedric, V. 1990. Simulation study of an automated guide-vehicle system in a Yugoslav hospital. *Journal of the Operational Research Society* **41**(4), 229–310.

Chaharbaghi, K. 1991. DSSL II: A powerful tool for modelling and analyzing complex systems, *International Journal of Operations and Production Management* **11**(4), 44–88.

Chaharbaghi, K., A. Goddard, R. Sayler, R. Buende 1990. A simulation methodology for evaluating the reliability, availability and performance of the next European Torus. *International Journal of Quality and Reliability Management* **7**(1), 30–55.

Chamberlin, E. 1933. *The theory of monopolistic competition.* Cambridge,Mass.: Harvard University Press.

Chernenko, I. V. 1989. A conceptual and a mathematical model of social production (in Russian). In Vladimir I. Paniotto (ed.), Experiences in modelling social processes: methodological and methodical problems of model building (in Russian), 173–81. Kiev: Naukova dumka.

Coelho, H., G. Gaspar, I. Ramos 1992. Experiments in modelling communication among autonomous agents. Paper presented at the IFIP WG 8.3, Working Conference on Decision Support Systems, Fontainebleau, France, 1–3 July.

Cohen M. N. 1985. Prehistoric hunter–gatherers: the meaning of social complexity. In *Prehistoric hunter–gatherers: the emergence of cultural complexity*, T. D. Price & J. A. Brown (eds), 99–119. New York: Academic.

REFERENCES

Cohen, M. 1986. Artificial intelligence and the dynamic performance of organizational designs. In *Ambiguity and command*, J. G. March & R. Weissinger-Baylon (eds), 53–71. Marshfield, Mass.: Pitman.

Cohen, M. D., J. G. March, J. P. Olsen 1972. A garbage can model of organizational choice. *Administrative Science Quarterly* **17**(1), 1-25.

Cohen, P. R. & H. J. Levesque 1990a. Intention is choice with commitment. *Artificial Intelligence* **42**, 213–61.

Cohen, P. R. & H. J. Levesque 1990b. Rational interaction as a basis of communication. In *Intentions in communication.*, P. R. Cohen, J. Morgan, M. E. Pollack (eds), 221–55. Cambridge, Mass.: MIT Press.

Cohen, P. R. & H. J. Levesque 1991. *Teamwork.* Technote 504. Menlo Park, Cal: SRI International.

Cohen, P. R. & C. R. Perrault 1979. Elements of a plan-based theory of speech-acts. *Cognitive Science* **3**, 177–212.

Collins, R. J. & D. R. Jefferson 1991. Representations for artificial organisms. In *From animals to animats*, J-A. Meyer (ed.), 383–90. Cambridge, Mass.: MIT Press.

Conte, R., M. Miceli, C. Castelfranchi 1991. Limits and levels of cooperation: disentangling various types of prosocial interaction. In *Decentralized AI*, vol. II, Y. Demazeau & J. P. Mueller (eds), 147–57. Amsterdam: Elsevier.

Corbara, B. 1991. *L'Organization sociale et sa genése chez la fourmi Ectatomma Ruidum Roger*, PhD thesis, Université Paris XIII.

Corbara B., D. Fresneau, J. P. Lachaud, Y. Leclerc, G. Goodall 1986. An automated photographic technique for behavioural investigations of social insects. *Behavioural Processes* **13**, 237–49.

Corbara, B., J. P. Lachaud, D. Fresneau 1989. Individual variability, social structure and division of labour in the Ponerine Ant Ectatomma ruidum Roger Hymenoptera, Formicidae. *Ethology* **82**, 89–100.

Cournot, A. 1838. *Recherches sur les principes mathématiques de la théorie des richesses.* Paris.

Crawford, V. P. & H. Haller 1990. Learning how to cooperate: optimal play in repeated coordination games. *Econometrica* **58**(3) 571–95.

Cyert, R. M. & J. G. March 1970. *Processus de décision dans l'entreprise.* Paris: Dunod.

Darwin, C. 1987. *The origin of species.* New York: New American Library.

Dolado, J. J. 1992. Qualitative simulation and system dynamics. *System Dynamics Review*, **8**(1), 55–81.

Doran, J. E. 1981. Multi-actor systems and the Maya collapse. In *Congres de l'Union Internationale des Sciences Prehistoriques and Protohistoriques*, 191-200. Colloquium 5 on data management and mathematical methods in archaeology (preproceedings).

Doran, J. E. 1982. A computational model of sociocultural systems. In *Theory and explanation in archaeology*, C. Renfrew, M. J. Rowlands, B. A. Segraves (eds), 375–88. New York: Academic.

Doran, J. E. 1987. Anthropological archeology, computational modelling and expert systems. In *Quantitative research in archeology: progress and prospects*, M. Aldenderfer (ed.), 73–88. London: Sage.

REFERENCES

Doran, J. E. 1989. Distributed artificial intelligence and the modelling of socio-cultural systems. In *Intelligent systems in human context: development, implications and applications*, L. Murray & J. Richardson (eds), 71–91. Oxford: Oxford University Press.

Doran, J. E. 1990. Computer-based simulation and formal modelling in archaeology: a review. In *Mathematics and information science in archaeology: a flexible framework*, A.Voorips (ed.). Studies in Modern Archaeology, vol. III, 93–114. Bonn: HOLOS-verlag.

Doran, J. E. (in press). DAI and emergent social complexity. In *Proceedings of the Conference on Dynamical Modelling and Human Systems*, Cambridge, December 1990, S van der Leeuw (ed.). Edinburgh: Edinburgh University Press..

Doran, J. E. 1992. A computational investigation of three models of specialization, exchange and social complexity. In *Representations in archaeology*, J-C. Gardin & C. S. Peebles (eds), 315–29. Bloomington: Indiana University Press.

Doran, J. E. & M. Palmer (in press). The EOS project: modelling prehistoric sociocultural trajectories. *Proceedings of the First European Symposium on Computing in Archaeology*, Saint-Germain-en-Laye, France, November 1991.

Doran J. E., H. Carvajal, Y. J. Choo, Y. Li 1991. The MCS Multi-agent Testbed: developments and experiments. In *Cooperating knowledge based systems 1990*, Proceedings of the International Working Conference on Cooperating Knowledge Based Systems, University of Keele, October 1990, S. M. Deen (ed.), 240–51. Berlin: Springer-Verlag.

Doyal, L. & I. Gough 1991. *A theory of human needs*. Basingstoke: Macmillan Education.

Drogoul A. & J. Ferber 1992. Multi-agent simulation as a tool for modeling societies: application to social differentiation in ant colonies. Paper presented at the MAAMAW 92, to be published as *Decentralized AI* vol. IV, C. Castelfranchi and E. Werner (eds). The Hague: North-Holland.

Drogoul A., J. Ferber, B. Corbara, D. Fresneau 1991. A behavioral simulation model for the study of emergent social structures. In *Proceedings of ECAL 91*, 161–70. Cambridge, Mass.: MIT Press.

Duncan, R. 1972. Characteristics of organizational environments and perceived environmental uncertainty. *Administrative Science Quarterly* **17**(3), 313–27.

Durfee, E. H., V. R. Lesser, D. D. Corkill 1987a. Coherent cooperation among communicating problem-solvers. *IEEE Transactions in Computers* **C36**, 1275–91.

Durfee, E. H., V. R. Lesser,D. D. Corkill 1987b. Cooperation through communication in a problem-solving network. In *Distributed artificial intelligence*, M. N. Huhns (ed.), 29–58. San Mateo, Cal.: Morgan Kaufmann.

Durham, W. H. 1991. *Coevolution: genes, culture, and human diversity*. Stanford, Cal.: Stanford University Press.

Dyson-Hudson R. & E. A. Smith 1978. Human territoriality: an ecological reassessment. *American Anthropologist* **80**, 21–41.

Eigen, M. & P. Schuster 1979. *The hypercycle: a principle of natural self-organization*. Berlin: Springer.

REFERENCES

Ennals, R. 1985. *Artificial intelligence applications to logical reasoning and historical research.* New York: John Wiley.

Entwisle, B. 1991. Micro–macro theoretical linkages in social demography. In Macro-micro linkages in sociology, J. Huber (ed.), Newbury Park, Cal.: Sage.

Fay, C. 1990. Systemes halieutiques et éspaces de pouvoirs: transformation des droits et des pratiques de pêche dans le Delta Central du Niger (Mali), 1920–1980, *Cahiers Sciences Humaines* **25** (1–2), 213–21.

Ferber, J. 1989. *Objets et agents: une étude des structures de representation et communication en intelligence artificielle.* These d'etat, Paris 6.

Flannery, K. 1968. Archaeological systems theory and early Mesoamerica. In *Anthropological archaeology in the Americas,* B. J. Meggars (ed.), 67–87. Washington DC: Anthropological Society of Washington.

Flannery, K. (ed.) 1986. *Guilá Naquitz: Archaic foraging and early agriculture in Oaxaca, Mexico.* New York: Academic.

Flannery, K. & J. Marcus 1983. *The cloud people.* San Diego, Cal.: Academic.

Flannery, K., J. Marcus, R. G. Reynolds 1989. *The flocks of the wamani.* San Diego, Cal.: Academic.

Fogel, D. B. 1993. On the philosophical differences between evolutionary algorithms and genetic algorithms. Paper presented at the Second Annual Conference on Evolutionary Programming, San Diego, Cal., 26–27 February.

Gleik, J. 1987. *Chaos: making a new science.* New York: Basic Books.

Forrester, J. 1968. *Principles of systems.* Cambridge, Mass: Wright-Allen Press.

Fox, B. & P. Glynn 1989. Simulating discounted costs. *Management Science* **35**(11), 1297–1315.

Freeman, S., M. Walker, R. Borden, B. Latané 1975. Diffusion of responsibility and restaurant tipping: Cheaper by the bunch. *Personality and Social Psychology Bulletin* **1**, 584–7.

Friedman, M. 1953. *Essays in positive economics.* Chicago: University of Chicago Press.

Galbraith, J. R. 1977. *Organization design.* London: Addison-Wesley.

Galliers, J. R. 1988. A strategic framework for multi-agent cooperative dialogue. In *Proceedings of the 8th European Conference on Artificial Intelligence,* 415–20. London: Pitman.

Galliers, J. R. 1991. Modelling autonomous belief revision in dialogue. In *Decentralized AI-2,* Y. Demazeau & J. P. Mueller (eds), 231–45. Amsterdam: Elsevier.

Gaspar, G. 1990. Communication and belief changes in a society of agents. Paper presented at Fifth Rocky Mountain Conference on Pragmatics in AI, Las Cruces (USA), 28–30 June.

Gaspar, G. & H. Coelho 1991. A modular architecture for agents living in society. INESC research Report.

Gasser, L. 1988. Distribution and coordination of tasks among intelligent agents. In *Proceedings of the 1st Scandinavian Conference on Artificial Intelligence,* 177–92. Amsterdam: Elsevier.

Griffin, L. J. 1992. Temporality events and explanation in historical sociology. *So-*

REFERENCES

ciological Methods and Research **20**(4), 403–27.

Guthrie, R. D. 1984. Mosaics, allelochemicals and nutrients: an ecological theory of late Pleistocene extinctions. In *Quaternary extinctions: a prehistoric revolution*, P. S. Martin & R. G. Klein (eds), 259–98. Tucson: University of Arizona Press.

Hammond, K. J. 1986. CHEF: a model of case-based planning. In *Proceedings of the 6th Conference of the American Association of Artificial Intelligence*, 267–71. San Mateo, CA: Morgan Kaufmann.

Herrnstein, R. J. 1991. Experiments on stable suboptimality in individual behavior. *American Economic Review* **81**(2) 360–4.

Hiller, H. 1991. Managing qualified nuclear decommissioning trust funds under uncertainty. *Energy Journal* **12**, 191–204.

Hillier B. & J. Hanson 1984. *The social logic of space*. Cambridge: Cambridge University Press.

Hillier B. & J. Hanson 1987. A second paradigm. *Architecture and Behaviour* **3**(3), 197–203.

Hillier B. & A. Penn 1992. Dense civilizations: the shape of cities in the 21st century. *Applied Energy* **43**, 44–66.

Hillier B. & A. Penn 1993. Natural movement: or, Configuration and attraction in urban pedestrian movement. *Environment and Planning B: Planning and Design* **20**, 29–66.

Hodder, I. (ed.) 1978. *Simulation studies in archaeology*. Cambridge: Cambridge University Press.

Hodder, I. 1985. Post-processual archaeology. In advances in archaeological method and theory, M. Schiffer (ed.), vol. VIII: 1–25. New York: Academic.

Hoffman, E., V. Jacob, J. Mardsen, A. Whinston 1986. Artificial intelligence in economics: expert systems modelling of microeconomic systems. In *Artificial intelligence in economics and management*, L. Pau (ed.), 1–9. Amsterdam: North-Holland.

Hogarth, R. 1986. Generalization in decision research: the role of formal models. *IEEE Transactions on Systems, Man and Cybernetics*, SMC–**16**(3), 439–49.

Hogeweg P. & B. Hesper 1985. Socio-informatic processes: MIRROR modeling methodology. *Journal of Theoretical Biology* **113**, 311–30.

Holland, J. H. 1975. *Adaptation in natural and artificial systems*. Ann Arbor, Mich.: University of Michigan Press.

Holland, J. H. & J. H. Miller 1991. Artificial adaptive agents in economic theory. *American Economic Review* **81**(2), 365–70.

Hosler D., J. A. Sabloff , D. Runge 1977. Simulation model development: a case study of the Classic Maya collapse. In *Social process in Maya prehistory*, N. Hammond (ed.), 552–90. London: Academic.

Isaac, G. 1978. The food-sharing behaviour of proto-human hominids. *Scientific American* **238**, 90–108.

Jackson, J. M. & B. Latané 1981. All alone in front of all those people: stage fright as a function of number and type of co-performers and audience. *Journal of Personality and Social Psychology*, **40**, 73–85.

REFERENCES

Johnson A. & T. K. Earle 1987. *The evolution of human societies: from forager group to agrarian state.* Stanford, Cal.: Stanford University Press.

Johnson-Laird, P. N. 1983. *Mental models: towards a cognitive science of language, inference and consciousness.* Cambridge: Cambridge University Press.

Johnson-Laird, P. N. 1988 Freedom and constraint in creativity. In *The nature of creativity: contemporary psychological perspectives*, R. J. Sternberg (ed.), 202–19. Cambridge: Cambridge University Press.

Kassibo, B. 1990. L'Organization sociale de la pêche dans le delta central du niger: genèse et évolution des systèmes de production halieutique. *Actes de l'atelier IER-ORSTOM*, Bamako.

Koyama, S. & D. H. Thomas (eds) 1981. *Affluent foragers: Pacific Coasts East and West.* Senri Ethnological Studies 9. National Museum of Ethnology, Osaka.

Krishnamurthi, L. & A. Rangaswamy 1987. The equity estimator for marketing research. *Marketing Science* **6**(4), 336–57.

Lachaud J. P. & D. Fresneau 1987. Social regulation in Ponerine Ants. In *From individual to collective behaviour in social insects*, Experientia Supplementum 54, 197–217. Basle: Birkhäuser Verlag.

Laë, R. 1990. Les Pêcheries artisanales du secteur de Mopti: ressource, communautes de pêcheurs et strategies d'exploitation. *Actes de l'atelier IER-ORSTOM*, Bamako.

Lant, T. & S. Mezias 1990. Managing discontinuous change: a simulation study of organizational learning and entrepreneurship. *Strategic Management Journal* **11**, 147–79.

Latané, B. 1981. The psychology of social impact. *American Psychologist*, **36**, 343–65.

Latané, B. 1991. *Dynamic social impact and the group mind.* Columbus, Ohio: Society for Experimental Social Psychology.

Latané, B. 1992. Strength from weakness: The fate of opinion minorities in spatially distributed groups. Unpublished paper.

Latané, B. & J. Dabbs 1975. Sex, group size and helping in three cities. *Sociometry* **38**, 180–94.

Latané, B. & J. Darley 1970. *The unresponsive bystander: why doesn't he help?* New York: Appleton-Century-Crofts (now Prentice-Hall).

Latané, B. & S. Harkins 1976. Cross-modality matches suggest anticipated stage fright a multiplicative power function of audience size and status. *Perception and Psychophysics* **20**, 482–8.

Latané, B. & T. L'Herrou 1992. Social clustering in the conformity game: dynamic social impact in electronic groups. Unpublished paper.

Latané, B. & S. Nida 1980. Social impact theory and group influence: a social engineering perspective. In *Psychology of group influence*, P. Paulus (ed.). Hillsdale, NJ: Lawrence Erlbaum.

Latané, B. & S. Nida 1981. Ten years of research on group size and helping. *Psychological Bulletin* **89**, 308–24.

Latané, B. & A. Nowak 1992. Self-organizing social systems: necessary and suffi-

REFERENCES

cient conditions for the emergence of clusters and polarization. Unpublished paper.

Latané, B. & A. Nowak 1994. Attitudes as catastrophes: from dimensions to categories with increasing involvement. In *Dynamical systems in social psychology*, R. Vallacher & A. Nowak (eds). New York: Academic.

Latané, B. & S. Wolf 1981. The social impact of majorities and minorities. *Psychological Review* **88**, 438–53.

Latané, B., H. Cappell, V. Joy 1970. Social deprivation, housing density and gregariousness in rats. *Journal of Comparative and Physiological Psychology* **70**, 221–7.

Latané, B., J. Liu, A. Nowak, M. Bonevento, L. Zheng 1992. Distance matters: physical space and social interaction. Unpublished paper.

Latané, B., A. Nowak, J. Liu 1992. Measuring emergent social phenomena: dynamism, polarization, and clustering as order parameters in dynamic social systems. Unpublished paper.

Latané, B., A. Nowak, J. Szamrej 1988. Computer simulations of social impact. Paper presented at the Eleventh International Conference on Groups, Networks, and Organizations, Nags Head, NC.

Latané, B., K. Williams, S. Harkins 1979. Many hands make light the work: causes and consequences of social loafing. *Journal of Personality and Social Psychology*, **37**, 822–32.

Lee, R. & I. DeVore (eds) 1968. *Man the hunter*. Chicago: Aldine.

Lesser, V. R. & D. D. Corkill 1987. Distributed problem-solving. In *Encyclopedia of artificial intelligence*, S. C. Shapiro (ed.), 245–51. New York: John Wiley.

Levesque, H., P. H. Cohen, J. H. T. Nunes 1990. On acting together. In *Proceedings of the 9th Conference of the American Association of Artificial Intelligence*, 94–9. San Mateo, Cal.: Morgan Kaufmann.

Lewenstein, M., B. Nowak, B. Latané 1992. Statistical mechanics of social impact. *Physical Review A***45**, 1–14.

Lindauer, M. 1986. Communication and orientation in honeybees. *Monitore Zoologico Italiano*N.S.**20**, 371–9.

Lowe, J. W. G. 1985. *The dynamics of Apocalypse: a systems simulation of the classic Maya collapse*. Albuquerque: University of New Mexico Press.

Lynch, K. 1960. *The image of the city*. Cambridge, Mass.: MIT Press.

Mack, D. 1991. *An investigation using computer models into the relationships between task uncertainty, complexity and organization*. MSc thesis, University of Essex.

Malone, T. W. 1987. Modeling coordination in organizations and markets. *Management Science* **33**(10), 1317–32.

March, J. G., & J. Olsen 1986. Garbage can models of decision-making in organizations. In *Ambiguity and command*, J. G. March & R. Weissinger-Baylon (eds), 11–35. Marshfield, Mass.: Pitman.

March, J. G. & R. Weissinger-Baylon (eds) 1986. *Ambiguity and command: organizational perspectives on military decision-making*. Marchfield, Mass.: Pitman.

Marimon, R., E. McGrattan, T. J. Sargent 1990. Money as a medium of exchange

REFERENCES

in an economy with artificially intelligent agents. *Journal of Economic Dynamics and Control* **14**, 329–73.

Martial, von F. 1990. Interactions among autonomous planning agents. In *Decentralized AI*, Y. Demazeau & J. P. Mueller (eds), 105–19. Amsterdam: Elsevier.

Masuch, M. & P. Lapotin 1989. Beyond garbage cans: an AI model of organizational choice. *Administrative Science Quarterly* **34**(1), 38–67.

Meadows, D., J. Richardson, G. Bruckmann 1982. *Groping in the dark*. New York: John Wiley.

Mellars, P. A. 1985. The ecological basis of social complexity in the upper paleolithic of Southwestern France. In *Prehistoric hunter–gatherers: the emergence of cultural complexity*, T. D. Price & J. A. Brown (eds), 271–97. New York: Academic.

Meyer, R., E. Johnson, K. Keller, R. Staelin 1989. Information overload and the nonrobustness of linear models. *Journal of Consumer Research* 15(4), 498–508.

Miller, R. M. 1968a. Markets as logic programs. In *Artificial intelligence in economics and management*, L. F. Pau (ed.). Amsterdam: Elsevier.

Miller, R. M. 1968b. On distributing the intelligence of economic processes: l'éonomique et l'intelligence artificielle. Paper presented at the Conference Internationale IFAC. 31 August – 4 September.

Mitchell, T. M. 1978. *Version spaces: an approach to concept learning*. PhD dissertation, Stanford University.

Mithen, S. J. 1989. Evolutionary theory and post-processual archaeology. *Antiquity* **63**: 483–94.

Mithen, S. J. 1990. *Thoughtful foragers: a study of prehistoric decision making*. Cambridge: Cambridge University Press.

Mithen, S. J. 1991. A cybernetic wasteland? Rationality, emotion and Mesolithic foraging. *Proceedings of the Prehistoric Society* **57**(2), 1–9.

Möhring, M. 1990. *MIMOSE: Eine funktionale Sprache zur Beschreibung und Simulation individuellen Verhaltens in interagierenden Populationen*. PhD thesis, Universität Koblenz.

Möhring, M. & V. Strotmann 1993. Modelling and simulation of multilevel models in the social sciences with MIMOSE. In *Catastrophe, chaos and self-organization in social systems*, K. G. Troitzsch (ed.), 47–80. Berlin: Akademie-Verlag.

Monteiro, J. C. 1989. Model of a society of intelligent systems. LNEC Report (in Portuguese).

Mosekilde, E., D. R. Rasmussen, T. S. Sorensen 1983. Self-organization and stochastic re-causalization in system dynamics models. Paper presented at the 1983 International System Dynamics Conference, Pine Manor College, Chestnut Hill, Mass.

Mosimann, J. E. & P. S. Martin 1975. Simulating overkill by Palaeoindians. *American Scientist* **63**, 305–13.

Murray, L. & J. Richardson (eds) 1989. *Intelligent systems in a human context: development, implications and applications*. Oxford: Oxford University Press.

Newell, A & H. Simon 1976. Computer science as empirical inquiry: symbols and search. *Communications of the ACM* **19**(3), 113–26.

REFERENCES

Nowak, A. & B. Latané 1994. Social dilemmas exist in space. In N. Schulz, W. Albers, R. N. Mueller (eds), *Social dilemmas and cooperation*. Heidelberg: Springer-Verlag.

Nowak, A., J. Szamrej, B. Latané 1990. From private attitude to public opinion: a dynamic theory of social impact. *Psychological Review* **97**, 362–76.

O'Leary, D. 1988. Methods of validating expert systems. *Interfaces* **18**(6), 72–9.

Padgett, J. 1980. Managing garbage can hierarchies, *Administrative Science Quarterly*, **25**(3), 583–604.

Palmer M. & J. Doran (in press). Contrasting models of Upper Palaeolithic social dynamics: a Distributed Artificial Intelligence approach.In *Computer Applications and Quantitative Methods in Archaeology, 1992*, J. Andresen, T. Madsen, I. Scollar (eds). Aarhus: Aarhus University Press.

Parunak, Van Dyke H. 1987. Manufacturing experience with the contract net. In *Distributed artificial intelligence*, M. N. Huhns (ed.), 285–310. San Mateo, Cal.: Kaufmann.

Parunak, Van Dyke H. 1990. Distributed AI and manufacturing control: some issues and insights. In *Decentralized AI*, Y. Demazeau & J. P. Mueller (eds), 81–101. Amsterdam: Elsevier.

Pau, L. 1986. *Artificial intelligence in economics and management*. Amsterdam, North-Holland.

Pave, A. 1989. Object centered representation and problems related to living systems in nature. In *Artificial intelligence in numerical and symbolic simulation*, A. Pave & G. C. Vansteenkiste (eds), 82–103. Lyon: Ecole Normale Superieure de Lyon.

Perrow, C. 1967. A framework for comparative analysis of organizations. *American Sociological Review* **32**(2), 194–208.

Piaget, J. 1977. *The development of thought: equilibration of cognitive structures*. New York: Viking.

Plott, C. R. 1982. Industrial organization theory and experimental science. *Journal of Economic Literature* **20**, 1485–1527.

Pooch U. W. & J. A. Wall 1993. *Discrete event simulation: a practical approach*. Boca Raton, Fla.: CRC Press.

Price, T. D. 1985. Affluent foragers of Mesolithic southern Scandinavia. In *Prehistoric hunter–gatherers: the emergence of cultural complexity*, T. D. Price & J. Brown (eds), 341–63. New York: Academic.

Price, T. D. & J. Brown (eds) 1985. *Prehistoric hunter–gatherers: the emergence of cultural complexity*. New York: Academic.

Prigogine, I. & G. Nicolis 1977. *Self-organization in nonequilibrium systems: from dissipative structures to order through fluctuations*. New York: John Wiley.

Prigogine, I. & I. Stengers 1984. *Order out of chaos: man's new dialogue with nature*, New York: Bantam.

Quadagno, J. & S. J. Knapp 1992. Have historical sociologists forsaken theory? *Sociological Methods and Research* **20**(4), 481–507.

Quensiere, J. 1990. Systemique et pluridisciplinarite: l'éxemple du programme

REFERENCES

d'étude de la pêche dans le delta interieur du Niger. In C. Mullon (ed.), *Seminfor ORSTOM* **4**, 560–81.

Radzicki, M. 1988. Institutional dynamics: an extension of the institutionalist approach to socioeconomic analysis. *Journal of Economic Issues* **22**(3), 633–65.

Radzicki, M. 1990. Institutional dynamics, deterministic chaos and self-organizing systems. *Journal of Economic Issues* **24**(1), 57–102.

Ramstad, Y. 1986. A pragmatist's quest for holistic knowledge: the scientific methodology of John R. Commons. *Journal of Economic Issues* **20**(4), 1067–1105.

Randers, J. 1973. *Conceptualizing dynamic models of social systems: lessons from the study of social change*. PhD thesis, Alfred P. Sloan School of Management, MIT.

Renfrew A. C. 1987. Problems in the modelling of socio-cultural systems. *European Journal of Operational Research* **30**, 179–92.

Renfrew A. C. (in press). Dynamic modelling in archaeology: what, when and where? In *Proceedings of the Conference on Dynamical Modelling and Human Systems*, Cambridge, December 1990, S. van der Leeuw (ed.). Edinburgh: Edinburgh University Press.

Renfrew, C. & K. Cooke (eds) 1979. *Transformations: mathematical approaches to culture change*. New York: Academic.

Reynolds, R. 1981. An adaptive computer simulation model of the acquisition of incipient agriculture in prehistoric Oaxaca, Mexico. In *Manejo de datos y Metodos Matematicos de Arqueolo gia*, G. L. Cowgill, R. Whallon, B. S. Ottaway (eds), 202–16. Paris: Union Internacional de Ciencias Prehistoricas y Protohistoricas.

Reynolds, R. G. 1986. An adaptive computer model for the evolution of plant collecting and early agriculture in the Eastern Valley of Oaxaca, Mexico. In *Quila Naquitz: archaic foraging and early agriculture in Oaxaca, Mexico*, K. V. Flannery (ed.), 439–500. San Diego, Cal.: Academic.

Reynolds, R. G. & W. Sverdlick 1993. Solving problems in hierarchical systems using cultural algorithms. Paper presented at the Second Annual Conference on Evolutionary Programming, San Diego, Cal., 26–7 February.

Rosenschein, J. S. & M. R. Genesereth 1988. Deals among rational agents. In *The ecology of computation*, B. A. Huberman (ed.), 117–32. Amsterdam: Elsevier.

Rowley-Conwy, P. A. 1983. Sedentary hunters: the Ertebølle example. In *Hunter–gatherer economy in prehistory*, G. N. Bailey (ed.), 111–26. Cambridge: Cambridge University Press.

Rozenblit, J., J. Hu, T. Kim, B. Zeigler 1990. Knowledge-based design and simulation environment: fundamental concepts and implementation. *Journal of the Operational Research Society* **41**(6), 475–89.

Sabloff, J. A. (ed.) 1978. *Simulations in archaeology*. Albuquerque: University of New Mexico Press.

Sabloff, J. A. 1990. *The new archaeology and the ancient Maya*. New York: Scientific American Library.

Sack, R. D. 1986. *Human territoriality*. Cambridge: Cambridge University Press.

Savatsky, K. S. & R. G. Reynolds 1989. A hierarchical model of the evolution of co-

REFERENCES

operation in cultural systems. *Biosystems* **23**, 261–79.

Schank, R. C. & R. P. Abelson 1977. *Scripts, plans, goals and understanding*. Hillsdale, N.J.: Lawrence Erlbaum.

Scheller, W. 1990. Using computer simulation in the management of missile production programs. *Industrial Management* **32**(5), 13–16.

Sernadas, C., H. Coelho, G. Gaspar 1987. Communicating knowledge systems: big talk among small systems. *Applied Artificial Intelligence* **1**(3 & 4), 233–60 and 315–35.

Shannon R. E. 1975. *Systems simulation: the art and science*. Englewood Cliffs, NJ: Prentice-Hall.

Shapiro, C. 1989. Theories of oligopoly behavior. In *Handbook of industrial organization*, Vol. I., R. Schmalensee & R. Dwilling (eds), 229–414. Amsterdam: Elsevier.

Shennan, S. 1992. Tradition, rationality and cultural transmission. In *Processual & post-processual archaeology: the current debate*, R. Preucel (ed.), 197–208. Carbondale, Il.: Center of Archaeological Investigations.

Simon, H. A. 1981. *The sciences of the artificial*. Cambridge, Mass.: MIT Press.

Simon, H. A. 1983. *Models of bounded rationality: behavioral economics and business organization*, vol. II. Cambridge, Mass.: MIT Press.

Smith, R. G. 1980. The contract net protocol: high level communication and control in a distributed problem solver. *IEEE Transactions on Computers*, **C–29**(12):1104–13.

Smith, V. L. 1982. Microeconomic systems as an experimental science. *American Economic Review* **72**, 923–55.

Sparkes, P. 1989. Simulation in the finance retail and services sectors. *Management Science* **33**(9), 20–27.

Star, S. 1986. Trader: a knowledge-based system for trading in markets. Paper presented at L'Economique et l'intelligence artificielle, Conference Internationale IFAC, 31 August–4 September.

Sterman, J. D. 1987. Testing behavioral simulation models by direct experiment. *Management Science* **33**(12), 1572–92.

Sterman, J. D. 1988. Deterministic chaos in models of human behavior: methodological issues and experimental results. *System Dynamic Review* **4**, 48–178.

Sterman, J. D. 1989. Deterministic chaos in an experimental system. *Journal of Economic Behavior and Organization* **12**(1), 1–28.

Theraulaz G., S. Goss, J. Gervet, J. L. Deneubourg 1991. Task differentiation in Polistes wasp colonies: a model for self-organizing groups of robots. In *From animals to animats*, J-A. Meyer (ed.), 346–55. Cambridge Mass.: MIT Press.

Thomas, D. 1972. A computer simulation model of Great Basin Shoshonean settlement patterns. In *Models in archaeology*, D. Clarke (ed.), 671–704. London: Methuen.

Thomas, D. H. 1973. An empirical test for Steward's model of Great Basin Settlement patterns. *American Antiquity* **38**, 155–76.

Vasani, S. 1993. *Learning the concept of cooperation*. MSc thesis, Wayne State Univer-

REFERENCES

sity, Detroit, Mich.

Villa, P. 1991. Middle Pleistocene prehistory in southwestern Europe: the state of our knowledge and ignorance. *Journal of Anthropological Research* **47**, 193–217.

Volterra, V. 1926. Variations and fluctuations of the number of individuals of animal species living together. In *Animal ecology*, R. N. Chapman (ed.), New York: McGraw-Hill.

Voorips, A. 1987. Formal and statistical models in archeology. In *Quantitative research in archaeology: progress and prospects*, M. Aldenderfer (ed.), 61–72. London: Sage.

Weidlich, W. & G. Haag 1983. *Concepts and models of a quantitative sociology: the dynamics of interacting populations*. Springer Series in Synergetics 14. Berlin: Springer.

Weidlich, W. & G. Haag (eds) 1988. *Interregional migration: dynamic theory and comparative analysis*. Berlin: Springer.

Werner, E. 1989. Cooperating agents: aA unified theory of communication and social structure. In *Distributed artificial intelligence*, vol. II, M. N. Huhns & L. Gasser (eds), 3–36. San Mateo, Cal.: Morgan Kaufmann.

Werner E. & Y. Demazeau 1992. *Decentralized AI* vol. III. The Hague: North-Holland.

Whitelaw, T. M. 1989. *The social organization of space in hunter–gatherer communities: some implications for social inference in archaeology*. Ph.D thesis, University of Cambridge.

Willey, G. R. & D. B. Shimkin, D.B. 1973. The Mayan collapse: a summary view. In *The classic Maya collapse*, T. P. Culbert (ed.). Albuquerque: University of New Mexico Press.

Winograd, T. & F. Flores 1986. *Understanding computers and cognition: a new foundation for design*. Norwood, NJ: Ablex.

Wobst, H. M. 1974. Boundary conditions for Palaeolithic social systems: a simulation approach. *American Antiquity* **39**, 147–78.

Wobst, H. M. 1978. The archaeo-ethnology of hunter–gatherers, or the tyranny of the ethnographic record in archaeology. *American Antiquity* **43**, 303–9.

Wolf, S. & B. Latané 1983. Majority and minority influence on restaurant preferences. *Journal of Personality and Social Psychology* **45**, 282–92.

Wolf, S. & B. Latané 1985. Conformity, innovation, and the psychosocial law. In Perspectives on minority influence., S. Moscovici, G. Mugny & E. Van Avermaet (eds). Cambridge: Cambridge University Press.

Wolfram, S. 1986. *Theory and applications of cellular automata*. Singapore: World Scientific.

Woodburn, J. 1982. Egalitarian societies. *Man* **17**, 431–51.

Zeigler B. P. 1976. *Theory of modelling and simulation*. New York: John Wiley (reissued by Krieger, Malabar, Fla., 1985).

Zeigler, B. P. 1990. *Object oriented simulation with hiearchical, modular models*. New York: Academic.

Zipf, G. K. 1949. *Human behavior and the principle of least effort*. New York: Hafner.

Index

Abbott, A. 36
Abelson, R. 187
Aborigines 170, 171
ABSIM 170
abstraction 10, 22, 203
actors 20, 22–5, 27, 29, 32–5, 133
adaptive process 243
Africa 95, 96
agency 15, 132
aggression 17, 263, 267, 280
agriculture 149, 171, 172, 175, 176, 220, 221
AI 3, 9, 10, 11, 17, 26, 32, 186–8, 200, 217, 264, 270, 281
Aldenderfer, M. 163, 169, 170, 174, 177, 178, 180, 182–4
alleles 220
Alterman, R. 267
Aminzade, R. 36
analogy 22
Anderson, P. 23, 24, 26, 28, 29
ant 5, 15, 17, 126, 137, 138, 140, 141
anthill 126
anthropology 1, 16, 142, 144, 164
anti-cognitive 271
archaeology 1, 16, 19, 31, 163, 165, 166, 177, 196
architecture 32, 85–124, 200, 253, 254, 262, 265

art 2, 14, 166, 194, 198
attitude 63–8, 74–84, 150, 152, 155, 156, 186, 265, 267, 268, 276
auction 31
autocatalytic 132
autocorrelation 52
automata 65, 83
automaton 69, 77

Bailey, G. 166
Baligh, H. 28, 30
Banerjee, S. 28, 29
behaviour 2–13, 17, 19, 20, 23, 27–40, 63–86, 96, 117, 125–38, 141–3, 146, 151, 152, 156, 160, 162, 165–70, 175–81, 184–92, 195–8, 201–208, 217–22, 226, 229, 241–5, 250–53, 258
belief 11, 28, 32, 38, 187, 202, 211, 219–29, 231–40, 267, 276–81
Berkes, F. 142
Bertrand, J. 242
Bhaskar, R. 197
Binford, L. 168, 174
biomass 146, 148, 149, 153, 160
biotope 148–56
blackboard 148
Blanning, R. 27, 28, 30
Bloch, M. 195
Blundell, R. 19

INDEX

Boden, M.   187, 188
Bond, A.   192, 197, 264
Bousquet, F.   17, 142, 146
Boyd, R.   188, 189, 220
browser   139
burials   164, 167

Caldas, J.   17, 241, 243
Cambier, C.   142, 146
Caniglia, A.   19
Carley, K.   25
Carlson, D.   28, 32
Castelfranchi, C.   17, 131, 263, 266, 268, 272, 279, 281
causality   38
causation   21, 34, 37
cause   34, 127, 180, 230, 238
cave   164, 165, 171, 177, 180, 194
Cedric, V.   19
ceremony   229, 230
Chaharbaghi, K.   19
Chamberlin, E.   242, 251
chaos   9, 20, 34, 36, 39
Chernenko, I.   41, 42, 43, 44, 45, 46
chiefdoms   32
City   106
city   5, 7, 8, 87, 88, 115, 117
clobbering   209, 216, 217
Coelho, H.   17, 241, 243, 244, 253
cognition   9, 15, 186, 187, 195–7, 201, 203
cognitive   15, 17, 25, 26, 28, 86, 130, 131, 177, 186–9, 192–7, 200, 201, 202, 204, 216, 217, 218, 263–7, 271, 273, 276, 277, 281, 282
Cohen, M. D.   23, 24
Cohen, M. W.   131, 193–6, 203, 265, 269, 278
Collins, R.   129
communication   15, 25, 32, 33, 66, 130, 157, 158, 184, 197, 222, 226–9, 264, 265
community   15, 20, 21, 29, 32, 115,

182, 202, 204, 207, 209, 210, 213–16, 230
competition   45, 53, 149, 242, 249, 250, 252, 254, 256, 258, 262, 280
conflict   3, 23, 25, 30, 34, 203, 216, 274, 275, 280, 281
consensus   23, 25, 178, 185
consumer   19, 246, 247
Conte, R.   17, 131, 263, 266, 268, 272, 275, 276, 280, 281
contingency   30
contract   32, 204, 264
Cooke, K.   163
co-operation   32, 53, 57, 60, 203, 236, 238–50, 254, 256, 258, 262, 263, 265, 268, 275, 280
Corbara, B.   137
Corkill, D.   146, 264
Cournot, A.   242
crossover   234, 235
crowding   64, 203, 209
culture   2, 4, 27, 28, 32, 125, 164, 175–7, 188–90, 219, 220, 231
Cyert, R.   244

Dalton, N.   16, 85
Darley, J.   64
Darwin, C.   53
Demazeau, Y.   130
demography   178
disorganization   35
distributed artificial intelligence (DAI)   9, 10, 13, 17, 130, 146, 162, 186, 192, 197, 243, 244, 263
Doran, J.   1, 3, 16, 17, 28, 31–3, 62, 129, 131, 181, 186, 187, 191, 192, 195–7
Doyal, L.   117
Drogoul, A.   17, 126, 133, 137, 140
Duncan, R.   30
duopoly   243–59
Durfee, E.   264
Durham, W.   219, 221

302

INDEX

Dyson-Hudson, R. 216

Earle, T. 193
ecology 143, 164, 189
economics 1, 19, 33–5, 116, 243, 262
economy 84, 97, 101–117, 143, 168, 195, 216, 220
ecosystem 143
ecotone 169
education 61, 76
efficiency 25, 30, 128, 172, 174, 177, 182–5, 216
egalitarian 167, 193
emergence 12, 18, 31, 63–84, 130–32, 194, 195, 229, 235, 282
Ennals, R. 21, 28
entropy 35, 52, 53
EOS 186, 192, 196–208, 218
equilibrium 35, 49, 64, 67, 83, 241, 242, 249, 251
ethnology 130
ethology 126, 130
evolution 17, 21, 29, 31, 35, 38, 40–42, 44–62, 79, 81–6, 115, 116, 126, 149, 156, 160, 164, 188–90, 219–21, 229, 239, 250, 252, 258–62
experiment 13, 17, 22, 24, 36, 62, 85, 89, 90, 118, 120, 122, 126, 129, 141, 146, 157, 192, 197, 198, 200, 202, 207, 215, 237–9, 244–52, 257, 258, 262, 282

Feldman, R. 220
Ferber, J. 17, 126, 133, 137, 146
Fischer, G. 24, 26
fishing 17, 153, 161
Flannery, K. 169, 171, 172, 175, 221, 229, 230
flexibility 50, 69, 197
Flores, F. 265
Fogel, D. 229

food 2, 7, 128, 136, 138–41, 170, 173, 182, 185, 194, 230
forager 170, 177, 183, 185
Forrester, J. 2
Fox, B. 19
Freeman, S. 64
Friedman, M. 243

Galbraith, J. 36
Galliers, J. 265, 267
games 242
Gaspar, G. 244, 253, 257
Gasser, L. 192, 197, 264
genes 189
Genesereth, M. 265
geometry 65, 89, 93
Gilbert, N. 1, 192
glaciation 177
Gleick, J. 68
Gough, I. 117
government 29
Griffin, L. 36
Guthrie, R. 182

Haag, G. 51, 61, 62
Hammond, K. 267
Hanson, J. 85, 89, 90, 95, 118
Harkins, S. 64
herding 229, 230
Herrnstein, R. 243
Hesper, B. 129
heuristics 118, 120, 122, 124, 188, 243, 247
hierarchies 208–217, 226, 233
Hillier, B. 85, 89, 90, 95, 116, 118
Hodder, L. 163, 178
Hoffman, E. 28, 31
Hogarth, R. 39
Hogeweg, P. 129
Holland, J. 219, 220, 229, 244
homeostasis 141
hominid 163, 165, 189
Hosler, D. 2, 3, 7, 10

303

INDEX

hunter–gatherer 16, 163–93, 220
hypercognitive 263, 265, 271, 281

ideology 84, 165, 179
intelligence 3, 9, 13, 16–19, 25–9, 37, 76, 130, 146, 162, 186, 189, 192, 195–7, 217, 243, 244, 263, 264
intention 32, 251
intentionality 269, 279, 281

Jackson, J. 64
Jefferson, D. 129
Johnson-Laird, P. 187, 188

Kassibo, B. 144, 156
kinship 232, 235–9
Knapp, S. 36
Koyama, S. 167
Krishnamurthi, L. 19

language 5, 10, 13, 15, 27, 51, 69, 133, 148, 166, 195–8, 244, 251–5
Lapotin, P. 20, 25, 26, 27
Latané, B. 16, 63, 64, 65, 66, 69, 71, 77, 79, 81, 84, 131
leadership 20, 251, 252
Lee, R. 167
Levesque, H. 131, 265, 269
Lewenstein, M. 64, 65, 81
Lindauer, M. 132
lithics 170
llamas 229, 230, 232, 234
logic 5, 9, 10, 24, 28, 85, 202
Lotka 127
Lynch, K. 86, 87, 116

Mack, D. 36
macro 12, 15–19, 45–8, 50–52, 55, 60–62, 64, 84, 126, 128, 130, 133, 141, 156, 157, 219–22, 235
Mali 17, 143
Malone, T. 36, 264

March, J. 23, 24, 244
Marcus, J. 221
Marimon, R. 244
markets 96, 241–58, 262
Markov 25, 179, 180
Masuch, M. 20, 25–7
Maya 2, 4
measurement 46, 64, 202
mechanism 25, 45, 51, 96, 125, 135, 254
Mellars, T. 192–8, 202, 203, 217
memory 51, 69, 86, 87, 120, 124, 125, 172, 184, 197, 200, 201
mesoamerican 2
Mesolithic 165, 167, 173, 174
metaphor 20, 26, 27
methodology 19, 30, 31, 33, 35–8, 127, 180, 243, 245, 282
Meyer, R. 19
Mezias, S. 20
microeconomics 144, 241
migration 148
MIMOSE 41, 47, 51, 62
mind 5, 16, 76, 116, 166, 187, 263, 266, 282
Mitchell, T. 221
Mithen, S. 16, 163, 169, 173, 177–83, 187, 195, 217
Möhring, M. 47, 51, 62
Monte Carlo 24, 26, 39, 74
Monteiro, J. 244
Morand, P. 142
Mosekilde, E. 35
Mosimann, J. 181
Mullon, C. 142

negentropy 35
Newell, A. 26, 27
Nicolis, G. 62
Nida, S. 64
Nowak, A. 16, 63–5, 69, 71, 76–9, 84, 131

INDEX

oligopoly 17, 241–3, 251
Olsen, J. 23, 24
organism 37, 129
organization 16, 19, 20, 23–7, 30–33, 36, 37, 64, 126, 135, 143, 146, 147, 152, 157, 159, 162, 165, 166, 168, 171, 179, 193, 195, 210

Padgett, J. 25
Palaeolithic 17, 131, 178, 192–218
Palmer, M. 69, 192
paradigm 229, 239
Parunak, V. 264, 269
Penn, A. 16, 85, 116
periodogram 52
Perrault, C. 278
Perrow, C. 30
phenotype 51, 220
Piaget, J. 28
Pleistocene 165, 181, 182
politics 271
Pooch, U. 8
precognitive 264–78, 280, 282
presocial 268, 271
prestige 2
Prigogine, I. 35, 62, 132
psychology 1, 19, 63, 68, 130, 186, 188

Quadagno, J. 36
Quensiere, J. 142, 143

Radzicki, M. 21, 33–6
Randers, J. 34
Randomness 68
randomness 68, 79, 118, 125
Rangaswamy, A. 19
reflexivity 15
Renfrew, A. 163, 195
Reynolds, R. 16, 163, 169–72, 175, 177–84, 187, 189, 191, 219, 220, 226, 234
Richerson, P. 188, 189, 220

ritual 2, 184, 229
robot 15, 270, 272, 275
Rosenschein, J. 265
Rowley-Conwy, P. 165, 167
Rozenblit, J. 19
rule-based 19, 28–30, 37, 39, 40, 118

Sabloff, J. 3, 4, 163
Sack, R. 216
Savatsky, K. 234
scheduling 172, 175
Scheller, W. 19
Schuster, P. 43, 44
sedentism 168, 194
semantics 247
Sernadas, C. 244
Séror, A. 16, 19
Shapiro, C. 242
Shennan, S. 188
Shimkin, D. 2
Simon, H. 26, 27, 149, 242
SITSIM 69–79, 82
Smith, R. 204, 216, 241, 244
sociogenesis 141
sociograms 141
sociology 19, 130, 142, 164
statistics 81, 82, 133, 174
Stengers, I. 35, 132
Sterman, J. 20, 35, 36
Strotmann, V. 47, 51, 62
structure 4, 5, 8–10, 13, 20, 21, 23–30, 32, 34, 38, 39, 53, 65, 69, 70, 87–91, 95, 96, 106, 108, 109, 111, 112, 116, 125, 128, 131, 141, 193, 198, 201, 220–27, 232, 235, 238–41, 254, 255, 272
subjectivism 265
subjectivity 117, 125
subsistence 163, 165, 168–70, 174, 177–9, 182, 185, 186, 221
sunãy 229–31, 235, 238, 239
supergames 242

305

INDEX

Szamrej 69

teamwork 32
territoriality 193, 216, 217
testbed 13, 192, 197–210, 212, 216,
217, 266, 282
Theraulaz, G. 135
Thorson, S. 28, 29
Troitzsch, K. 16, 41

unconscious 88, 116

variables 6, 7, 9, 13, 21, 22, 26, 34,
38, 39, 42, 67, 68, 74, 76, 79, 81,
83, 114, 127, 137, 138, 170, 173,
176, 178, 181, 186, 187, 190, 269

VIP Protocol 227, 229, 233, 234
Volterra, V. 127
Voorrips, A. 22

Wamani 230
Weidlich, W. 51, 61, 62
Werner, E. 130, 265
Whitelaw, T. 168
Willey, G. 2
Winograd, T. 265
Wobst, H. 167, 178
Wolf, S. 64
Woodburn, J. 168

Zeigler, B. 196
Zipf, G. 66